Coping
with Computers
in the Elementary
and Middle Schools

Coping
with Computers
in the Elementary
and Middle Schools

C. Alan Riedesel
State University of New York at Buffalo

Douglas H. Clements
Kent State University

105074

Prentice-Hall, Inc., Englewood Cliffs, New Jersey 07632

Library of Congress Cataloging in Publication Data

RIEDESEL, C. ALAN.
    Coping with computers in the elementary and middle
schools.

    Includes bibliographies and index.
    1.–Education, Elementary—Data processing.   2.–Middle
schools—Data processing.   3.–Microcomputers.   4.–Education—Computer programs.   I.–Clements, Douglas H.
    II.–Title.
LB1028.43.R54 1985   372.13′9445   84-6928
ISBN   0-13-172420-7

Cover photo: Ken Karp
Editorial/production supervision and
interior design: Joyce Turner
Cover design: Wanda Lubelska
Manufacturing buyer: Ron Chapman

Printed in the United States of America

10   9   8   7   6   5   4   3   2   1

ISBN   0-13-172420-7   01

Prentice-Hall International, Inc., *London*
Prentice-Hall of Australia Pty. Limited, *Sydney*
Editora Prentice-Hall do Brasil, Ltda., *Rio de Janeiro*
Prentice-Hall Canada Inc., *Toronto*
Prentice-Hall of India Private Limited, *New Delhi*
Prentice-Hall of Japan, Inc., *Tokyo*
Prentice-Hall of Southeast Asia Pte. Ltd., *Singapore*
Whitehall Books Limited, *Wellington, New Zealand*

**To our Wives
and to the Teachers
and Children
who learn to
"Cope with Computers"**

Contents

PREFACE

Coping with Computers in the Elementary and Middle Schools is designed for pre-service and in-service teachers, as an introduction to the use of computers in the classroom. No computer background is assumed.

The authors have made the following assumption in writing this book:

1. There is a need for a book which primarily addresses the classroom use of microcomputers in the elementary/middle school. This book is such a text. Therefore, it does not attempt an exhaustive coverage of every topic but rather tries to give you enough to get a good start.
2. The computer is like the TV. Each is a valuable tool for learning and understanding. However, each can do psychological damage or misuse time. Each can subtly affect the way we think and act. For each, the majority of people need to know and understand proper uses of the machine. However, not all persons need to know all about the machines' workings.
3. As with all elementary school learning, children learn best when (1) they are faced with a problem which they believe needs to be solved, and (2) they have an opportunity to discover the solution.
4. Some of the material in this book will become dated before the book is printed. Therefore, we have tried to deal with classroom situations and applications of computers that will serve teachers as examples for their use of any materials, old or new.

Like TV, computers will have a great effect upon our society. It is up to us as teachers to exercise wisdom in using computers to provide the best education for elementary/middle school students.

Alan Riedesel

Douglas Clements

Coping
with Computers
in the Elementary
and Middle Schools

1

Why Computers in the Elementary School

Nancy James, principal at Lincoln Park school, went to see her graduate advisor, Dr. Kent. They were to discuss several questions she had concerning the role of computers in her elementary/middle school. (Ms. James's school was small and contained classes K through 8.)

Nancy began, "A group of parents has raised $5,000 and has given me permission to buy equipment to begin the use of computers in our school. I checked with the central administration, and they will support the purchase if I will send in a description of the equipment and how we plan to use it. What shall I buy?"

Dr. Kent knew Nancy did not have a background in microcomputers but was an excellent principal who had a very fine understanding of children and of approaches to teaching. With this in mind he asked, "How do you plan to use microcomputers in your school?"

"I'm not sure—that's what I want to talk to you about."

"OK, before we decide how to spend the money, let's look at some of the options. Take a look at this material." Dr. Kent handed the material that appears below to Ms. James.

Computers in the Elementary/Middle School

1. *Computers are in the everyday life of the children.* Daily our children have contact with computers or with the results of computers. A form letter arrives

at the house, and the child wonders how the company made the letter seem to be personal. A mother or father says, "This magazine subscription is fouled up again. It must have been the silly computer." Some children are addicted to "video" games, which are in reality computer games.

Almost every day there are comments about computers made on the television news. The newspapers report on some new computer uses. Computers are becoming as much a part of life as is television.

Many children and adults have not learned to make the best use of television. We cannot afford to have children and adults who are not able to use computers wisely. Thus, we need to help children learn when to use and when not to use aspects of computer technology.

These aspects of computers can be taught without a great deal of contact with computers. However, we need to consider a number of issues, teaching strategies, and materials in developing lessons dealing with what is now called *computer literacy*. Whether a school is large or small, computerized or without any computers, it needs to deal with many aspects of computer literacy. (Chapter 2 explores this topic further.)

2. *Children can be taught to use computers.* Another aspect of computer literacy is the actual operation of microcomputers. Children at a very early age can be taught, and in many cases discover on their own, how to use microcomputers for a variety of uses.

There are several "computer languages" to choose among when this phase of computer literacy is taught. A scope and sequence chart of topics children should study concerning computers, needs to be carefully considered before making any purchases.

It is difficult to decide when children should have the opportunity to operate computers and learn one of the languages of computers. (This topic will be developed further in Part Three.)

3. *The computer can be used for instruction.* There are packaged programs for the microcomputer that help teach new concepts, practice on concepts already developed, or simulate a situation. The quality of such materials varies greatly. There is a need for careful study of computer-assisted-instruction (CAI) material and of good methods of using CAI. Also, the selection of microcomputers for a given school should be partially based upon the availability of quality CAI materials. (We look at these applications in chapters 3 and 6.)

4. *The computer can be used as a teacher aid.* The teacher can use a microcomputer for a variety of professional chores. There are teacher grade books which keep records on individual children and perform a variety of time-consuming operations such as averaging, weighting scores, and so forth. Also, there are programs for helping individual teachers make vocabulary games, mathematics practice materials, and tests.

Computers can also be used to help "manage instruction." There are programs which give tests and provide suggestions for assignments on the basis of these tests. Once again, this is an area that requires some study. (See Chapter 7.)

5. *The computer can be used in written communication.* Microcomputers can be used as super-supertypewriters which aid both teacher and student in improving their written communication. This is one of the most exciting uses in the upper elementary and middle schools. Many children have found that by using a micro-word processor, they now really enjoy writing.

In addition to helping in the development of written materials, there are programs that can be used to check spelling errors. With proper teaching, this use can actually improve the spelling of the children (and the teacher). (See Chapter 12.)

6. *Use the computer as a "problem-solving" tool.* There are a number of ways in which the microcomputer can help teach mathematical concepts, improve the logical thinking pattern of children, and solve problems posed in science and social studies. (Chapters 13 and 14 focus upon some of these applications.)

7. *Use the computer to aid the handicapped.* There are a number of special uses that can be designed to aid in the education of children with hearing, seeing, speaking, and other physical or mental difficulties. (Chapter 16 gives suggestions for this use.)

8. *The computer can help the gifted.* Microcomputers provide a number of ways of challenging gifted students. The uses are almost unlimited. Exploring ways in which the program can be enriched by micros is a challenging activity for teachers and administrators.

9. *The computers can help parents.* There are many home uses for computers that children can learn and can then help their parents explore. Children can have a part in better home financial management, better shopping practices, and perhaps even better security. Also, a school that is well versed in the use of microcomputers can be a real help to parents. Today many parents are being encouraged to buy microcomputers to "teach" their children at home. Much like the encyclopedia salesperson of a few years back, today's microcomputer salesperson may encourage a sincere parent to purchase a package that is not the best one for his or her particular use or financial situation.

10. *Use the computer in the school library.* There many ways the microcomputer can be used to improve both school and classroom libraries. Not only are there programs for book circulation, but filing system programs can be effectively used to sort and manage the books.

11. *Use the computer in the office.* Micros can be used to keep attendance records, process letters to parents, keep track of a variety of financial transactions, and in many ways ease the burden of the school office.

Uses for the microcomputer in the elementary/middle school are almost endless. Should every school immediately buy as many microcomputers as they can? Probably not. It takes time to develop many of the uses of microcomputers. A school or teacher would be wise to jump in with enthusiasm and with their minds in full gear. There are many decisions concerning microcomputers that can only be made by persons who know well what should be taught to children and how it should be taught.

The use of computers in the elementary/middle school is a wide open, somewhat scary field. However, there is no reason why any elementary teacher (even one without mathematical talent and with an "all thumbs" approach to machines) cannot become a skilled user of computers in the elementary school.

When she had finished reading the material, Nancy went back to see Dr. Kent. She said, "I see that I have a lot of 'homework' to do before I can make a good choice. In fact, I'm going to have a committee of teachers, parents, and children help me. Will you please suggest some books and journals that I can obtain to help the committee in its study of the issues."

"Certainly, here's a start," said Dr. Kent as he handed Nancy a list of articles, books, and magazines. "You'll need to get some of the latest issues of the magazines, for there are new products appearing all the time. However, you will find that the basic ideas and principles needed to decide what to buy, and how to use what you buy, will remain quite stable. Be sure you don't disregard a sound article that may be a few years old.

I'd be happy to meet with your committee when they have had a chance to do some study. Also, you will want to visit some schools that have begun good programs. If you want, I'll arrange for you to visit several schools in the area."

The suggested references Dr. Kent gave to Nancy are listed at the end of the chapter.

MYTHS ABOUT COMPUTERS

Like any new field, computers are surrounded by many myths the non-computer-oriented person often believes. Here are a few you may need to think over.

1. Myth: Only math people like and can work well with computers.

Response: Mathematics is only one function that computers can perform. In many ways the math function is not as impressive at the elementary/middle school level as are some of the other functions. The language arts uses are endless. In fact, while the authors deal with elementary school mathematics a good portion of their professional time, they find that they use microcomputers much more often for activities that are associated with the language arts (like writing this book).

**2. Myth: I don't get along with machines
and technology. I couldn't use a computer
in my classroom.**

Response: After just a bit of instruction and a few months in the classroom, almost all teachers see the computer's potential to expand their abilities as teachers. Many say they are not sure how they ever got along without the computer.

Also, remember that the microcomputer differs from the larger computers of the past. It is personal; no one else can look over your shoulder. Your information is not stored in a central place. You can decide when and when not to use a computer. With the large mainframe computers, businesses, schools, and governments were locked into a rather rigid use of computers. The authors agree with a recent statement in *Classroom Computer News*, where the author states:

> Lately, I have been giving a small sermon whenever any "humanist" asks, "What's the big fuss about computers anyway?" I talk about Luther and the Reformation, the goal of putting people in direct contact with the Deity and doing away with all the high priests, scribes and interpreters that had kept people down during the Middle Ages. The computer—particularly the microcomputer—has inadvertently done what the Reformation set out to do; put the individual in charge. It has been likened to that instrument of the Reformation, the Gutenberg press, but it goes much further. Everyone cannot and will not run a press, nor does running a printing press necessarily empower an individual. Everyone who gains access to a computer in some measure takes charge of his/her own life. The attraction of computers for adults and children is the feeling of control that comes from success in the programming—or even just operating—a powerful tool that serves one's own purposes. (Naiman, 1982)

With that feeling of individual control comes the need for individual responsibility. I find that I take much more responsibility for my spelling, grammar, and general writing now that I use a microcomputer. Before, I would make the typist or secretary responsible for my errors. Certainly, in a democracy, individual responsibility is to be encouraged.

**3. Myth: Computers are another educational fad.
They'll be the rage, then go into the closets
alongside the video players and the teaching
machines. Why waste my time on a fad?**

Response: Computers are becoming increasingly prevalent in society, in children's lives, and in schools. It is estimated that by 1990 over half of all homes will have a microcomputer. If the economy improves, this may well be a conservative estimate. Whether schools use them or not, children will have a great deal of contact with them, and professionals need to take the lead. Educators need to be involved as much as, if not more than, technical persons.

Computers are a new dimension in educational technology because they're interactive. There is the danger that they can be misused in the same manner as the teaching machine and programmed instruction. The programmed instruction movement focused primarily on the teaching of facts and content details. It tried to develop entire subject matter curriculums based upon a single type of learning that was applicable to only a portion of the material. Computers will be important in education. We must ensure that their use is backed by sound educational practice. This is the responsibility of the teacher and of other professional educators.

4. Myth: They're too expensive.

Response: Microcomputers range in price from $50 to a few thousand dollars—and the price is still coming down. In fact, it was necessary to change the figure from $100 to $50 over a period of six months. A machine that was nationally promoted as a bargain at $750 now sells for $100.

5. Myth: You have to know how to program a computer—and I don't.

Response: Exciting and worthwhile activities can be conducted without the teacher programming in BASIC or some other computer language. The computer is a tool; if you want a job done, it is very likely that there are programs written to help you do it. For instance, you can use a file program to keep notes and bibliographies for your social studies materials. Or you can use a grade book to keep records, average and weigh grades, and determine marks. Also, using the computer as a word processor to help you and your students with what you want to write can be done without programming a line. New programs for children and teachers are being written every day. In fact, it's almost a full-time job keeping up with the programs that are coming out for school use. Adam Osborne, who has written widely on computers and developed the Osborne microcomputer (one of the most cost-productive microcomputers), indicated in an interview on public television that he believed that the computer industry should be taken to task if there still existed any need to know computer programming by 1990. Osborne believes that computers will accept natural language—both written and spoken—in a manner that requires only that the "programmer" know how to think through the problem he or she wishes to program.

6. Myth (and a big one): I can't . . . program a computer. How can my children learn from me?

Response: New computer languages such as LOGO are written for children (although they're great for anyone). You and your children can be writing simple programs the first day. One author believes that the best LOGO language lesson he has taught to his college class was the first one. He had just gotten a copy of the LOGO language, and he said to the class, "I don't know this language—here are a few commands to get us started. Let's see what we can do." Such a nice graphic pattern design was developed that one of the class members, who was a quilter, copied it from the screen so that she could use it for a pattern.

Languages such as LOGO will not become outdated in the same way BASIC may, because problem solving is learned in a natural manner.

7. Myth: There are no good educational programs around.

Response: This myth has a kernel of truth. That is, there are many educational programs around that aren't of high quality. (There are also many low quality books around.) While much that is available is not good, much is interesting, worthwhile, and even fascinating. Some programs one of the writers demonstrated for teachers proved so interesting that I have had trouble getting the teachers to stop and go on to preview other programs. Also, programs won't get better until more superteachers get involved.

8. Myth: All the games are those "shootem-up" games—I don't want to encourage that.

Response: Many nonviolent, challenging educational games are being produced. In truth, there are too many of the violent variety. Educators need to ask for quality teaching games which motivate by the quality of the educational content itself.

9. Myth: Computers will replace me!

Response: Experienced educators know that computers, like any tool, help us do better what we are already doing well. Properly used, the microcomputer should open the way for the teacher to be able to spend time motivating, working with individuals, and conducting creative discussions. There is no way at the present time that a computer program can conduct a high-level class discussion with kindergarten children. However, a computer program can help with letter and numeral identification and may do as well in conducting practice for these skills as can the teacher.

10. Myth: Children can't do it.

Response: There is more evidence coming in all the time that children can run computer programs, that they can learn to program, and that they can learn to pace their own education. They benefit from all these skills.

REMEMBER . . . REMEMBER

1. The microcomputer should be considered a tool as much as a hoe, a fork, a drill, or an automobile. Thus, it is possible to know how to use the tool effectively without having a thorough grasp of all aspects of its design, its workings, and the theory of its operation. The majority of skilled users of electric sewing machines know little of the internal workings of the machine. You can be a state award winner in sewing without knowing how the machine works. Much of the early writing on computers in the elementary/middle school has been done by computer-oriented educators who may place too much emphasis on knowing all the technical aspects of computers.

2. Many of the materials for use with computers in schools have been designed by persons with little real experience in education. It is more important to know what to teach, when to teach, and how to teach than it is to know every aspect of computer programming if you are going to work with computers in the elementary school.

3. While you can learn how to program a computer (and probably will want to enjoy this aspect), there are many, many things you can do with computers in the elementary/middle school before you learn to program. A teacher who became quite interested in computers for children called the largest and most respected developer of computer-assisted-instruction material and asked what she had to do to become an author of such materials. They suggested that the most important thing for her to do was to be able to think through all the ways she could teach a concept to children and to be sure that if given the right tools, she could teach the concept to almost any child. Given this ability, she could then study ways in which a microcomputer could be used to teach the material. However, they felt that she would only need a little knowledge of computer programming.

4. To discover the best use of microcomputers for a given school will require a team effort. It will require the best thinking of teachers who know what to teach and how to teach, of administrators who can help organize the school, of computer programmers, and of parents and children.

Computers are here to stay—like it or not—and they can be fun. A particular lady was very much a non-computer person and would probably have liked to get rid of them. But when she looked at ways in which she could use a filing system to help her find recipes, she became excited. She had over 300 cookbooks and often could not remember where a particular recipe was located. With the filing system she can ask for a location by name, or by recipe, or by ingredient. (Of course, she is only using this system with some of her recipes; for most things the books work well.) Yes, computers are here to stay, and teachers need to develop the best uses of them for elementary/middle schools.

One elementary school teacher entered the computer world in the following manner: In the late spring the principal called the teacher to the office and mentioned that the school would be buying one microcomputer for the building. This computer would be available to any of the teachers to try out during the summer. Our friend signed up for the first week after school and took the computer home at the end of the school year. She was told by the principal that she could keep the machine until another teacher signed up.

When she got home with the machine, she called a friend who owned the same make computer and asked for help in getting started. The friend came over and unboxed the computer, the disk drive, and the assortment of cords. It looked like an impossible task. However, in a few minutes the machine was running and the two were trying out some of the programs contained on the master disk. With a friend to help, things went along quite well.

A word processing program disk was borrowed and with the help of the friend, the teacher was writing letters to friends in about an hour. Sure, she made mistakes and once or twice forgot to save some of her writing; but by the end of the first week, she could use the computer for any writing she wished. She then borrowed two computer disks on BASIC and worked with them. Another teacher came over with a LOGO disk, and together the two explored drawing figures on the screen. A few minutes after they began, they were making boxes, triangles, and the like.

After two weeks another teacher checked out the computer. However, later in the summer the first teacher was able to use the computer for two weeks more and had the opportunity to go over several of the computer-assisted-instruction programs available to this particular computer. By the end of the summer, the teacher was ready to have her children work with the computer. She did have two suggestions for anyone starting out: Try to work with someone; and don't be afraid to ask questions. She found that there are many little things that can be learned only through experience and experimentation.

Study Suggestions

1. Visit at least two computer stores. Talk with several clerks. Are they knowledgeable? Ask about the computers. Ask about their ideas on educational uses. Check their teaching philosophy.

2. At the computer store skim through several magazines. Note which ones seem to tell the most about "everyday use." Note those that seem technical. Which magazines seem to have educational applications?

3. Look over the computer-oriented magazines at locations such as supermarkets, bookstores, and magazine stands. Which magazines do these stores sell?

4. Get several friends to go with you to buy at least four different computer-oriented magazines. Compare the information these magazines contain and the approach they take.

5. To keep up-to-date in such a rapidly developing field as computers in the elementary/middle school, it is necessary to read periodicals as well as books. Subscribe to the magazine that you feel will be most useful to you. Before subscribing, check libraries and teachers' lounges for availability of key magazines.

Suggested Readings

Evans, Christopher. *The Micro Millennium.* New York: Viking, 1979 (now in paper).

Evans looks at many interesting ideas. He explores artificial intelligence and suggests where we will be going in the future. Make up a study guide for reading the book. Get another teacher and a parent to read the book. What are their reactions?

Moursund, David. *Introduction to computers in education for elementary and middle school teachers.* Eugene, Oreg.: International Council for Computers in Education, 1981.

Moursund is one of the leaders of the microcomputer-in-schools movement. Read this small booklet as an overview to this field. Does his approach agree with that presented in this book?

Papert, Seymour. *Mindstorms: Children, computers and powerful ideas.* New York: Basic Books, 1980.

Papert suggests ways of using the computer with children. As a computer scientist and student of Piaget, he presents some unique insights. What is his view of CAI? What is his view of computer programming for children?

Watson, Nancy (ed.). *Microcomputers in education: Getting started* and *Microcomputers in education: Uses for the 80's.* Tempe, Ariz.: Arizona State University, 1981, 1982.

Watson edits the presentations from two conferences at Arizona State. What do the speakers say about micros in the various subject areas? What are their views on computer literacy?

Weizenbaum, Joseph. *Computer power and human reason.* New York: W. H. Freeman and Co., 1976.

Weizenbaum is one of the pioneers in the field of computers and in the use of artificial intelligence languages. Although the book is several years old, it looks at a number of very important ideas. Also, his chapter on how computers work is one of the best. How do you react to his story of Eliza?

Computer Journals for Educators

The appendix contains a listing of journals that deal with computers, and computers in education. Check the journal section and become familiar with as many as possible. The need to check current journals cannot be overemphasized.

Bibliography

NAIMAN, ADELINE. On video arcades: A microsermon. *Classroom Computer News,* September/October 1982, p. 35.

Introduction to Computer Literacy

This entire book deals with computer literacy; however, the next four chapters will focus on computer literacy for children, attempting to answer the following questions:

1. Why should it be taught?
2. What should be taught?
3. How should it be taught?

There are no universally accepted answers to these questions. Therefore, you will be introduced to several viewpoints, including that of the authors. Some computer literacy content is discussed specifically, concentrating on those areas not dealt with in other chapters.

WHY SHOULD WE TEACH COMPUTER LITERACY?

The United States is experiencing another "revolution." The Industrial Revolution changed the country from a basically agricultural society to an industrial society. The economic emphasis is presently changing from the production of industrial goods and services to the provision of science and knowledge. The United States is rapidly moving from being an industrial society to being an information society. Over half the labor force holds information-related jobs (Molnar, 1981). However, other nations are surpassing ours in this move. If as a nation we fail to become computer literate, they will continue to surpass us. According to a National Science Foundation report, we as a nation are becoming technologically illiterate. Arguing that every educated child needs to understand the uses and applications of computers in society, Molnar stated:

> A nation concerned with its social needs and economic growth cannot be indifferent to the problems of literacy. If we are to reap the benefits of science-driven industries, we must develop a computer-literate society. (p.36)

From another perspective, we must consider the issue of human waste. Those children who are not equipped to cope with an information society will not be employable, useful members of that society—an unacceptable social and psychological cost. It has been said that ignorance of computers will render people as functionally illiterate as does ignorance of reading, writing, and arithmetic (Michaels, 1968). Such illiterates will not only be cut off from thousands of careers, but they will be excluded from a repository of massive quantities of the world's knowledge, as well as from the use of a powerful problem-solving tool which many consider to have the ability to amplify human thinking, expand the intellectual capabilities of learners, and liberate human potential. Some fear that the gap between those working creatively with the computer and the rest of the population is growing.

Computer literacy for all children has been advocated by many educational organizations (National Council of Supervisors of Mathematics, 1978; National Council of Teachers of Mathematics, 1980), including those—like the National Council for Social Studies—that are concerned with areas other than mathematics. The National Assessment of Educational Progress (NAEP) now includes computer questions in their nationwide assessments. Likewise, several professionals have stressed the urgent need for teaching computer literacy in the schools (Molnar, 1981), citing computer literacy as the next great crisis in American education (Luehrmann, 1980; Molnar, 1978). Former Governor Brown of California has stressed the importance of computers to children and society and has taken strong steps to ensure support for the cause of computers in education (Brown, 1982). Minnesota has made a statewide push for computer literacy (Rawitsch, 1982). Many colleges are including minimal computer literacy as a requirement for graduation; some are even demanding that their students own a computer.

Is this urgent push for computer literacy necessary? There are those who argue that just as people no longer need to know anything about how automobiles or televisions work in order to use them, children need not learn how computers work. Some educators skeptically point to the "technological revolutions" of the past—teaching machines and language laboratories—which gather dust in storage rooms. They suspect that commercial interests lie behind the pressure to place computers in classrooms and agree that all students need not be "computer literate." Others fear that computers will dehumanize education and lead to a further erosion of basic skills.

These arguments raise important issues that must be considered carefully. However, they also rest on questionable assumptions. Marshall McLuhan pointed out that computers are not new kinds of engines; they are not part of the "Gutenberg technology." They serve as extensions of human minds rather than of human muscles. They can manipulate information, and can do so in increasingly intelligent ways. They are not restricted to a narrow range of applications but are "general purpose" machines which are almost infinitely adaptable. For these reasons, they will have a profound effect on almost every area of human endeavor, including education.

The main point is that computers *will* be used in all areas of society, including education. The only reasonable course for educators to take is to meet this challenge in ways that will improve education for children. Given that children will use computers, educators need to decide what type and level of use is appropriate for individual children. It is true that society is moving away from knowing about computers in the technical sense and toward knowing about how to use computers; still, some basic knowledge about how computers work may be necessary to fully understand the many ways in which these machines can be used. It is these uses—finding and manipulating information, solving problems, creating, communicating, and learning—that must be the central concern of those responsible for children's learning. The fears of losing competence in basic skills or mechanizing children and their learning will then be unfounded. Research indicates that—*used wisely*—computers can help humanize and improve the intellectual quality of educational environments.

Educators must accept the responsibility of meeting this challenge. If we do not, others will. If other sources accept leadership, then computer education will be in the hands of those without dedication to, and expertise in, the provision of educational opportunities befitting a democracy. The first ramification of giving over control in this area is the possibility of a decrease in the quality of education for every child. The second is the possibility of a societal movement toward overreliance on and submission to the "expert" (either computer or technocrat), what Hansgen (1982) has termed "the tyranny of expertise." "Those who use the computer, if left unchecked, will probably acquire a great amount of power" (Frates and Moldrup, 1980, p. 18).

Unfortunately, even those children who have grown up with video games are strikingly ignorant of basic computer literacy.

WHAT IS COMPUTER LITERACY?

Computer literacy is "an awareness and understanding of the computer, its role in society, and its impact on education" (Holly O'Donnell).

"If you can tell the computer how to do the things you want it to, you are computer literate" (Arthur Luehrmann).

"I expect a literate person to have a general command of language and literature with all that entails, but not necessarily to have achieved mastery of all language and literary skills" (Daniel Watt).

"Computer literacy refers to a knowledge of the non-technical and low-technical aspects of the capabilities and limitations of computers, and of the social, vocational, and educational implications of computers. Not only programming, computer literacy should include the use of "information retrieval, word processing, statistics, and other application systems" (David Moursund).

"The ability to use suitably programmed computers in appropriate ways in accomplishing tasks and solving problems; and ability to make informed judgments about social and ethical issues involving computer and communications systems" (Beverly Hunter).

"Computer literacy . . . is whatever understanding, skills, and attitudes one needs to function effectively within a given social role that directly or indirectly involves computers" (Ronald Anderson and Daniel Klassen).

"Computer literacy is the part of computer science that everyone should know or be able to do" (Ronald Anderson).

"Computer literacy is the ability to function in a computer and technology oriented society" (William Zachmeier and others).

"(a) Computer literacy deals with a spectrum of computer users, users' needs, and delivery systems.
(b) The spectrum can be naturally divided into two areas dealing with learning *with* computers and learning *about* computers" (Ramon Zamora).

As these definitions indicate, there is no agreement—even among the experts—concerning an answer to the question. Possibly a look at what has been suggested in terms of a curriculum for computer literacy is most useful to teachers, as it helps establish both what it is and what might be introduced to students to help them attain literacy. As you are reading, it will be useful to notice that some professionals have made a distinction between computer awareness and computer literacy. Awareness usually means becoming knowledgeable about the effects of computers on our lives and on our society. Literacy, on the other hand, includes awareness but also implies some ability to use, program, or control the computer. This would necessitate hands-on experience with computers and practice in their use.

The rest of this chapter will present an overview of computer literacy curricular topics. First, a framework will be introduced which includes four basic categories of topics and subtopics for each. A brief description will acquaint the reader with the topics and specify the chapters in which they will be discussed. Next, a table will be presented which will list the topics and show which ones have been considered for inclusion in the curriculum by several authorities on computer literacy.

What is a computer? This topic includes basic vocabulary and concepts, the history of computers, different types of computers and their uses, and computer systems, which consist of a computer, other electronic equipment such as printers and television sets, and computer programs—all of which operate together. These topics, first addressed in Chapter 3, provide a conceptual basis for understanding the origins and nature of computers.

How does a computer work? The way hardware and software work is also introduced in Chapter 3. *Hardware* is the physical equipment of a computer system, such as keyboards, the internal parts of the computer, printers, television sets for viewing, and so on. *Software* is the name for the computer programs which actually tell the computer what to do. They are lists of instructions which might tell the computer how to present a math lesson, draw a picture, or keep track of files. Teaching suggestions for these and other topics are included in Chapter 5. The evaluation of software is discussed in Chapter 8. Several later chapters deal with aspects of these subjects and discuss various computer languages—the words or instructions a computer can "understand" or carry out (Part Four).

What can a computer do (awareness)? This category deals with the awareness of how we use computers and the influence of computers in our lives. The advantages and disadvantages of computers and of using computers is discussed. Many of the disadvantages have to do with the limitations of intelligence characteristic of present-day computers. Artificial intelligence, the study and development of computers that "think," represents a field of endeavor which attempts to ameliorate these problems. Three other subtopics—computer careers, misuses of the computer, and computers and the future—concern the social impact of computers. Background on the first two subjects is provided in Chapter 4; teaching suggestions are described in Chapter 5. The chapters in Part Five look forward to the future.

What can a computer do? This extensive topic concerns the abilities and skills necessary for the development of full computer literacy—using the computer as a tool to accomplish goals. The subtopic on getting ready to use computers includes the attitudes, skills, and higher-level abilities which will contribute to successful use of computer technology. *Computer programming* involves creating a list of instructions for a computer. Children and adults must "teach the computer" to accomplish a specific task; for example, drawing a picture, printing words and sentences, solving a mathematics problem, or asking questions and printing responses. These topics are addressed in Chapter 5 and, more extensively, in the chapters in Part Four. Using computers as tools includes learning how and when to use computers, learning from computer-assisted-instructional programs, using utility programs (for filing, keeping track of figures, and so forth), and other uses. This important area is discussed in Part Three and in Chapter 20 (Utilities).

Table 2-1 lists the computer literacy topics described above. To construct this table, an illustrative sample of the curricular suggestions of several authorities was reviewed and placed within the framework of computer literacy topics as accurately as possible. However, it should be clear that because these authorities did not agree on a definition of computer literacy—much less specific content—this placement is approximate at best. It represents an interpretation of the authors' intentions; that is, while the authors may not have specifically mentioned a topic, other statements they made led to the conclusion that they would include the topic in a curriculum. Many mentioned topics not considered in the framework presented here. Therefore, the checklist should be viewed as an attempt to illustrate emphases rather than specifics; as an overview rather than as a critical review. With these points in mind, kindly study Table 2-1.

Examination of the table reveals that there is diversity of opinion (for those interested in a lucid presentation of opposing viewpoints, see the debate in Luehrmann, 1981; and Anderson, Klassen, and Johnson, 1981), yet several professionals agree on many of the topics the teacher might include in a study of computer literacy. The main goal of this book is to help you as a teacher guide children in using the computer as a tool in solving problems ("Man is a tool-using animal. . . . Without tools he is nothing, with tools he is all"—Carlyle). To do this intelligently, you should have an understanding of its history, development, and impact. You as a teacher need to have this information; but you must decide what you want to teach your children. Professional educators are constantly making such choices on the basis of time constraints, availability of materials, and,

TABLE 2-1 What Should Be Included in a Computer Literacy Curriculum

Topic		Bitter	O'Donnell	Rosenblum & Frye	Zachmeier et al.	Walkington	Anderson et al.	Luehrmann	Darmstadt	Hino & Boss	Olds	Sadowski	Doerr	Hunter
What is a computer?														
Basic explanations	K-8	x		x	x	x	x			x		x	x	x
Vocabulary/concepts	K-8	x		x	x	x	x			x		x		x
History	3-8	x			x	x	x		x	x		x		
Types of computers	5-8	x		x	x	x	x							x
Computer systems	7-8	x		x	x	x	x						x	x
How Does a Computer Work?														
How does a computer work? Introduction	3-8	x		x	x	x	x			x		x	x	x
Hardware	4-8	x		x	x	x	x			x		x	x	x
Software	4-8	x		x	x	x	x					x	x	x
Computer languages	4-8	x		x	x	x	x			x		x	x	x
What Can a Computer Do? (Awareness)														
What does a computer do?	1-8	x		x	x	x	x			x		x	x	x
How do we use a computer?	1-8	x	x	x	x	x	x			x		x	x	x
Computers in our lives	2-8	x	x	x	x	x	x		x	x		x	x	x
Advantages/ disadvantages (limitations)	2-8	x		x	x	x	x					x	x	x
Artificial intelligence and robotics	5-8	x					x							x
Computer careers	6-8	x	x		x	x	x					x	x	x
Misuses of the computer Computer ethics (fraud and other crimes)	4-8	x	x		x	x	x					x		x
Invasion of privacy	5-8	x	x		x	x	x					x		x
Computers and the future	2-8	x			x	x	x		x	x		x	x	
What Can a Computer Do? (Abilities/Skills Level)														
Getting Ready to Use Computers Behaving responsibly toward other users, their material, and equipment	K-8	x	x			x						x		x

17

TABLE 2-1 (cont.)

Topic		Bitter	O'Donnell	Rosenblum & Frye	Zachmeier et al.	Walkington	Anderson et al.	Luehrmann	Darmstadt	Hino & Boss	Olds	Sadowski	Doerr	Hunter
Keyboard/ touch typing	1-4	x			x									x
Communicating effectively	K-8		x		x	x	x	x	x		x			x
Clear and logical thinking	3-8	x	x		x	x	x	x	x		x			x
Systematic problem solving; flow charting	4-8	x	x	x	x		x	x	x		x	x	x	x
Mathematics of computing	4-8	x		x	x	x	x				x		x	x
Computer Programming														
Programming programmable devices	K-2	x						x			x			x
LOGO														
Turtle geometry/ shapes	K-2	x			x						x			x
Moving shapes	1-3	x									x			x
Programming and Problem solving	3-8	x			x						x			x
BASIC														
Graphics	4-8	x												
Sound and color	4-8	x							x					
Programming and Problem solving	5-8	x		x	x	x	x				x	x	x	
PILOT	5-8	x			x									x
Pascal	8-8	x												x
Using Computer Tools														
Select and use appropriate computer applications	K-8		x	x	x		x	x			x	x		x
Loading and running simple programs	K-8		x	x	x	x	x	x			x	x	x	x
Classroom/educational management (used by the children)	K-8			x	x		x							x
CAI materials	K-8		x	x	x		x				x	x	x	x
Modify programs	1-8		x	x	x		x	x					x	x
Use and evaluate documentation of programs	2-8		x	x	x		x				x		x	x
DBMS	2-8		x	x	x		x					x		x
Word processing	4-8	x	x		x		x					x		x
Data processing	4-8		x	x	x		x	x				x		x

most importantly, knowledge of what *their* children need and want to know and to be able to do. On the whole, children need to be able to use the computer as a tool, and they need to know the social and personal implications of computers. Exactly what content and activities they should experience is best decided by their teacher.

Remember, too, that while much of the content discussed below could be contained in a separate "computer literacy unit," there is also much that could (even more profitably) be included in the language arts, social studies, science, and mathematics curricula. This points to the need for *every* teacher to be computer literate and to contribute to the computer literacy of his or her students.

This book is based on the belief that it is necessary for students to achieve computer literacy. However, the focus should be on the use of computers to achieve broader educational goals, including the abilities of problem solving; understanding oneself and others within one's society; communicating; and thinking mathematically, scientifically, poetically, and artistically. Each of these areas involves creating, working with, and communicating information. Attaining competence in these abilities should be the goal of education. Children can learn to use computers, can learn about all the possible uses of computers, and can learn about computers as one way of achieving this goal. Computer literacy, and computers themselves, become not the goal, but rather powerful tools used to achieve the goal.

Self-Test (True-False)

Use this self-test as a review and for study purposes.

1. By the time our students graduate, more will be working (in some way) with a computer than not.
2. There is a danger that people who are not computer literate will be overly dependent on those who are.
3. Fortunately, there is a consensus on what it means to be computer literate.
4. Computer literacy means being able to read about computers and understanding what is read.
5. Since many children play video games, we do not have to worry much about their being computer literate!
6. Children should become computer literate to be prepared for their future jobs and to develop their abilities to solve problems.
7. The computer probably is best viewed as a powerful tool.
8. Most professionals believe that only those preparing for highly technical jobs need extensive computer education.
9. "Computer awareness" is the same as "computer literacy."

Think About

1. What definition of computer literacy seemed most valid for you? For your students? Why?
2. Is "computer literacy" a useful term? What does "literacy" mean? Is there a word or phrase you think would better serve educational purposes?
3. Reexamine Table 2-1. Which parts of it do you believe should be given priority for *your* children's introduction to computer literacy? Why?
4. Which parts do you think you would treat as a separate unit or course of study? Which would you integrate into other coursework?
5. Do you really believe there is a need to understand computers more than, say, radio or microwave ovens? Why or why not? How much need adults in our society understand? When and how should they learn this information?
6. Will all future citizens need to be able to control computers? In what sense?

Suggested References

Watt, D. Computer literacy: What should schools do about it? *Instructor,* October 1981, pp. 85–87.
Watt presents a lucid account of the schools' need for a comprehensive program of computer literacy instruction. Good reading for parents of your students.

Molnar, Andrew R. The next great crisis in American education: Computer literacy. *AEDS Journal,* 1978, 12, 11–20.

Molnar, Andrew R. The coming of computer literacy: Are we prepared for it? *Educational Technology,* 1981, 21(1), 26–28.

Michaels, D. *The unprepared society.* New York: Basic Books, 1968.
Other good readings for anyone who is concerned about the need for computer literacy training include Molnar (1978, 1981) and Michaels (1968).

Bitter, Gary G. The road to computer literacy: A scope and sequence model. *Electronic Learning,* September 1982, pp. 60–63.

Hunter, Beverly. *My students use computers: Learning activities for computer literacy.* Reston, Va: Reston Publishing Co., 1983.

Zachmeier, William, et al. K-8 computer literacy curriculum. *The Computing Teacher,* March 1983, 10(7), 7–10.
Bitter (1982), Hunter (1983), and Zachmeier et al. (1983) present a fairly extensive scope and sequence model for computer literacy.

Olds, H. How to think about computers. In B. R. Sadowski (ed.), *Using computers to enhance teaching and improve teacher centers.* Houston: National Teacher Centers Computer Technology Conference, 1981.
If you want to think a little deeper about the role of microcomputers in education and society, read Olds.

Luehrmann, Arthur. Computer literacy—What should it be? *Mathematics Teacher,* 1981, 74, 682–686.

Anderson, Ronald E., Klassen, Daniel L., and Johnson, David C. In defense of a comprehensive view of computer literacy—A reply to Luehrmann. *Mathematics Teacher,* 1981, 74, 687–690.
Try to resolve the debate presented in Luehrmann (1981) and Anderson et al. (1981).

Gawronski, J. D., and West, Charlene. Computer literacy. *ASCD Curriculum Update,* October 1982.
J. D. Gawronski and Charlene West present several views of computer literacy and attempt to arrive at a consensus. After reading their article and this chapter, do you agree with their choice of topics? They list numerous references. Write to several promising ones for information.

Corbitt, Mary Kay. *Guide to resources in instructional computing.* Reston, Va: National Council of Teachers of Mathematics, 1982.
For more resources see Corbitt.

Anderson, Ronald, and Klassen, Daniel. A conceptual framework for developing computer literacy instruction. *AEDS Journal,* 1981, 14, 128–150.
Anderson and Klassen describe a useful framework for developing computer literacy instruction.

Bibliography

ANDERSON, RONALD, AND KLASSEN, DANIEL. A conceptual framework for developing computer literacy instruction. *AEDS Journal,* 1981, 14, 128–150.

ANDERSON, RONALD E., KLASSEN, DANIEL L., AND JOHNSON, DAVID C. In defense of a comprehensive view of computer literacy—A reply to Luehrmann. *Mathematics Teacher,* 1981, 74, 687–690.

BITTER, GARY G. The road to computer literacy: A scope and sequence model. *Electronic Learning,* September 1982, pp. 60–63.

BROWN, EDMUND G., JR. Computers and the schools. *T.H.E. Journal,* 1982, 10(1), 99–100.

CORBITT, MARY KAY. Guide to resources in instructional computing. Reston, Va: National Council of Teachers of Mathematics, 1982.

DARMSTADT CAREER CENTER. *Goals for computer education.* New York: Author, n.d.

DOERR, CHRISTINE. *Microcomputers and the 3 R's.* Rochelle Park, N.J.: Hayden Book Co., 1979.

DWYER, T. Solo-mode computing. In R. Taylor (ed.), *The computer in the school: Tutor, tool, and tutee.* New York: Teachers College 1980.

FRATES, JEFFERY, AND MOLDRUP, WILLIAM. *Introduction to the computer: An integrative approach.* Englewood Cliffs, N.J.: Prentice-Hall, 1980.

GAWRONSKI, J. D., AND WEST, CHARLENE. Computer literacy. *ASCD Curriculum Update,* October 1982.

HANSGEN, R. The consequences of a technological society: The tyranny of expertise. *Technology Concentration Papers.* Toronto: National Council of Teachers of Mathematics, 1982.

HINO, J., AND BOSS, JACKIE. Summer fun on micros for kids and parents. *The Computing Teacher,* May 1982, pp. 26–30.

HUNTER, BEVERLY. Computer literacy in grades K-8. *Journal of Educational Technology Systems,* 1981/82, 10(1), 59–66.

HUNTER, BEVERLY. *My students use computers: Learning activities for computer literacy.* Reston, Va: Reston Publishing Co., 1983.

LUEHRMANN, ARTHUR. Computer illiteracy—A national crisis and a solution for it. *Byte,* July 1980, pp. 98; 101–102.

LUEHRMANN, ARTHUR. Computer literacy—What should it be? *Mathematics Teacher,* 1981, 74, 682–686.

LUEHRMANN, ARTHUR. Computer literacy: What it is, why it's important. *Electronic Learning,* May/June 1982, p. 20; 22.

McISAAC, DONALD N. Impact of personal computing on education. *AEDS Journal,* 1979, 13, 7–15.

MICHAELS, D. *The unprepared society.* New York: Basic Books, 1968.

MOLNAR, ANDREW, R. The next great crisis in American education: Computer literacy. *AEDS Journal,* 1978, 12, 11–20.

MOLNAR, ANDREW R. The coming of computer literacy: Are we prepared for it? *Educational Technology,* 1981, 21(1), 26–28.

MOURSUND, D. What is computer literacy? *Creative Computing,* November/December 1976, pp. 2; 6; 55.

NATIONAL COUNCIL OF SUPERVISORS OF MATHEMATICS. Position paper on basic skills. *Mathematics Teacher,* 1978, 71, 147–152.

NATIONAL COUNCIL OF TEACHERS OF MATHEMATICS. *An agenda for action: Recommendations for school mathematics in the 1980's.* Reston Va: National Council of Teachers of Mathematics, 1980.

NATIONAL INSTITUTE OF EDUCATION. *Automated dictionaries and word processors.* Washington, D.C.: National Institute of Education, 1980.

O'DONNELL, HOLLY. Computer literacy, part I: An overview. *Reading Teacher,* 1982, 35, 490–494.

OLDS, H. How to think about computers. In B. R. Sadowski (ed.), *Using computers to enhance teaching and improve teacher centers.* Houston: National Teacher Centers Computer Technology Conference, 1981.

RAWITSCH, D. G. Minnesota's statewide push for computer literacy. *Instructional Innovator,* 1982, 27(2), 34–35.

ROSENBLUM, JANIS, AND FRYE, SHIRLEY. Computer literacy as content. In N. R. Watson (ed.), Microcomputers in education: Uses for the '80's. (Publication No. 3). Proceedings of the Second Annual Microcomputer Conference, Arizona State University, July 15 and 16, 1982.

SADOWSKI, BARBARA. Computer literacy for students and teachers. In B. Sadowski and C. Lovett (eds.), *Using computers to enhance teaching and improve teacher centers.* Houston: University of Houston, 1981.

WALKINGTON, PATRICIA A. Curriculum guide for beginning computer literacy and programming in BASIC. In N. A. Watson (ed.), Microcomputers in education: Getting started (Publication No. 2). Proceedings of the Ninth Annual Math/Science Conference, Arizona State University, January 16–17, 1981.

WATT, D. Computer literacy: What should schools do about it? *Instructor,* October 1981, pp. 85–87.

WINKLE, LINDA W., AND MATHEWS, WALTER M. Computer equity comes of age. *Phi Delta Kappan,* 1982, 63, 314–315.

ZACHMEIER, WILLIAM, ET AL. K-8 computer literacy curriculum. *The Computing Teacher,* 1983, 10(7), 7–10.

ZAMORA, RAMON. Computer and other literacies. In M. Grady and J. Gawronski (eds.), *Computer in curriculum and instruction.* Alexandria, Va: Association for Supervision and Curriculum Development, 1983.

3

Hardware and Software

WHAT IS A COMPUTER?
HOW DOES A COMPUTER WORK?

A computer is a machine that can accept and store large amounts of data, process it according to specified arithmetical and logical instructions (with minimal human intervention), and produce the results of such processing. You might feel inclined to say, "Great, next time I want my data processed, I'll let you know." Try not to let "computerese" (technical jargon) put you off or make you feel that your world and the world of the computer are far apart. We process data every day.

An analogy between computers and people might be useful in illustrating that point and in showing how such concepts might be explained to older students. For instance, given an addition problem to solve, a student first looks at the problem (visual input of data). The student's brain translates the visual image into neurological impulses. The computer takes coded data in the form of magnetic disks or typed in directly from a keyboard, which it then translates into electrical impulses. The student then remembers the process that she must follow. Add the digits in the left hand ("ones") column, rename (carry) if necessary, and so on. Especially if the problem is long, she will probably have to record each part of her answer. The computer follows steps, too. These steps, the computer program, must be supplied in exact detail by a programmer. Once they are supplied, the computer follows the instructions, adding the numbers and recording the result (information). Finally, the student produces the result. She might write her answer on the chalkboard, tell it to the class, or use it to solve the original problem (for example, cut off the needed amount of material for a project). The computer might show the result on a CRT, print it on paper, or use it to solve a more complex problem.

There are differences, of course; and a review of these differences actually emphasizes the importance of the computer to people. For instance, the computer is not able to solve problems without being told how to do so. People can create solutions. At this time most computers also think "linearly." They follow only set sequences of steps. People can think in divergent ways. However, people tire of interminable, repetitious tasks, their accuracy often is less than perfect, and their memory can fail; computers excel in these very areas. Thus, computers can be a valuable tool for people to use in intellectual activities.

HARDWARE

Hardware is the physical equipment of a computer system. A school microcomputer system is often made up of the computer itself, which contains a keyboard; a cassette tape or disk drive; a TV-type monitor; and possibly a printer of some sort. What is the purpose of each of these pieces of equipment? Let's look and see.

For most microcomputers used in the elementary/middle school, the typewriter-type keyboard is the *input device.* The input device is a means of giving the computer instructions. This keyboard is usually much like a typical typewriter keyboard. However, on some inexpensive micros the keyboard is a flat pressure-sensitive typing face rather than the more typical board of keys.

As more and more devices are added to a basic computer system, the input may also include devices which allow a voice transmission of commands. With the addition of a device, many of the current crop of micros have a capability of responding to between twenty and one hundred words, if such words are properly pronounced. If input is desired from other computers or from some outside source, the computer may be attached to a telephone or telephone cable. Some micros have the capacity to use a reader which will interpret the dark marks on paper. Such devices are often used in correcting multiple-choice tests. The "readers" are known as optical scanners. In the past punched cards were often used as the input device.

The input device for a micro is similar in function to the microphone of a tape recorder. Its job is to be sure that the messages get to the computer itself.

The Hardware Components

Overview: The physical components of a computer system are called *hardware*. The external hardware of a microcomputer system consists of input units—devices which allow people to communicate with the computer—and output units—devices which allow the computer to communicate with us. The internal hardware consists of units that control the work the computer does. This illustration shows the typical input and output units (also called I/O devices) of a microcomputer system.

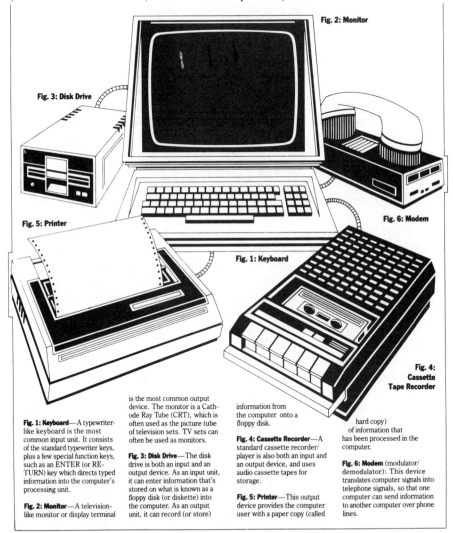

Fig. 2: Monitor

Fig. 3: Disk Drive

Fig. 6: Modem

Fig. 5: Printer

Fig. 1: Keyboard

Fig. 4: Cassette Tape Recorder

Fig. 1: Keyboard—A typewriter-like keyboard is the most common input unit. It consists of the standard typewriter keys, plus a few special function keys, such as an ENTER (or RE-TURN) key which directs typed information into the computer's processing unit.

Fig. 2: Monitor—A television-like monitor or display terminal is the most common output device. The monitor is a Cathode Ray Tube (CRT), which is often used as the picture tube of television sets. TV sets can often be used as monitors.

Fig. 3: Disk Drive—The disk drive is both an input and an output device. As an input unit, it can enter information that's stored on what is known as a floppy disk (or diskette) into the computer. As an output unit, it can record (or store) information from the computer onto a floppy disk.

Fig. 4: Cassette Recorder—A standard cassette recorder/player is also both an input and an output device, and uses audio cassette tapes for storage.

Fig. 5: Printer—This output device provides the computer user with a paper copy (called hard copy) of information that has been processed in the computer.

Fig. 6: Modem (modulator/demodulator): This device translates computer signals into telephone signals, so that one computer can send information to another computer over phone lines.

25

Let's take a simple use. A few minutes ago I wrote a letter using a micro. I used the typewriter keyboard on my micro as the *input.* Once I began to enter the data, there was a need for *storage.* My typing didn't go directly to the paper on which the letter was to be printed. The typing keys are connected to the memory in the computer itself, so that each letter I type in is converted to a code number and temporarily stored in the main portion of the computer. This portion is usually directly in back of the keyboard. However, on some micros the keyboard may be a separate unit, and the storage and operation of the computer may be housed in a box that may or may not be attached to a TV-type screen.

This temporary storage within the computer is known as random access memory, often called RAM. The letter I type into my computer would be lost if I just turned off the electricity. When I am finished with my letter, I indicate to the machine that I wish to save the material. The computer moves the letter from the temporary storage (RAM) to a disk that I have in the disk drive. Thus, a magnetic disk acts as more permanent storage. A cassette tape could also be used but would greatly slow down the operation. If I did not want to store my letter on a disk or tape, I could print the letter directly with a printer attached to my micro. On some occasions I will print the letter immediately upon completion. On still other occasions I will store the letter on a disk as a record for myself and print the letter to send.

What happens between the time I hit the keys and the time the letter is stored on a disk or printed out on paper? This is where the "main works" of the computer come in. The heart of the computer is called the *central processing unit,* which consists of memory and arithmetic/logic circuits. The latter look at the information being typed in and manipulate the symbols. It is helpful to think of a computer as fundamentally a symbol manipulator. It interprets symbols fed into it in terms of on and off switches: 0 = off, and 1 = on.

For example, if we consider about 128 symbol possibilities from the keyboard (there are actually more because of the use of special keys), we can think of the computer checking the information as it comes in through the keys. First, yes or no—upper or lower case; then coding of the letter. It continues until the message is clear and the coding for a particular letter is temporarily locked into place. Each letter requires a string of eight yes-no decisions. In terms of 0 and 1, a touch of a key could produce 00101010. Each eight-digit string is called a *byte,* while each of the digits is called a *bit.* The word *take* would have four bytes. *Take* would be T—84 in base ten, A—65 in base ten, K—75 in base ten, and E—69 in base ten. The computer would change each to binary code. This coding is stored in the computer or on a disk. It is the job of the arithmetic/logic unit to manipulate the symbols so that the letters I type in come out on the printer. (In a somewhat similar fashion to a tape recorder changing sound to magnetic markings and back to sound.) While I am typing, the letters I hit will appear on the screen on a TV set called a *monitor output*. It acts in the same way as a pair of earphones might function in my tape recording example. However, I am able to keep my writing on the screen.

Back to my letter. We have my letter stored temporarily in the computer and/or on a disk. Suppose I want to print it out. I turn on the attached printer and give the order to print the letter by indicating these instructions on the keyboard. The printer then gives me a copy of the letter. In this case the printer is an *output* device.

The big difference between today's microcomputer and the huge computers of the late 1960s is in the capacity to keep track of on-off commands. The old machines made use of tubes or transistors, and the new ones make use of silicon (sand) chips on which thousands of on-off switches are photographically printed. Thus, a little Apple is not much bigger than a typewriter, but it has twelve times the storage capacity of a 1966 machine that took up a good-sized room.

You may find the accompanying diagram helpful.

The majority of today's microcomputers make use of a TV-type screen as the preliminary input. Many years ago the first input was on cards or by a typewriter device putting the input on paper.

The *output* is through the TV-type monitor or through *hard copy* with a printer. Printers come in many sizes, shapes, and prices. The typical home or small school printer will usually be the type called *dot matrix*. This is the sort that gives you the typical "computer look." The letters or pictures are formed by a head composed of small cylinders that strike the ribbon. The quality of the print greatly depends upon the printer. You can get rather good quality print for between $300 and $500. There is a great deal of difference in speed between one dot matrix printer and another. However, your speed in printing is usually much faster than that of the fastest typist.

In addition to reasonably low cost, the dot matrix printer has the advantage of being able to print anything you can get on the monitor screen. Thus, if you make a drawing using graphics, you can print it.

One kind of type used by many businesses and schools for the word processing of letters is that of the *daisy wheel*. The daisy wheel printer can give type that is of equal or better quality than that of an electric typewriter. It is called a daisy wheel because the device that strikes the ribbon is a cluster of typewriter-type keys that are set in a circular manner and look like a daisy. The daisy wheel printer is priced from a low of about $600 to well over $2,000.

Selection of hardware is a difficult task. We found out something about this in Chapter 1. Every few months the prices of computers change (usually getting less expensive). However, since it is necessary to "cope" with computers at the present time, it probably is not wise to wait too long before getting involved.

Overview: The "real" computer in any microcomputer system is actually no bigger than a dime. (*Fig. 1*). It consists of thousands of transistors (electronic on/off switches) which, through the miracle of microphotography, have been squeezed onto a slice or "chip" of silicon. This chip, which is encased in a rectangle of plastic, is called a microprocessor.

Although there are other chips within a microcomputer, the microprocessor has features that set it apart from all the others. These features include a Control Unit, which handles or controls the operation of all of the computer's parts, and an Arithmetic/Logic Unit, where arithmetic and logical operations are performed. As such, the microprocessor is the Central Processing Unit (CPU) of a computer (*Fig. 2, A*).

The other chips within a microcomputer perform other specific functions. One group provides a space, called memory, where information that is to be used by the computer is stored. These memory chips (*Fig. 2, B*) are known as Random Access Memory (RAM).

Another group of memory chips provides a place where certain information is stored permanently. This information is built into the computer by the manufacturer and includes such things as instructions that trans-

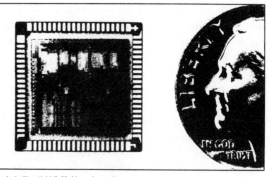

Fig. 1: *A silicon "chip": No bigger than a dime*

late the computer language BASIC into the only language a computer can understand, called machine language. These chips (*Fig. 2, C*) are known as Read Only Memory (ROM).

All of these chips plug into a plastic board,

called a mother board (*Fig. 2, D*), which provides an interconnecting network for them.

There are also additional Input/Output ports (*Fig. 2, E*) which electronically connect computer peripherals (or accessories) to the CPU.

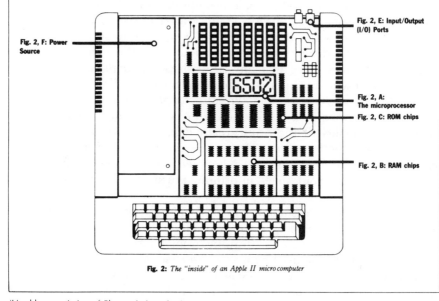

Fig. 2, F: Power Source

Fig. 2, E: Input/Output (I/O) Ports

Fig. 2, A: The microprocessor

Fig. 2, C: ROM chips

Fig. 2, B: RAM chips

Fig. 2: *The "inside" of an Apple II micro computer*

(Used by permission of *Electronic Learning.*)

Several articles concerned with the selection of hardware are mentioned in the topical appendix. While the hardware they mention will in many cases be outdated, the criteria for selection will still be valid.

Here are a few things to keep in mind when you buy hardware:

1. *Be sure you know what you want the computer to be able to do.* It doesn't make any difference if the computer has all kinds of features at a low price—if these are not the features you need. A computer that allows programming in

Overview: Software refers to step-by-step instructions that tell a computer what to do and how to do it. Those step-by-step instructions are called a *program*.

Today there are hundreds of different kinds of commercially available programs, called applications software. Programs that drill students on basic number facts, help balance a checkbook, or turn the computer into a word processing (or text editing) terminal are three examples of applications software.

These programs are stored outside the computer in one of two basic ways: on an ordinary audio cassette tape, or on what is known as a floppy disk. The illustrations on this page provide a detailed look at a floppy disk.

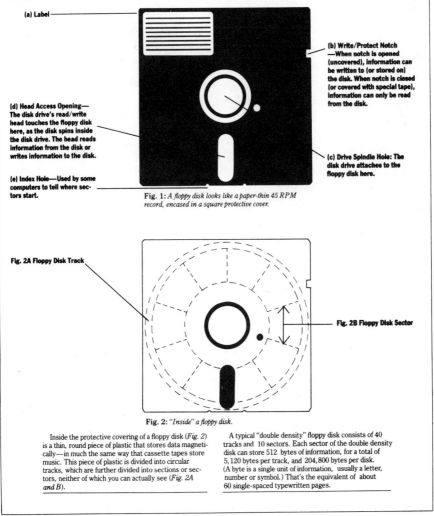

(a) Label

(b) Write/Protect Notch
—When notch is opened (uncovered), information can be written to (or stored on) the disk. When notch is closed (or covered with special tape), information can only be read from the disk.

(d) Head Access Opening—The disk drive's read/write head touches the floppy disk here, as the disk spins inside the disk drive. The head reads information from the disk or writes information to the disk.

(c) Drive Spindle Hole: The disk drive attaches to the floppy disk here.

(e) Index Hole—Used by some computers to tell where sectors start.

Fig. 1: *A floppy disk looks like a paper-thin 45 RPM record, encased in a square protective cover.*

Fig. 2A Floppy Disk Track

Fig. 2B Floppy Disk Sector

Fig. 2: *"Inside" a floppy disk.*

Inside the protective covering of a floppy disk (*Fig. 2*) is a thin, round piece of plastic that stores data magnetically—in much the same way that cassette tapes store music. This piece of plastic is divided into circular tracks, which are further divided into sections or sectors, neither of which you can actually see (*Fig. 2A and B*).

A typical "double density" floppy disk consists of 40 tracks and 10 sectors. Each sector of the double density disk can store 512 bytes of information, for a total of 5,120 bytes per track, and 204,800 bytes per disk. (A byte is a single unit of information, usually a letter, number or symbol.) That's the equivalent of about 60 single-spaced typewritten pages.

BASIC and LOGO, has a variety of educational software available, and has a capacity for expansion may cost more than one with more memory but less versatility.

2. Find out what packaged programs are available. A good computer may not be of great use to your room if it won't run the programs you want.

3. Very few computers are compatible with other computers. Thus, if you get a Radio Shack computer, you will not be able to run Apple or Texas Instruments programs unless you buy special versions of the programs you want.

The VIC, an inexpensive computer with a keyboard. (Courtesy of Commodore.)

4. Get advice from several sources. Check with computer people on the quality of the machine. Find out from educators the quality and quantity of programs available for the machine. Find out what computers friends and nearby schools are using.

We know of one school district that bought a large number of inexpensive, but very good, computers, but did not have in mind how to use them. Since there were few packaged programs available, it took a long time to get started. Often the best computer for an elementary or middle school may cost more than a computer for secondary school computer science courses; the elementary/middle school needs it for a variety of functions, while the computer science course needs it only for programming.

HISTORY

As mentioned above, processing data is neither unfamiliar nor new. Humans, blessed with intelligence and the ability to manipulate symbols—but not with unlimited storage capacity—quite early developed memory aids, recording information on walls, stones, and trees. The growth of agriculture and trading necessitated the use of measurement and uniform written records, such as knotted cords, clay tablets, papyrus, and finally paper. The increased need for counting led to the development of the abacus, counting boards, and more advanced symbol systems like Hindu-Arabic numerals and logarithms. The latter was invented by Napier in 1614. He also developed a primitive form of slide rule called Napier's bones, based on the ideas underlying logarithms. This was a mechanical arrangement of strips of bones on which numbers were printed. When brought into combination, they would perform multiplication. The slide rule (perhaps the first analog computer) was invented by William Oughtred (1575–1660).

Many dreamed of machines to replace the human effort that went into these early calculating systems. Leonardo da Vinci made drawings of such machines but never attempted a working model. The first working machine was constructed by Blaise Pascal, who in 1642 at nineteen years of age invented a device to add long columns of numbers at his father's tax office. His machine was gear driven, with rows of wheels containing teeth numbered 0 to 9. It was a simple device, similar to a supermarket "counter" or the odometer of a car. However, it embodied two principles utilized by later workers in the field: that renaming or "carries" could be done automatically, and that multiplication could be performed through repeated addition. Few of Pascal's machines were sold, since the employers could hire accountants to do the computation for little pay. There was also (as there is today) resistance to the machines from the workers, who feared that their jobs would be stolen. The modern computer language Pascal is named after this mathematician.

Gottfried Wilhelm von Leibnitz improved Pascal's device so that it could multiply, divide, and calculate numerical roots. In 1820 Charles

Pascal's Adding Machine. (Smithsonian Institution Photo No. 53100.)

Thomas constructed the first successful calculating machine, an improvement on that of Leibnitz. Charles Babbage, in the early part of the nineteenth century, worked on two machines—the difference engine and the analytical engine—that closely parallel the design of modern computers. The latter contained four parts: a storage unit, a mill for performing computations, a system of gears for transferring data between these two systems, and a separate component for getting data into and out of the device.

Ada Lovelace, daughter of the poet Byron, developed mathematical ideas of computer programming for the Babbage engines. She is viewed as the first computer programmer; a modern computer language is called

Babbage's Difference Engine. (Smithsonian Institution Photo No. 53190.)

Ada in her honor. She was also the first to argue that computers could not be creative—they do only what we know how to order them to do. The machines were never completed, even though the designs were workable.

Babbage died a sad and disappointed man. He was ahead of his time—the technology was not up to producing the gears, and there was no demand yet for the product. Burroughs successfully marketed a machine to assist with bookkeeping in 1891. The Monroe calculator was introduced in 1911, the first keyboard rotary machine to be successful. The first machine to become automated and to use data processing techniques was the weaving loom. Joseph Marie Jacquard developed an automated loom that used punched cards to produce intricate patterns in cloth.

The first use of punched cards for processing data was in the com-

Jacquard's Loom. (Smithsonian Institution Photo No. 45599.)

piling of statistics for the 1890 census. It was feared that if the pace of the 1880 census—involving repeated hand sorting and counting—was not improved upon, the 1890 census would not have been completed in a decade. The Census Office held a competition to select a more efficient system. Herman Hollerith, a statistician from Buffalo, New York, won with a mechanical system for recording, computing, and tabulating census data. Data was recorded by punching holes in cards, which were then "read" by a tabulating machine which brought down telescoping pins on the card. Hollerith started his own company, later to become IBM. Through the years improvements were made on punched card systems, but today they are gradually being replaced by electronic storage, which we will now explore briefly.

In 1937 Howard Aiken invented the Mark I computer, which consisted of seventy-eight adding machines and desk calculators wired together and controlled by a roll of punched tape. It had 800 km (497.1 miles) of wires connecting the relays and switches. Mechanical registers were used to store numbers. John Mauchly and Prosper Eckert created the first electronic computer during World War II. ENIAC (Electronic Numerical Integrator and Calculator) used vacuum tubes instead of me-

(Courtesy of Intel Corporate (CA).)

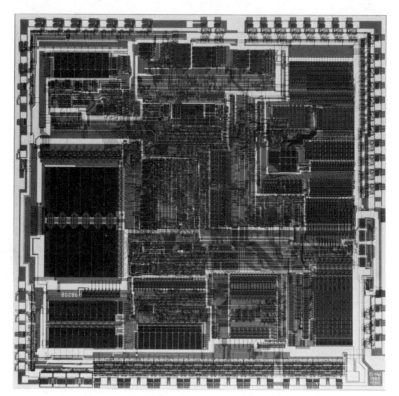

chanical relays and was controlled by wires. This represented the first of the *first-generation* computers.

This computer still had to be programmed externally. In 1945, John Von Neuman proposed the internally programmed computer, EDVAC (Electronic Discrete Variable Automatic Computer). This meant that the computer could be programmed by a set of cards before it started processing data, and therefore it required no human direction. Mauchy and Eckert later built the first commercial computer, UNIVAC (Universal Automatic Computer).

Second-generation computers, first appearing in 1959, replaced the bulky, hot, energy-greedy vacuum tubes with transistors, allowing for smaller, faster, and more powerful computer systems. This solid-state technology concentrated on modular (block-building) concepts, permitting systems to be expanded without being replaced.

The further miniaturization of electronic circuits, integrated circuits, brought on *third-generation* computers. These were smaller and more powerful, with operating speeds measured in billionths of a second. Simultaneously, the development of optical scanners, larger and faster storage systems, and magnetic ink readers expanded the capabilities of the computer system. More computer languages were developed.

The 1970s saw the introduction of the fourth generation of computers. Large-scale integrated circuits (LSIC) permitted even faster, smaller, more powerful computers. Microprocessors, entire computers on one integrated circuit chip, are so small that thousands can fit in a teaspoon. Each contains minute switches etched into a tiny piece of silicon by a photoelectric process. The fantastic growth of computer technology and production is summarized by Christopher Evans:

(Courtesy of International Business Machines Corporation.)

ENIAC Computer. (Smithsonian Institution Photo No. 53192.)

Suppose for a moment that the automobile industry had developed at the same rate as computers and over the same period: how much cheaper and more efficient would the current models be? . . . Today you would be able to buy a Rolls Royce for $2.75, it would do three million miles to the gallon, and it would deliver enough power to drive the Queen Elizabeth II. And if you were interested in miniaturization, you could place half a dozen of them on a pinhead. (1979, p. 76)

Many of today's microcomputers, then, have as much capability as the huge mainframe computers of twenty years ago; so teachers do not have to feel that the machines are not powerful. However, each computer should be evaluated separately. Mainframes of today are, of course, much more powerful than microcomputers. Also, some very small and inexpensive microcomputers may not be capable of doing the jobs you want done (for example, they may be limited to short programs in only one language).

This area offers an excellent opportunity to integrate computer literacy, language arts, science, and social studies as children research and report on topics that interest them. The history of computing can be dramatized through student presentations—from book reports to models of Napier's bones.

SOFTWARE

Software is the instruction given to the computer that makes it perform. As we mentioned before, an old computer saying is *"Garbage in—Garbage*

UNIVAC I Computer. (Smithsonian Institution Photo No. 72-2616.)

out"—the software is the key to computing. You can either develop your own software—if you have the time, interest, and expertise—or you can buy packaged software and pay to have it done for you. For most micro-computer users the answer is somewhere in between. They will buy some and develop some.

Very few persons would want to program their own word processing program. But many might program their own record-keeping system. Chapter 6 provides a rather thorough guide for selecting software.

Self-Test

1. The most expensive computer is almost always a better buy.

2. Computers for the elementary school usually cost less than those needed for secondary school computer science courses.

3. You can tell the power of a computer by looking at its size.

4. A speech synthesizer can only be an output device.

5. For the best analysis of available computers, we need to ask the computer science teacher.

6. A daisy wheel printer, in general, produces a higher quality of print than a dot matrix.

7. To print graphics material, I would use a daisy wheel printer.

8. Programming is the key to good computer usage.

9. A single device cannot be both an input and an output device.

10. We use ROM memory to store material that we develop.

Think About

1. List the steps you would take if you were given $3,000 and required to spend the money buying yourself a computer and computer materials.
2. Study four current microcomputers. Make a list of advantages and disadvantages.
3. Discuss: Is it important for teachers to have computers of the type the school is using?
4. How important is getting specific hardware?
5. When should you wait for improvements in hardware? When should you go ahead and purchase?
6. Study a particular bit of hardware you do not know much about. For example, there are a number of different types of speech synthesizers.
7. Some people compare a computer to a stereo system to explain the workings of the various parts. What other devices could you use to explain the workings of a computer?

Suggested References

(Also check the magazines listed in the appendix.)

Benson, Terry. Printer buyer's guide. *Interface Age*, April 1983, pp. 73–84.
Benson discusses a number of printers. Study his suggestions and compare the printers with those that are current.

Franz, Fredrick. Inside microcomputers. *Today's Education*, April/May 1982, pp. 17–19.
Franz gives a good overview of microcomputers and how they work. Study it carefully.

Hawkins, William J. New personal computers. *Popular Science*, 219(5), November 1981, 93–97.
Compare the current crop of computers with those analyzed by Hawkins.

Immel, Richard A. When to buy at discount. *Popular Computing*, August 1983, pp. 48–54.
What are Immel's suggestions about buying at discount. When should you?

Meilach, J. Ten Steps to take before you buy a computer. *Interface Age*, June 1982, pp. 66–69.
What ten steps does Meilach suggest you follow before buying a computer? Do you agree?

Bibliography

EVANS, CHRISTOPHER. *The micro millennium.* New York: Viking Press, 1979.

MAYER, RICHARD E. Contributions of cognitive science and related research on learning to the design of computer literacy curricula. Report No. 81-1. Series in learning and cognition. Santa Barbara, Calif.: University of California, Department of Psychology, 1980. (ERIC Document Reproduction Service No. ED 207 551)

Computers and Society

WHAT CAN A COMPUTER DO? (AWARENESS LEVEL)

Microprocessors are appearing everywhere, from automobiles to ovens. They help people weld metal, saw wood, design products, and compose music. As with computer history, educators should be familiar with both the uses of the computer and the ramifications of these uses for society. Educators must strive to (a) integrate this knowledge into the existing curriculum, for example, in a social studies unit; (b) plan special lessons on these topics where that is appropriate; (c) add depth and insight to any work they do with computers in the classroom; and (d) be prepared to answer queries and lead discussions about this important and crucial issue.

As we have seen, the first computers were used for specific purposes. They were designed to solve special problems, and their high cost made them unavailable to most people and organizations. With the development of increasingly lower-cost, general-purpose computers, almost every business (and many individuals) started to use computer technology to help solve their varied problems. There is presently a great diversity of applications, most of which fit into one or more of the following categories.

Data summarization, or data reduction, is the condensation of large amounts of detailed data, or raw information, into a more useful form. It usually involves tabulating the number of items within each of several categories, or the totals of amounts within categories.

Computation is the application of mathematical or statistical formulas to data. In business this might involve payrolls, sales predictions, or tax preparations. Researchers often use statistical "packages" to analyze the data they collect.

File maintenance has been a common computer application and is becoming more prevalent in recent years. The computer is used to store, maintain, and retrieve information. Serving as a large, automated system of file cabinets, the computer can change, add, and delete information. It can also produce reports, sorting and retrieving according to a prescribed rule. It might place files into order, such as alphabetical order. These jobs are called information retrieval and data arrangement.

Data management systems are programs which aid in the manipulation of computer files and the extraction of data from the files for the preparation of reports. Users need only specify the data files to be used, and the programs will produce detailed programs which can be used to access the data files. Thus, those with little programming experience can virtually write programs which manipulate data files. So as not to waste storage space, data base management systems have been created which provide for the storage, maintenance, and retrieval of data from a single, combined collection of files known as a data base. A school has a noncomputerized "data base" if it keeps all the records of all its students in one location, such as in a set of file cabinets. Anyone who wants to add information to these records, or copy information from them, uses this single set of records.

Operations control involves the monitoring and control of several phases of production in manufacturing.

Simulations are representations of physical conditions or situations according to a mathematical model. Like a model airplane, they have characteristics in common with the real object or situation. Even though they are not the real object, models of airplane wings, in the simulated flight of an air tunnel, can tell us much about how a real airplane's wings would perform. Thus, in simulations a "copy" of reality is obtained to learn more about a situation that might be impractical, expensive, or dangerous to experience directly. For example: An executive might want to predict the effects on business of hiring ten new salespersons; a city planner wishing to construct a new building might want to know whether this would result in overcrowding; or a scientist with a particular experiment in mind might need to learn the results of mixing a specific combination of chemicals. Computer simulations can help them answer their questions.

Word processing, discussed more fully in other sections, is an invaluable aid to business. In *language translation* the computer converts material written in one language into another.

How would these applications help a person in business? Computers increase a business's profit margin through efficient solution of inventory, ordering, accounting, billing, taxation, and payroll problems. Even microcomputers can maintain files on business sales. They have the additional capability of performing graphic and statistical analyses of production, buying, and selling trends to assist in wise decision making. They can help analyze personnel or material requirements for jobs. Products can be designed with the aid of a computer, tested with computer simulations, modeled, and then evaluated for effectiveness or for their ability to "sell." Computers play a major role in financial transactions of all types. EFT, Elecronic Funds Transfer, is a computerized system of transferring credit—rather than money—between banks. Many believe we may well become a completely cashless society. Computers also read coded lines on products—ABC or Alphanumeric Bar Code—such as those in a supermarket, which allow automatic tabulation of inventory, prices, sales, and tax.

The transportation industry relies heavily on computers. They are used to plot paths for shipping; plan efficient use of personnel, time, and materials; control railroad trains and yards; and control air traffic, train pilots, and design and construct safe aircraft.

Health organizations use computer systems extensively. On the more mundane level, computers assist with such tasks as room and bed assignments. However, they are increasingly being used to determine kinds and amounts of medicine, to conduct laboratory tests, and to plan meals nutritionally designed for specific patient needs. New medical techniques are tested via simulations. Computers monitor the health of patients through the use of analog-to-digital conversion devices that signal staff immediately when sudden changes occur which are out of the range of normal bodily functions. The advent of "expert" computer systems which can make decisions in ways similar to humans has led to the utilization of computers for diagnosis. Provided with symptoms, the computer will output possible causes and cures. The system is actually a simulation of the mental processes of a physician analyzing a difficult case. It generates and tests hypotheses. It informs the doctor what data it is disregarding and what it is considering. It questions the doctor as to other observations and laboratory tests. Unlike the human clinician, however, it has the advantage of being available twenty-four hours a day, being current, and having an excellent memory. The incredible speed with which computers can search huge banks of files makes them admirably suited to matching donors to users of blood or organs.

As discussed above, government was one of the first users of computers. It is still the largest user. Like the Census Bureau, the Internal Revenue Service collects and must process large amounts of data from individuals and businesses. The Bureau of the Budget depends on computers to predict how much money various agencies will need and how much will be available. Virtually all governmental record keeping is done with computers. Networks provide information for informed decision making. The court system is beginning to manage information and time with the aid of the computer, and national records are being kept concerning crime.

The Postal Service is a major user of computer technology. Letters and parcels are sorted, addresses read, and mail moved with the help of machines. Computers help schedule transportation, regulate the working environment, inspect mail, and even keep track of how many computers are being used. Probably in the very near future, the Electronic Mail and Message will to a great extent replace paper mail. Messages will be transported almost instantly. They will be read, replied to, sent to other parties, discarded, and filed with a flick of a computer key. Taking even greater advantage of computer technology, they will be searched, scanned, and altered *automatically* with little or no intervention by the user. For example, a computer might receive a message of cancellation regarding a dinner party and automatically issue an invitation to another guest.

Mail ordering will be drastically different. Specifications for a consumer item might be typed in, whereupon the computer would search all available sources for the best match. With your approval, the item would be automatically ordered and your account charged. Or you—or even your computer—might request more information about certain items. Bills would be checked, paid, and recorded, automatically. Difficult to believe? On a limited basis, every one of these services is already being performed by computers (Nelson, 1981). After discussing illustrations such as these, a class might brainstorm on computer applications for our daily lives. Children might then be challenged to design their own "computer services," describing how they would work. Projects of this nature could first be researched and then written up as compositions. Older students might wish to write their own computer program to accomplish such a task. For example, they might create a simple electronic mail program (for a model, see Muller and Kovacs, 1983).

At state, city, and local levels, computers are used to solve problems of transportation flow, housing, management of services, environmental design, and so on. Libraries use computers to manage and control large data networks of holdings, book circulation, statistical studies, fee calculations, and general data searches. Children could be led to discuss what information they sometimes seek out. Do any of the sources of this information utilize computers? Could they? How?

Computers are, of course, a "natural" in science. Yet the variety of applications is impressive. They have been used to uncover sites and facts in archaeological studies. Volcanic activity is monitored by scanning devices that send data to computers for analysis. Computers analyze soil samples and movements of the earth to locate probable oil deposits. They are used to study the communication of porpoises. They are used to determine the proportion of pollutants present in water or air. Simulations of waterways have been constructed to examine their effects. Computers are responsible in part for the more accurate weather predictions we now enjoy. They analyze soil, rainfall, and other factors to maximize agricultural output. In the social sciences computer simulations have been developed in the areas of sociology, psychology, anthropology, economics, and history. Although these models cannot predict the behavior of individuals, they provide insights into various trends affecting group behavior. A discussion of the problems and limitations of such simulations can be found in Kaufman (1976). A science fiction trilogy, *The Foundation Trilogy,* by Isaac Asimov, presents an interesting futuristic look at such applications.

Not to be constrained by "typical" applications, computers have entered the world of the arts. They have helped artists draw, create cartoons, produce graphic images as well as television commercials and movies, design sculptures, compose traditional and computer-generated musical compositions, and construct multimedia pieces (see Chapter 15).

Computer Careers

It has been estimated that by 1985, 75 percent of all occupations will involve computer use in some way. Job security and computer literacy are becoming increasingly linked. Of course, many of the people who use computers are not technicians. Most computer careers require that the employee solve problems with the assistance of the computer. As outlined above, almost every area of human activity utilizes computer capabilities in some way. Here we will discuss only career opportunities which are directly related to the computer industry. There are five basic categories of computer and data processing employees.

Personnel in computer operations prepare and input data, monitor computer operation, and deliver output for the users. They include computer terminal operators, who need only minimal technical knowledge; operations supervisors, responsible for keeping the data processing system running efficiently; and computer systems operators, responsible for the technical functioning of the CPU.

Computer technicians service and repair hardware.

Computer programmers must have formal educational training and technical expertise. They develop, "debug," test, implement, and maintain computer programs that meet the needs of users. They are usually competent in several computer languages.

Computer systems analysts study computer systems and the needs of an organization to determine what data processing techniques and hardware are necessary to complete the task at hand.

Computer specialists have highly technical backgrounds in hardware, software, communication, or systems engineering.

Other sources provide more extensive listings of computer careers (for example, Quick scan of computer careers, 1982; Kennedy and Winkler, 1982; Mandell, 1982).

Undoubtedly, computers will eliminate jobs, especially those that are time consuming, tedious, and laborious. There is disagreement as to whether an equal number of service- or knowledge-oriented jobs will be created. Leisure time may, by necessity, increase. Educators need to prepare children for both the careers and the leisure time; computer literacy is essential for each of these areas.

ADVANTAGES AND DISADVANTAGES/LIMITATIONS OF COMPUTERS

This area provides an excellent springboard for discussions involving students' perspectives on capabilities: their own and those of computers.

Advantages

1. Speed: Computers can perform millions of calculations per second. Large amounts of data can be searched incredibly quickly.
2. Reliability: Computers work for unlimited lengths of time with little human supervision. With children, then, they can be extremely "patient."
3. Accuracy: Computers do this work accurately; with correct data and programs, the result is virtually free of error.
4. Memory: Computers can store large amounts of information and can retrieve it quickly.
5. Generality: Computers can, at least theoretically, solve any problem if it can be expressed in a logical form.
6. Arithmetic and logic: Computers can solve complex problems involving arithmetic and logic—determining what is true and what is false.
7. Computers can calculate an optimum strategy for decision making if sufficient information is provided.

Disadvantages/Limitations

1. Limited intelligence or creativity: The computers of today are not capable of solving problems requiring creative intelligence without specific instructions from people. They are not yet able to recognize patterns as people do.
2. Complexity: Since people have to design programs for computers, much effort goes into solving new problems. If a program is not reused, it is usually not cost-efficient.
3. Cost: Computers are getting less expensive, but they are not yet available to everyone. This creates another problem, which is that the gap between "haves" and "have-nots" may widen in a computerized society.
4. Less capable in decision making involving judgment: Computers cannot yet determine goals and values.
5. Improvise poorly: Today's computers cannot work well with incomplete information or instructions or adapt well to new situations.

Reviewing the list of limitations, you might make two observations. One concerns the frequent use of the qualifying word *yet*. The other is that the things computers cannot yet do well are things that people do well—they are intelligent behaviors. Some would argue that computers will never be creative or truly intelligent. However, there are those who disagree and are working to build such intelligence into computers. While it is good practice to discuss the limitations of present-day computers with students, it also behooves educators to know that these limitations may *not* be permanent. The next section discusses artificial intelligence, the study of the "smart machine."

Before leaving this section, there are two more points to be made. First, in an era in which several computers are available for less than $100, many argue that cost cannot be considered a limitation. However, it should remain on the list until full computing facilities—hardware, software, data, and so forth—are equally available to all students. This includes those from rich suburbs, from poor inner cities, and those living in poverty both here and in other countries. Such equity will not be achieved in the foreseeable future.

Second, wise teachers might consider using the computer characteristics listed above in planning their guidance of children. For instance, children often overvalue the fast, "correct-the-first-time" answer. The teacher might lead them to see that when programming computers—giving them instructions on what to do—almost no one "gets it right" the first time. Good computer programmers are usually good "debuggers"; they examine their work carefully to locate and fix errors. Similarly, with children who tend to blurt out answers, the teacher might discuss or demonstrate how a logical sequence of steps must be performed by the computer before it can come up with an answer. In the same way, students may benefit in many situations from using such a sequence. Directly working on a computer might benefit a passive child; the computer will wait forever, doing nothing until the child takes the initiative.

ARTIFICIAL INTELLIGENCE

Artificial intelligence is the study and development of computer systems which can perform intelligent tasks; in other words, computer simulations of human intellectual activities. This makes computers appear to think. This type of research may help us learn more about the "thinking" processes of both machines and people.

Is it absurd to think that computers can think? It has been said that they cannot write novels like Hemingway or music like Bach. However, on that basis most of us would not be judged capable of thought either! Probably, the fear that machines will surpass our capabilities keeps people from evaluating this issue clearly.

Most of the activities in which the computer has appeared to be intelligent have been gamelike. For example, quite powerful programs have been written for chess, checkers, and bridge. Computers do well on these games because they can examine millions of possibilities in seconds.

A game of chess has about as many possible opening moves as there are atoms in the universe. A way of selecting the best among these possibilities is devised by a programmer. Some believe that the intelligence of the computer is only a reflection of the intelligence of the programmer; others, like Marvin Minsky and Christopher Evans, tend to believe that truly intelligent machines can be developed—we have just not gotten that far yet. It is not certain which opinion is correct; however, it *is* true that Dr. Arthur Samuel of IBM has written programs that have beaten state champions in chess matches.

You are already familiar with several "intelligent" machines. Your thermostat makes decisions—when the temperature drops below a certain point, it senses this and turns on the heat. When a higher temperature is reached, it turns it off again. Not impressed with the intellectual brilliance of the device? You shouldn't be; any one-celled organism is smarter. However, in the future, thermostats will be a bit more intelligent. With built-in microprocessors, they will control heat flow differently for different rooms at different times of day. They might sense the presence of people in rooms and direct infrared lights to warm them, allowing the air in the house to remain cool—thereby saving money and energy resources—while keeping the people comfortably warm. Other examples of computerized *process control* in our world include sensing devices that tell a computer about the relative traffic flow on city streets, allowing it to make the lights stay green longer on the streets that are busier at that time; and steel mill machinery that measures the temperature and thickness of the metal, adjusting the heat and the pressure to produce a plate of precise thickness.

Evans (1979) pointed out that while computers are not yet as intelligent as humans, they are (on a rating scale that is explained in detail in *The Micro Millennium*) more intelligent than a tapeworm. And while humans reached their state of intelligence over several hundred million years, the computer has had only a quarter of a century of development. Evans goes on to debate common objections to the notion that a computer can think; for example, the Shock/Horror Objection (not logical—actually just a feeling), the Personal Consciousness Objection (one can never even prove the consciousness of another human), the Ah, But It Can't Do That Objection (a never-ending objection, which is forced to continually create new challenges as computers consistently master those set before), and Lady Lovelace's Objection that a computer can do only what it has been programmed to do. In answer to this last objection, Evans argues that humans are "set up" through our genetic history and through learning, just as computers are set up through programming. He draws an analogy between the reflexes and involuntary motor behaviors of humankind and the built-in programming of the computer, and between the individual learning of people and the destructible software of computers. Second, he reports that computers have accomplished tasks, have "thought creatively," in areas beyond human achievement. For example, a computer surpassed man in solving the famous "four-color problem," proving that on any two-dimensional map you would need only four colors to ensure that no two territories of the same color adjoin each other. Another constructed new proofs in Euclidean geometry.

As a final argument, Evans discusses what is often accepted as the best test of computer intelligence presently devised—the Turing test, after its inventor, brilliant scientist Alan Turing. Here a person is screened off from a computer and a normal thinking human being while establishing communication with each through a terminal. This person is to carry out conversations with each in an attempt to determine which is which. If the person cannot do this, the computer passes the test as an intelligent machine. While no computer has yet passed this test absolutely, Evans notes that on several occasions this has almost occurred. Once, at MIT, two scientists were talking via the network, when one left without telling the other—who carried on a conversation with the computer, unaware that it was not still his friend. Evans concludes that the difference between computers and people is one of degree, not of kind. As you might imagine, other people's opinions differ. Religious thinkers maintain that intelligence is not all there is to humanity or to the making of wise decisions. Others have argued that it is the responsibility of humans to limit the power of any tool.

Is this branch of computer science helpful at all in working with children? Besides its importance as content for the study of computer literacy, the main subject of this chapter, computer simulations of game playing have been created by children. These start off as fairly "dumb" programs, and the children describe why the programs are dumb ("It could have beat me on the last move and it didn't") and how they could improve them (Papert and Solomon, 1970). For instance, they might alter the program so that it responds correctly to an opportunity to win on the last move, then extend this so that it can "force" a win from the second last move. Through a repetition of this process, they come to a high level of understanding of their *own* thinking, while they gain experience in programming, problem solving, and artificial intelligence. With good teaching, such experiences can be invaluable.

A machine that closely simulates human behavior is called a *robot*. There are three categories of machines: simple machines (extensions of human muscle power), programmable machines (which can do a number of tasks, like Jacquard's loom), and robots. A robot usually consists of a programmed general-purpose computer with memory, sensing devices such as photoelectric cells, and effector equipment such as mechanical arms. Thus, its actions are determined not only by programming but also by the information it gets from the world which is relevant to the task it is performing; in effect, robots make decisions (Evans, 1979). The first robots were designed to handle radioactive materials for atomic bombs. Later, self-propelled robots whose sole purpose was to recharge themselves were developed. Robots that respond to human commands and solve simple problems have been constructed. Presently, however, it is in industry that the most work on robots has been done. Television gives them vision. Touch sensors respond to pressure and points of contact. Distance is sensed through laser beams, sound through microphones. Complex chemical-analysis sensors can even provide a sense of smell. Robots have helped explore the moon, repair technical equipment, and assemble machines. They are also being developed as toys.

Does robotics have any educational implications? Educators should be aware that this type of research is valuable in producing prosthetic devices for handicapped children. Again, besides being fascinating content for study and discussions, some of the robot toys provide a superb introduction to simple programming for young children. For example, the toy Big Trak is programmable and can be attached to a personal computer with a wireless remote control to enhance its educational value (see Ciarcia, 1981). While still somewhat expensive, simple robots which can be controlled by programs written by students on a microcomputer are available.

You might also try "playing robot" in your class to illustrate some of their characteristics. One student plays the robot, one the programmer. The programmer directs the robot to do some task, say, getting paper for a class project from the cupboard. The instructions must be precise, or the robot should not follow them. For example, "Go to the cupboard" is not in the robot's repertoire; it must be told exactly how many steps to take in what direction. Similarly, even the directions "Open a space between your fingers and thumb" is not sufficient, since right or left is not specified. You can equip your classroom "robot" with sensing devices— "Look to see if anything is in front of you"—but you must remember to give it detailed instructions on what to do in *each* case; for example, "If there is nothing there, take one step forward; if there is, turn right 90 degrees," and so on.

How much can robots ever do? Should robots' programs have built-in safeguards so that they can't hurt people? These questions have poten-

(Courtesy of RB Robot Corporation, Golden, Colorado.)

tial for excellent classroom discussions, library research, reporting, and reading. See Isaac Asimov's *I, Robot* for a fictional, but thoughtful, development of "the three laws of robotics"—laws that he believes must be built into every robot. Have your students create their own set of "laws" that they believe all robots should obey, along with explanations and possibly fictional accounts of how their robots would operate. Compare them to Asimov's. There are many other readings about robots that might excite your students' imaginations. Some are listed at the end of this chapter. Remember that good science fiction, like good fiction of any kind, is a worthwhile area for children to explore. It can help them see the challenge of today's technology and inspire them to dream about tomorrow.

MISUSES OF THE COMPUTER

Like most human tools, computers can be misused. Because computers are complex, they are vulnerable to many types of abuse. Unfortunately, computer crimes also pay well; where the average noncomputer embezzlement involves about $100,000, those involving computers average over $1,000,000. On the other hand, if "computerized money" replaces cash, direct theft of money may decline.

One of the most frequently occurring types of abuse involves theft of computer time. For example, one fifteen-year-old Californian illegally used over 200 hours of the University of California's computer time (worth over $24,000), using under $100 worth of equipment and a telephone.

Programs and data are, of course, valuable assets in an information society. Another common theft is the piracy of software or data such as lists of customers. The magnitude of the crime can be better visualized if it is remembered that some programs may cost hundreds of thousands of dollars to develop. Programs and data may also be altered; for instance, there are cases of students' changing other students' grades on transcripts. Credit ratings or voting results may be changed.

Computer crimes are difficult to uncover, partially owing to the nature of the crime—little or no physical evidence is created. Also, most computer criminals do not have a history of illegal activities; and laws are not always clear. Further, large companies do not want to publicize the ease with which their computers were vandalized.

Can these crimes be prevented? As with all crime, the most effective prevention involves moral education, along with the knowledge of computer/information ethics. That this is true is supported by the fact that many computer criminals believe they are just playing a challenging "game" when they tamper with passwords and access to others' systems. Also, researchers have found that organizations that demand high standards of business ethics have employees who tend not to commit computer fraud, presumably because they value the organization and protect its information. Beyond this, procedures such as frequent changes in passwords and regulation of computer documentation can be carried out with little expense. Hardware and software security can be tightened, and auditing increased. However, special "Tiger" teams have shown that even specially protected programs can be broken into in minutes by experts. Again, computer crimes, in the end, are human crimes, and necessitate human solutions.

The issue of piracy is not unique to the world of the computer. Yet the need to store huge volumes of information about people in computer data banks causes many people to fear that their privacy has been seriously threatened. While we should maintain vigilance concerning our right to privacy, at least one expert has concluded that it is the record-keeping practices of organizations, not their use or misuse of computers, that causes the problems that occur (Frates and Moldrup, 1980).

We are an information society, and that information must be safeguarded. Active roles must be assumed by individuals regarding the use of computers. Education must play an essential role in producing a literate, concerned population. Because computer crimes are *human* problems, discussions and debates are excellent vehicles for value clarification exercises, as well as lessons in an important aspect of computer literacy.

ATTITUDES TOWARD COMPUTERS

As discussed in Chapter 1, there are many widely held attitudes and beliefs about computers that, regardless of their accuracy, influence public opinion as to computer applications. One of these beliefs is that computers are incapable of error, in the sense that whatever a computer "says" is correct and not open to question or change. Another is the fear that the computer is stripping away our privacy. Many think of the computer as the ultimate intelligence or brain which can operate without people and which will surpass them in capability. People often feel the computer is strange and complex—too strange to be comprehensible. The most difficult attitude to deal with is fear—of depersonalization, of over-centralization, of being replaced, and of losing our place as the "rulers" of our world.

Most of these beliefs and attitudes stem from basic misunderstandings of the roles of humans and machines. Unfortunately, most people receive their information about computers from the mass media, which has tended to emphasize the sensational, although recently informative documentaries are being produced.

The public must receive accurate, and preferably firsthand, information about computers, so that the citizens of tomorrow will neither be intimidated nor misinformed about computers and their potential: for societal good, for misuse, and for personal growth and enrichment. Educators must ensure that this information is provided.

Self-Test *(True/False)*

1. Computers are reliable and fast.
2. Computers have no real intelligence.
3. Computers are actually more intelligent than people, but they're not creative or compassionate.
4. Computers can figure out the best way of doing some things, if given enough information.
5. Robots seem intelligent, but actually they cannot react to things in the environment.
6. Having a computer solve a single complex problem is not an efficient use of the computer.
7. Today's computers cannot improvise solutions.
8. People who "break the code" of a large computer and use this time without permission are actually not hurting anyone. They are just meeting a challenge.
9. Computers have committed serious crimes.
10. Computers can create art.
11. Computer simulations are used in business and science as well as in education.
12. Robots are just like mechanical people.
13. To solve ethical issues, we need only teach our students more about computer technology.
14. All computer scientists agree that computers cannot be more intelligent than people.
15. Computers can only solve problems that humans have already solved; they just do it faster and more accurately.
16. Computers cause crimes to be committed.
17. Most people who work with computers must learn to program them.
18. Electronic mail involves the delivery of letters and packages by robots.
19. To prepare children for careers with computers, we must educate them all in high-level mathematics.
20. Schools need to prepare children for changes in work and leisure—computers are altering the future of both.
21. Computers can think of more things simultaneously than a person can.
22. Computers are faster and more accurate than humans in many tasks.
23. Computers are used mainly to help people do math quickly.
24. Government is the largest user of computers.
25. Simulations are fun and can be educational, but they are of little use in the real world.
26. A computer can perform some diagnosis of a sick person's illness.
27. Computerized file maintenance is much like the file keeping that most schools do every day.
28. Data summarization is the arrangement and indexing of vast amounts of information.

Think About

1. A human can be thought of as a complex information processing machine. Explain this analogy, naming the input, storage, processing, and output "devices." Criticize the analogy.

2. What do you use that could be thought of as secondary storage, such as printed material?

3. Boys seem to use computers more than girls. While boys *should* be allowed to learn from computers, girls should not be forced to use them if they don't want to.

4. Why do you write some things down to remember them and memorize others? Which method of information storage and retrieval serves you better in which situations?

5. Do you think people could live knowing that other beings or machines were more intelligent than they were?

6. Do you agree that children should be taught that computers are like people, and people are like computers?

7. Should a computer in the classroom be personalized by calling it a name? Will this help students understand the way computers work, or will it block true understanding?

8. Do you think a law should be declared that guarantees equal access to computers for everyone?

9. Do you think women will have fewer opportunities for jobs in the future if they don't become computer literate?

10. What will robots do for you in your home and school by the next century?

11. Two people are engaged in a heated discussion. "No machine will ever be as intelligent as a person. There's a lot more to intelligence than going fast." "There *is* a lot more to intelligence than going fast, but computers can do a lot more than that. They can store and retrieve incredible amounts of information. They can be constructed to learn and design new systems which are even smarter. They may not ever appreciate a handsome face, but they will be smarter than we are soon." The two turn to you. One says, "You're interested in computers. What do you say?"

12. Is it possible to create thinking machines without fully understanding our own thought processes?

13. What jobs are computers ideally suited for?

14. List all the places records about you are kept. What is in them? Who has access to them? How would you feel if everyone could see them?

15. Who should teach computer literacy, those who know computers, or those who know society and people? Or is there a better option?

16. Make a list of all the computer applications in your life. Do this with your students or with colleagues. Where else would you benefit from the use of this technology? Does using a microprocessor in, say, your microwave oven scare you? If not, why do any microcomputers make you anxious?

17. Reread the section on the disadvantages of computers. Which will cease to be disadvantages as technology, and our ability to use technology, increases? Which (if any) are inherent in the use of machines?

18. Computer crimes, it was concluded, are human crimes. What does this mean for a computer literacy curriculum? Should we teach ethics within such a curriculum? Or should such ethics be dealt with in other, specifically de-

signed coursework—or, should this be the domain of schools at all? What do you do in school that would form the foundation for ethical use of all devices and tools?

19. What attitudes would you want your students to have toward computers? What are your attitudes? Do you feel leery, anxious, even a bit resentful? Try to sit back a bit and examine why you might feel that way. What could you do to try to discover if these feelings are valid? If they are not, what could you do to change them? If any of them are, what should you do about *that*?

20. Read Christopher Evans's book concerning artificial intelligence. Take a position in support of or against his viewpoint, and defend your position.

21. Many available texts, such as several of those listed below, discuss societal uses and misuses of the computer, as well as the impact of computers on society.

22. Of the computer uses discussed in this chapter, which would benefit you the most? Why?

23. Is computer art really art? Why or why not?

Suggested References

Frates, Jeffery, and Moldrup, William. *Introduction to the computer: An integrative approach.* Englewood Cliffs, N.J.: Prentice-Hall, 1980.

Rothman, Stanley, and Mosmann, Charles. *Computers and society* (2nd ed.). Chicago: Science Research Associates, 1976.

Sanders, Donald. *Computers in society* (2nd ed.). New York: McGraw-Hill, 1977. These readings will increase your awareness of the role of computers in our lives.

Krutch, J. *Experiments in artificial intelligence for small computers.* Indianapolis: Howard W. Sans & Co., 1981.
For the reader who wishes to pursue the area in more depth, Krutch provides some understandable artificial intelligence programs that can be typed into your microcomputer—including programs that play games, solve problems, and converse in the manner of a Rogerian psychotherapist (a modification of the original ELIZA program).

Joseph Weizenbaum. *Computer power and human reason: From judgment to calculation.* San Francisco: W. H. Freeman and Co., 1976.
Weizenbaum, the creator of ELIZA, presents a stimulating discussion of the thinking of machines and people, including a critique of the applications of artificial intelligence.

Moursund, David. Introduction to computers in education for elementary and middle school teachers. Chapter 7. *The Computing Teacher,* 1981, 9(2), 15–24.
Moursund provides background information and activities for teaching these topics. What suggestions would you use?

Some books about robots that you and your students might enjoy include

Frankenstein (the famous first man-made "monster"—have your students compare the creature to that of the movies)

R.U.R. (a 1923 play that coined the word *robot*)
The Nine Billion Names of God
Men Are Different
The Feeling of Power
Maxon's Master
Hardcastle
The Answer
Epicac
The City and the Stars
Who Can Replace a Man?

You might also be interested in other stories by Asimov, Bradbury, Clark, Heinlein, and others. Some of the issues raised above may spark worthwhile class discussions.

Bibliography

ASIMOV, ISAAC. *I, Robot.* Garden City, N.Y.: Doubleday, 1950.

CIARCIA, S. A computer-controlled tank. *Byte,* February 1981, pp. 44–48; 50; 52; 54–55; 58; 60; 62; 64; 66.

EVANS, CHRISTOPHER. *The micro millennium.* New York: Viking Press, 1979.

FRATES, JEFFERY, AND MOLDRUP, WILLIAM. *Introduction to the computer: An integrative approach.* Englewood Cliffs, N.J.: Prentice-Hall, 1980.

KAUFMAN, D. T., JR. *Teaching the future: A guide to future-oriented education.* Palm Springs, Calif.: ETC Publications, 1976.

KENNEDY, JOYCE L., AND WINKLER, C. *Computer careers: The complete pocket guide to America's fastest growing job market.* Cardiff, Calif.: Sun Features Inc., 1982.

MANDELL, PHYLLIS LEVY. Computer literacy, languages, and careers. *School Library Journal,* 1982, 28(8), 19–22.

MULLER, B., AND KOVACS, D. An electronic mailbox. *Teaching and Computers,* Spring 1983, pp. 38–41.

NELSON, TED. Mail chauvinism: The magicians, the snark, and the camel. *Creative Computing,* November 1981, pp. 128; 130; 134–135; 138; 140; 142; 144; 150; 156.

PAPERT, SEYMOUR, AND SOLOMON, C. NIM: A game-playing program. Memo 254, MIT Artificial Intelligence Laboratory, 1970.

QUICK SCAN OF COMPUTER CAREERS. *Changing Times,* June 1982, pp. 50–51.

ROTHMAN, STANLEY, AND MOSMANN, CHARLES. *Computers and society* (2nd ed.). Chicago: Science Research Associates, 1976.

SANDERS, DONALD. *Computers in society* (2nd ed.). New York: McGraw-Hill, 1977.

JOSEPH WEIZENBAUM. *Computer power and human reason: From judgment to calculation.* San Francisco: W. H. Freeman and Co., 1976.

Approaches to Computer Literacy

Having discussed in previous chapters why computer literacy should be taught and what should be taught, this chapter suggests *how* it might be taught. Following are materials and approaches you might wish to try.

What Is a Computer? How Does a Computer Work?

Introducing Computers. A sound-filmstrip series, *Math Matters* (by Guidance Associates, 1975)—including *Computers: From Pebbles to Programs, Computer Software: What It Is and How It Works, Numbers: From Notches to Numerals,* and films on topics such as programming—provides a good vehicle for the initial presentation of many computer literacy concepts. Although somewhat old and not geared to microcomputers, the movie *Computers: Challenging Man's Supremacy* contains exciting discussions of computer applications and an interview with science fiction writer Arthur C. Clark.

Other children's books concerning computers are Marion Ball's *What is a Computer* and *Be a Computer Literate* (Ball, 1972; Ball and Charp, 1978), and Jean Rice's *My Friend the Computer* (1976). At the time of this writing, there is not a lot of material in this area on the market, so these may be useful to you. However, they do have faults; for example, some concentrate almost exclusively on numerical data (not words), reinforcing the erroneous concept of many children that computers are fancy calculators. Also, explanations may have to be supplemented. Other books for children include *Exploring the World of Computers* (Spencer, 1982); *Microcomputer Coloring Book* (Spencer, 1983); *Computer Awareness Book* (Spencer and Beatty, 1978); *Computers—A First Book* (O'Brian, 1978); *Computer Alphabet Book* (Wall, 1979); *COM-LIT: Computer Literacy for Kids* (Horn & Collins, 1983); and, for older beginners, *Exploring With Computers* (Bitter, 1981) and *Are You Computer Literate?* (Billings & Moursund, 1979). You and your students might also look up the word *computer* in your school's encyclopedia. Vocabulary and spelling games, such as Concentration and "I am thinking of a word" might be used to practice these skills.

New material is being produced constantly. Dataflow, a game by Systems Incorporated, tries to give the "feel" of a computer in operation. Flow charts, vocabulary, and problem solving are involved. Visual masters, games, and a host of books are available for helping teachers teach flow charting and programming (some are listed in Part 4).

Here is how one fourth-grade teacher helped her students understand the functions and interactions of the components of computer systems. The class had recently taken a field trip to a nearby fast-food restaurant. They were now acting out the system they had seen, relating it to their school's microcomputer system. The input, or data, were ten youngsters standing in line to be served, one at a time. The control unit was represented by the store's manager, who was directing the staff in serving the customers. The arithmetic/logic unit was the staff. As each customer came forward, the manager took the order and wrote it on an erasable board (short-term memory). This signaled to the cooks that they should make the food. The orders were assembled and given in order to the customers (output). Another day the children acted out the same roles, but this time they dramatized a simple program they had designed to run on their school's computer.

Notice that this simple dramatization can be expanded for older children, and more vocabulary can be introduced. For instance, the cook is a *processor*, but considering the cashier, we have a multiprocessor, and the implicit definition of a system as a collection of related processes. If many customers are at the counter, the board may fill with orders. This illustrates the concept of the *buffer*. If the buffer board is full, the waiter may not proceed. If it is not full, it is all right to proceed. Although the board was erased for each customer, the tapes from the cash register kept a permanent record of the orders and the flow of money, which were stored in the back room by the manager (long-term storage). The process can be diagramed for students (see Figure 5-1); and the analogy to computer systems can easily be seen (Figure 5-2).

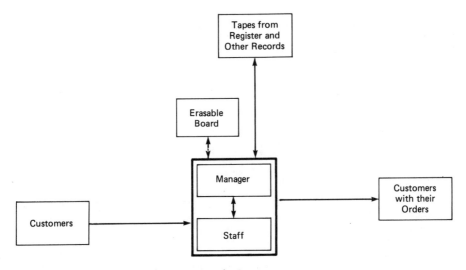

FIGURE 5-1   Functions and Interactions of a Restaurant.

There is evidence that these approaches, providing learners with concrete models of computer operations and encouraging them to dramatize them and restate the information in their own words, result in broader, more effective learning (Mayer, 1980).

Children in the elementary grades may enjoy being introduced to the "world inside the computer" through an entertaining and educational picture book, *Katie and the Computer* by S. Frederick D'Ignazio. In it a little girl types *flower* on her new computer, falls into it in "through the looking glass" style, and begins an adventure in the world of Cybernia, complete with Flower Bytes who live in RAM Tower, the Colonel (control), and the mean and tricky program "Bug." Katie tries, despite the bug, to get the computer to paint a picture of a flower. She has to bobsled up to the CPU and help the Bytes line up. The story familiarizes children with the key words associated with computer components and with the major processes. The components are metaphorically represented as landmarks, and the processes appear as episodes in the story. It should be noted, however, that the allegory is not specific enough to allow children or adults to understand how computers work; teachers would need to find this out on their own and help children understand it in ways other than reading the book.

Analogies between parts of computers and familiar objects can help students conceptualize and remember computer components and their functions. For example, the permanent Read Only Memory, or ROM, might be thought of as a book describing a computer language. It contains information about the language, and this information does not disappear when the book is closed. The erasable Random Access Memory, or RAM, can be seen as "magic slates"—the self-erasing pads that can be

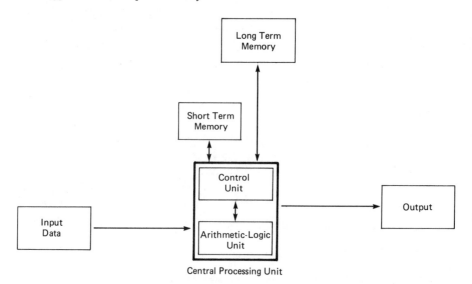

FIGURE 5-2   Functions and Interactions of a Computer System.

written on, and then erased by lifting the plastic top sheet. Anything can be written on them, but when you are done with them, all the information is erased forever. Disks and tapes—used to store information and programs so they are not lost—can be thought of as phonograph records and tape cassettes.

After dramatizing the workings of a computer, one teacher created a large bulletin board with a simple representation of the basic components of a computer. Children chose a problem from the pocket near the "input devices" and traced the solution through the arrows connecting the components. At each one they had to write "What should happen here?" Different answers were compared and discussed. Students should be able to describe the components in their own words; for example: "A TV (monitor) shows words, numbers, and pictures," or "A disk drive can save information such as programs, pictures, or stories on a disk." Research has shown that providing students with a concrete model and encouraging them to put it in their own words can have a strong positive effect on their learning (Mayer, 1982).

Because hardware is changing so rapidly with technological advances, it may not be wise to study it for its own sake. Rather, as students discover the various applications of computers, it will be natural to study the functions of the parts of computer systems. Again, this integrated study—computers in context—is more useful and more meaningful.

What Can the Computer Do (Awareness)?

Books, television programs, magazines, newspapers, and local industries provide a variety of resources for teachers introducing computer applications and careers. Helpful books include Gloria and Esther Goldreich's *What Can She Be? A Computer Scientist* and Berger's *Computers In Your Life*. These topics might best be taught as part of a social studies unit. For instance, one first-grade class took a walk to see how computers were used in a nearby supermarket. They observed the markings on products and how the computer "read" these, printing the name of the item and the price on a receipt and a display. They also heard the manager explain how she used a small computer to take inventory. The computer stored the information about items that were needed. At the end of the week, the manager called a larger computer on the telephone (!) and had her computer "talk" to the other computer, transferring her order for goods. A fourth-grade teacher had his students survey every person and source of information they could to uncover computer uses in their community. Hundreds of applications were found in a rural setting. Each group of students presented a report on (a) who used the computer; (b) why they used it; (c) what information they gave to the computer; (d) what information the computer gave them; (e) how they used this information; and (f) the kind of information the computer stored and the kind of processing it did.

A class library might also be created. Students can use these sources to construct reports, collages, and scrapbooks. Wall collages can brighten the classroom; computer literacy terms might be written on punched cards and displayed. Displays might include a microprocessor under a microscope; computer art, poetry, graphics, drafting, mathematics, business, and medical applications; computer receipts and ABC labels from supermarket products; a tape recording of computer-generated music; and so on. Sixth-grade students in one class did individual investigations concerning how information was stored and retrieved in areas such as journalism, medicine, law enforcement, business, and government. Notice that the emphasis in all these investigations was on *information*.

Field trips can provide invaluable experiences for children, especially if computers are not readily available. Trips to local microcomputer stores can provide hands-on experience and exposure to different types of computers, software, and literature. One third-grade class planned such a field trip together. After initial discussion their teacher wrote down those items they wanted to learn:

What We Want to Learn on Our Trip to the Computer Store

1. What kinds of microcomputers are there? How are they different? What can each kind do?
2. What computer programs are there? What do they do? How much do they cost? Can they teach us reading, social studies, math, and other subjects? Can they teach us about computers? Are there good games?
3. What books and magazines are there that could help us learn about computers and how to use them? How much do they cost?
4. How can we learn to program the computers ourselves? Is it hard? What are the different languages?

The class decided that since they only had about an hour to spend at the store, they had better split into four groups, each tackling one of the areas. The children chose an area they were most interested in and spent the rest of the period organizing their groups so that they would know exactly what they wanted to find out and how they would go about doing so at the store.

After a profitable visit, each group did more library research and finally organized a report, for presentation to the class, on what they had discovered. After that experience excitement was high, and several individuals and groups planned to investigate specific interests at greater depth. Knowledge and abilities in language arts, social studies, science, mathematics, and computer literacy had all increased. Just as important, the children had increased their self-concept, their independence, and their good feelings about school and learning.

University or college computing centers also can provide concrete experiences that relate to later lessons. Local libraries are beginning to add microcomputers to their resources. A local engineering company might illustrate present-day use of automation. Many times authorities from these and other businesses—such as banks, stores, police, post office, government offices, libraries, travel agencies, and newspapers—will be happy to come in and speak to your class about their use of computers. Discuss with the class what our society would be like without computers. One middle school science class discussed the use of computers by scientists. Their teacher guided them to understand how the computer is used in each of the stages of the scientific process.

Don't forget your own students as resources. Ask if anyone has a microcomputer at home. Have students who respond positively explain how they are used.

Computer Capabilities

A third-grade teacher overhears a boy complain, "The computer won't let me play the writing words game!" His friend explains in an exasperated tone, "You didn't load the program. It doesn't know how to do *anything* without a program." The teacher smiles, knowing that her informal discussions about computers, which she initiates during the class's work with computers, are having the desired effect.

After students have become partially aware of what a computer can and cannot do, teachers of older children may wish to conduct a group discussion, listing on the overhead projector or chart paper either "What a Computer Can Do Well . . . What People Can Do Well"; or possibly, "What a Computer Can Do Well . . . What a Computer Can *Not* Do Well." Students can be encouraged to provide examples of tasks for which the computer's speed, memory, and precision are appropriate and necessary. The information presented in the previous two chapters—the sections on advantages/disadvantages and artificial intelligence especially—might give you the background you would need to start such an activity. As a follow-up, children might write a futuristic story in which they describe the "computers of tomorrow," including their specific application(s). Discuss science fiction books and movies. Are any ideas too fantastic? Remember, if aerodynamics had advanced at the pace of computer technology, we could have landed on the moon ten years after Kitty Hawk! What tasks would your students like a computer to do for them today. Is it possible?

If you have a computer in the classroom, you can effectively dramatize advantages and disadvantages. For the former, have your students write the sentence "This is a speed test" twenty times, as fast as they can. Or they might add a long column of six-digit numbers. Compare their time to that needed by the computer for the same task, and compare the number of errors. To highlight disadvantages, ask the students to solve a word problem. Then (verbally) "ask" the computer. Can the computer solve the problem without a person programming it to do so? In the same way, compare the speed of a person working alone and a person using a computer—or if none is available, a calculator—on a test of fifty basic addition facts, including $1+4$, $6+6$, $9+0$, and so on. Which completed the test faster? When should a computer be used? When is it smarter *not* to use the computer? Or compile a list of questions a computer cannot answer: Which is your favorite flavor of ice cream? Do you feel sad? When? What makes a good mother?

After basic vocabulary and concepts have been introduced, interesting discussions—actually centered on the concepts of artificial intelligence—can compare computer and human activities with regard to memory, debugging, input and output, and even programming or solving problems. A game could be played to dramatize the Turing test of intelligence discussed in Chapter 4. Instead of "blind" questioning of a computer versus a human, one student or a class can pose questions to two students who differ—for example, one boy and one girl. Questions can be written to each of the two students, who sit in a different room. One of the two—let us say the boy—is free to make whatever response he believes will fool the questioner(s). The other must tell the truth. Can their identities be determined?

Discussions about "smart" machines can be profitable. How smart is a thermostat? An elevator? A microwave oven? Students might contribute to a bulletin board containing pictures and descriptions of a smart machine, specifying what the machine does that makes it appear intelligent. For example, what decisions and what consequent actions do each of the three named devices make?

Branching off from discussions of computer capabilities, investigate with students stories concerned with computer errors and computer crimes. Who committed them? What do people *feel* toward computers which might influence what they believe or perceive to be the role of computers in errors and crimes? Discuss different types of computer crime, the difficulty of preventing and tracing it, and possible preventive measures. "Software piracy," the illegal copying of the computer programs of others, is an important and interesting topic. Computer magazines will provide a readily available supply of information and opinions on this matter. You may wish to have students write essays concerning these topics. The MECC Computer Literacy Instructional Modules include information and teaching suggestions on most of these societal issues.

What Can a Computer Do? (Use)

Problem Solving and Thinking Strategies. What if no computers are available? First, it should be noted that many of the topics outlined in Table 2-1 and discussed above require no computer. Yet the importance of the computer in facilitating logical thinking was also stressed.

Taylor (1975) has provided examples of some activities that can help solve the problem of "Computerless Computing for Young Children, or What to Do Till the Computer Comes." He suggests that teachers conduct activities that prepare children for the types of thinking computer programming will demand. For example, classifying and reclassifying sets of foods might build a data base perspective: Children can put all the foods together that go together by color, type—such as fruit, vegetable, cereals, and so on—preference, texture, sweet/sour, origin, how eaten, when eaten, and so on. This will build important readiness skills, helping children understand how a computer filing system would work: The computer could also sort any information it has stored by a variety of attributes and could very quickly tell the user all the foods that were, for example, fruits, or yellow fruits, or yellow fruits that were smooth. Treasure-hunting games can help develop debugging skills. If children can be led to create a set of treasure-hunt directions to swap with another team, both teams will discover where their directions were incomplete or erroneous. They can debug these directions for another team. Similarly, children might write directions on, for example, how to make a peanut butter and jelly sandwich—a favorite among students and teachers (the activity, not the sandwich!). Seeing others attempt to follow their directions precisely would help them correct, or debug, any errors. Other debugging exercises might involve finding the errors in compositions, recipes for playdough, or in computations such as

$$
\begin{array}{r}
218 \\
-129 \\
\hline
99
\end{array}
\qquad
\begin{array}{r}
405 \\
-148 \\
\hline
267
\end{array}
$$

There are several types of bugs that are worth looking out for and discussing explicitly. These include giving incomplete instructions or instructions that are out of sequence, forgetting to establish some initial state (What does she need to do or know or have before she starts?), using unclear descriptions, leaving out a step, and so on.

Some teachers have developed childrens' ability to construct and follow specific directions by playing games such as May I?, Scavenger Hunt, or Simon Says (". . .all the girls with red pants hop three times and then sit down"). Students might draw maps without words or write directions without drawings to give explicit directions on how to get somewhere in the school. Beyond the concept of specific directions is the essential idea of the *procedure*—a step-by-step set of instructions to accomplish a certain class of tasks. Children learn many procedures—for example, getting ready when first entering the classroom, cleaning the room, doing arithmetic exercises, and so on. Just helping them to understand that these *are* procedures and to understand the nature of procedures is an important goal. Teachers can then encourage children to describe many types of procedures—how to eat cereal, clean a car, play a game, milk a cow, and so on. The important process of breaking a problem down into manageable parts can be highlighted. Children might describe the procedure for taking a bath as follows:

1. Go to the bathroom.
2. Fill the bathtub.
3. Get undressed.
4. Get in the water.
5. Wash all over.
6. Rinse off.
7. Get out.
8. Dry off.
9. Get pajamas on.

The teacher might then pretend she is a robot following this procedure as her instructions. She walks to a make-believe bathtub. She receives the next instruction but freezes—how *does* she fill the bathtub? She leads students to see that *subprocedures* are needed. Every numbered instruction can be further described as a procedure. Number 2, Fill the bathtub, might be described by the students:

2. Fill the bathtub.
   a. Turn the hot water faucet all the way on.
   b. Check to see if the water is hot.
   c. When it is, turn the cold water on until a warm temperature is reached.
   d. Add bubble bath.

Did you locate bugs in this program? One of the most disastrous omissions is neglecting to close the drain. Students might also discuss the problems of what a "warm" temperature is, how much bubble bath should be added, and so on. Of course, even these procedures could be broken down. What would be your procedure for turning the hot water faucet all the way on?

Students might be challenged to write down a procedure for looking up any word in the dictionary. They can exchange procedures and evaluate how well others' procedures work. Activities such as this are helpful in pointing out to students that although people can often perform a task, they may not be able to supply a complete description of how they do it. In working with computers, however, the exact steps must be specified.

Students can give and receive directions in the Step-on Game, in which foam rubber shapes differing in shape, color, size, and thickness are placed on the floor. One first grader told her classmates to first step only on the shapes that were large squares, then only on the shapes that were not thin green circles. Both following directions and multiple classifications were being exercised in that lesson.

A sixth-grade class wanted to take a poll of the entire school. In order to tackle this substantial task, their teacher helped them break it down into manageable pieces, for example: what questions to ask, how to collect the information, how to tabulate and analyze the results, and how to present them. These tasks, too, were broken up. In tabulating and analyzing the results, they asked: What is it we want to know—totals, totals within categories, averages, medians? Each of these tasks also presented questions: What is the best way to perform these mathematical operations? Would a calculator or computer help? What would it have to do? Are certain things better done with paper and pencil?

Simulations and Models. When teachers first read about complex computer simulations of medical diagnoses or business transactions, they often think there is little that could be done in the elementary school to illustrate and explain simulations and models. Actually, however, most teachers use models every day. They ask students to draw diagrams and pictures and then write number sentences as an aid in solving mathematical story problems. Or the earth's water cycle might be illustrated through evaporating a pan of water and collecting water droplets on a cold object. These are models. The real objects do not exist in the classroom; only a "simulation" of the objects exists. Discussing such models with students may improve their understanding of computer simulations and their own use of models in solving problems.

Similarly, games such as Life or Monopoly are simulations which are familiar to students and which therefore can serve as illustrations and catalysts for discussions. The strategies children use to win these games can be compared. Older students can be challenged to examine the *assumptions* that underlie the games—for example, the relative cost of houses and hotels as compared to the rent charged, the match between these aspects and the real world, and so on.

Other school activities can help children understand other uses of the computer. For instance, the card catalog or the filing system used in the office illustrates information storage and retrieval, a topic discussed more fully in Chapter 17.

Objections might be made to these lessons: "What does this have to do with computing?" "I don't know if there would be transfer from these activities to learning about computers." These are valid concerns. Certainly, the teacher should make every attempt to explicitly discuss and demonstrate the connections between these activities and computer activities. Yet there are strong arguments for suggesting activities such as these. First, despite the proliferation of the technology in our society, many students and classrooms will *not* have easy access to computers in the near future. Second, it should be remembered that the primary goal is not the development of computing skills but rather the development of problem-solving abilities. Therefore, these types of activities should be conducted throughout the curriculum. Of course, the topic "What can a computer do? (use)" is best approached through hands-on activities with computers. It is primarily these types of activities we will discuss in the remainder of this book.

Integrating Computer Literacy Content
Into the Curriculum

The teaching of much of the content of computer literacy discussed in Part 1 might best be done in conjunction with other studies. Bell's (1979) research indicated that you can have "Computer Literacy, School Mathematics, and Problem Solving: Three for the Price of One." Incorporating computer literacy into high-level problem solving had no negative effects on students' attitudes and achievement in mathematics and had a positive effect on their attitudes toward computers.

Remember, too, that many have argued that you do not have to be a mathematics teacher to teach computers. In fact, it is the opinion of several (Bell, 1980; Luehrmann, cited in Ahl, 1981; Wilson, 1981) that as experts in teaching clear, concise, logical communication, English teachers—and therefore most elementary teachers—would be best equipped to instruct children in computer literacy. Just as it would be ineffective, and almost pointless, to teach children to read and write without providing important *content* for that reading and writing, so is it ineffective and meaningless to teach children to use computers in an isolated, unconnected fashion.

In the study of such topics as history and development, it has been suggested that teachers exploit the potential for simultaneous work in the areas of science, social studies, and language arts. When using the computer as a tool by running programs or programming, worthwhile content should be considered. For example, if children are learning to program a computer, why not have them write a program that can enable the computer to generate its own random sentences? There is no better way to learn grammar than to have to use it, functionally, for a purpose. Or children could be challenged to write programs that drill users on social studies, science, or arithmetic content. In using each other's programs, valuable practice will be gained, but in *constructing* the programs, children will come to understand much more: the content itself, the nature of practice and feedback, the problem-solving nature of programming, and so on. Specific suggestions will be provided in the content chapters of this book.

APPROACHES TO COMPUTER LITERACY
FOR TEACHERS

Resources to help teachers themselves become computer literate are increasingly available. This is a hopeful sign, for faculty must understand computers in order for computers in education to work (Luehrmann, 1980; Parkhurst, 1979). In addition, teachers need to be computer literate to answer children's questions on computers and their effects, on information processing, and on the course of study (Beck, 1980). The importance of computer literacy demands that children—especially females and minorities—have equal access. This requires individualized instruction and, therefore, computer literate teachers. Most teachers favor the teaching of computer literacy but do not feel competent to teach it themselves (Stevens, 1980). Yet by virtue of their knowledge of children and education, teachers are the ones who are best suited to decide how computers should be used in the schools.

Those who wish to expand their competence can find helpful guidelines. For example, Dennis (1978) has provided a list of important facts and skills for those interested in using computers in instruction. Computing magazines are being published in abundance; a trip to a microcomputer store will allow you to survey a few. Single worthwhile issues might be purchased, and if a particular magazine serves your needs, subscriptions are (as usual) welcomed. In addition, magazine articles provide lists of references for help with computer literacy for teachers (for example, O'Donnell, 1982; Mandell, 1982; Rosen and Hicks, 1977). Large sections of educational magazines are often dedicated to computer literacy (for example, *Arithmetic Teacher*, February 1982; *Instructor*, October 1981; *Teacher*, January 1982; and *AEDS Journal*, Fall 1979). Articles that describe computer literacy curricula are available. Besides those listed in Table 2-1 (several of which provide exhaustive listings of objectives—for example, see Anderson and Klassen, 1981; Bitter, 1982; and other references from Chapter 2), there are references for the elementary school (for example, Anderson and Klassen, 1981; Hunter, 1983; Moursund, 1980, 1982) and the middle school (for example, Gress, 1982; Rogers, 1980–1981). Suggestions concerning methods of teaching computer literacy can be found in Mayer (1980).

For sufferers of computer phobia or computer anxiety—and teachers suffer more frequently than others—Stevens (1980), Bell (1981), and Jay (1981) offer comforting words and information designed to combat these maladies. You can undoubtedly guess what the suggestions involve—personal education and hands-on experience. Milner (1980) provides descriptions of courses fitting the needs of teachers with different interests and positions in computer literacy instruction. Teachers need to demand such courses if they are not available. Indeed, they are not; a survey showed a dismal picture of college training in computing for teachers (Dickerson and Pritchard, 1981), although many colleges are attempting to remedy that situation (for example, Bitter, 1982; Castek, 1975; Denenberg, 1980). Several excellent, readable introductory texts on computers and data processing are available (for example, Frates and Moldrup, 1980).

The fact that you're reading this book is an indication of your concern and desire for professional growth. If you use the resources that suit your needs and are willing to learn alongside your students, computer literacy offers a fascinating and rewarding field of inquiry.

FINAL REMARKS

Efforts to achieve widespread computer literacy have been state- (Brown, 1982; Kirchner, 1981) and nationwide (Linderholm, 1981). Other innovative approaches have been attempted on smaller scales. The annotated bibliography at the end of this chapter briefly describes some of these approaches. While you might not want to implement these specific approaches, reading about them increases one's awareness of computer literacy and methods of teaching it. This must become an educational priority:

> Universal computer literacy is a basic skill of the 1980's and deserves a major role in the school curriculum. To educate students for computer literacy, schools must develop leadership, curricula, and computer-literate teaching staffs. . . . The failure of schools to make a major commitment in this area now can have disastrous consequences for both the education of the public and the future of public education. (Watt, 1981, pp. 86–87)

Think About

1. Do you think students who are not computer literate will be significantly disadvantaged in our society at the time of their graduation?

2. Answer the following statement of an annoyed parent: "We didn't teach television literacy and kids never suffered. Who needs to know this literacy and 'computers in society' stuff? Why don't you teach them to read and write?"

3. One educator has argued that computers make calculations of square roots and logarithms as ancient as using a washboard. Another maintains that these algorithms (procedures) teach a child the meaning of mathematics, and besides, we shouldn't depend too much on machines. Who is "right"?

4. Should we teach computers as a separate subject, or are they rightly a part of other subject domains? For example, should we use them for computing in math, and study their societal implications in social studies?

5. Defend or attack the following statements:

    A. A computer literate student knows how to program the computer to do what he or she wants it to do. Anything else is just rote knowledge.

    B. I would rather have a child know why and where to use a computer—to understand how it could and should fit into his or her life—than to know what a byte is.

    C. Computer literate students will use the computer as a tool. They don't have to know trivial historical facts like the name of the first electronic computer, and most will never use programming. They need to know how to use the programs of others to accomplish their goals.

6. Should every student have a computer at his or her disposal at home and at school?

    Would you deny anyone access to a pencil or a book?

    Do you ever learn much about or from anything that was not close at hand? For example, would you look up an interesting word you came across in a dictionary that was upstairs? In the library across town? Right next to you? What if you could (verbally) ask a computerized dictionary and it would answer you instantly?

7. Should children work with calculators or computers first?

8. Is computer literacy (however *you* define it) a "basic"?

9. Construct a course outline for computer literacy at your grade level. Could you teach it?

Suggested References

Asimov, Isaac. **The feeling of power. In C. Fadiman (ed.),** *The Mathematical Magpie*. New York: Simon & Schuster. 1962.
Asimov compares and contrasts human and computer capabilities in an entertaining and thought-provoking story of a man of the future who discovers that he can actually work arithmetic *without* a computer, giving him a *feeling of power*. This would serve as an excellent introduction to the other activities on computer capabilities described in this chapter.

Hansen, T., Klassen, D., Anderson, R., and Johnson, D. **Computer literacy courses.** *AEDS Monitor*, November 1979, pp. 29–30.
The authors present a survey of computer literacy courses across the country.

Hunter, Barbara. *My students use computers: Learning activities for computer literacy.* Reston, Va.: Reston Publishing Co., 1983.
Hunter provides an excellent set of computer literacy objectives and activities for grades K–8. The objectives are classified into six strands: procedures, using programs, fundamentals, applications, impact, and writing computer programs. Lesson plans are comprehensive and well written. The book would serve as an excellent resource for teachers.

Dyrli, Odvard E. **The MUCK approach, or everything you shouldn't know about teaching with computers.** *Learning*, August 1982, pp. 76–79.

Fox, David, and Fox, Annie. **The Marin Computer Center: A "new age" learning environment.** *Creative Computing*, April 1979, pp. 116–118.

Garrison, Paul E. The world of scouting and computing. *Creative Computing,* July 1979, pp. 46–48.

Hirshberg, Peter. Compu-tots and other joys of museum life. *Instructional Innovator,* 1981, 26, 28–30.

Loop, Liza. ComputerTown, USA! *Instructional Innovator,* 1982, 27(2), 22–23.

Powell, James D., and Speece, Herbert E. Computer awareness laboratory. *Journal of Education Technology Systems,* 1977/1978, 6(1), 45–50.

Wrege, Rachael. Hands on! *Popular Computing,* June 1982, pp. 110–114; 116; 120–122.

Approaches to computer literacy have included computer parks and museums (Loop; Wrege), privately operated computer centers (Fox and Fox), computer centers in museums (Hirshberg), merit badges in computer scouting (Garrison), traveling vans (Powell and Speece), and MUCK, "an amazing hands-off, thought-proof way to computer literacy" (a satire by Dyrli). Reading about these will provide you with a clearer picture of activities on computers that are appropriate and interesting to children, as well as ideas for teaching computer literacy. An additional model for teaching computer literacy, Computeronics, was originally developed for gifted students. For information write Gifted Child Project, Leon County School Board, 2757 West Pensacola, Tallahassee, Florida 32304. Both MECC and TIES from Minnesota produce computer literacy materials for teachers and students.

Bibliography

AHL, DAVID H. Pascal, Ada, and Computer Literacy. *Creative Computing,* July/August 1981, pp. 116; 118; 120; 122–123.

ANDERSON, R. E., AND KLASSEN, D. L. A conceptual framework for developing computer literacy instruction. *AEDS Journal,* 1981, 14, 128–150.

BALL, MARION. *What is a computer?* Boston: Houghton Mifflin, 1972.

BALL, MARION, AND CHARP, S. *Be a computer literate.* Morristown, N.J.: Creative Computing Press, 1978.

BECK, JOHN J., JR. Computer literacy for elementary and secondary teachers. Paper presented at the Annual Meeting of the Texas Association for Supervision and Curriculum Development, Houston, Texas, November 5, 1980. (ERIC Document Reproduction Service No. ED 208 868)

BELL, ARTHUR H. Computer anxiety. *Media and Methods,* 1981, 18(3), 4–5; 25.

BELL, F. H. Computer literacy, school mathematics, and problem solving: Three for the price of one. *AEDS Journal,* 1979, 12, 163–170.

BELL, KATHLEEN. The computer and the English teacher. *English Journal,* 1980, 69, 88–90.

BERGER, MELVIN. *Computers in your life.* New York: Thomas Y. Crowell, 1981.

BILLINGS, KAREN, AND MOURSUND, DAVID. *Are you computer literate?* Beaverton, Oreg.: Dilithium Press, 1979.

BITTER, GARY. *Exploring with computers.* New York: Messner, 1981.

BITTER, GARY. Creating an effective computer literacy training model. *Educational Computer,* September/October 1982, pp. 42; 74.

BROWN, EDMUND G., JR. Computers and the schools. *T.H.E. Journal,* 1982, 10(1), 99–100.

CASTEK, JOHN, ET AL. *The LACE (La Crosse Computers in Education) Project.* La Crosse, Wis.: Wisconsin University, 1975. (ERIC Document Reproduction Service No. ED 117 116)

DENENBERG, STEWART A. An alternative curriculum for computer literacy development. *AEDS Journal,* 1980, 13, 156–173.

DENNIS, J. R. Training preservice teachers to teach with computers. *AEDS Journal,* 1978, 11, 25–30.

DICKERSON, LAUREL, AND PRITCHARD, WILLIAM H., JR. Microcomputers and education: Planning for the coming revolution in the classroom. *Educational Technology,* 1981, 21(1), 7–12.

D'IGNAZIO, FRED. Katie and the Computer. Morristown, N.J.: Creative Computing Press, 1979.

FRATES, JEFFREY, AND MOLDRUP, WILLIAM. *Introduction to the computer: An integrative approach.* Englewood Cliffs, N.J.: Prentice-Hall, 1980.

FRIEL, S., AND ROBERTS, N. Computer literacy bibliography. *Creative Computing,* 1980, pp. 92–97.

GOLDREICH, GLORIA, AND GOLDREICH, ESTHER. *What can she be? A computer scientist.* New York: Lothrop, Lee, and Shepard, 1979.

GRESS, EILEEN K. A computer-literacy module for the junior high school. *Arithmetic Teacher,* 1982, 29(7), 46–49.

HANSEN, T., KLASSEN, D., ANDERSON, R., AND JOHNSON, D. Computer literacy courses. *AEDS Monitor,* November 1979, pp. 29–30.

HORN, CARIN, AND COLLINS, CARROLL. *COM-LIT: Computer literacy for kids.* Austin, Tex.: Sterling Swift, 1983.

JAY, TIMOTHY B. Computerphobia: What to do about it. *Educational Technology,* 1981, 21(1), 47–48.

KIRCHNER, ALICE M. One state's approach to computer literacy. *Technological Horizons in Education,* 1981, 8(4), 43–44.

LINDERHOLM, OWEN. A beginning for Britain and computers—With the BBC. *Creative Computing,* October 1981, 122–123.

LUEHRMANN, ARTHUR. Computer illiteracy—A national crisis and a solution for it. *Byte,* July 1980, pp. 98; 101–102.

MANDELL, PHYLLIS LEVY. Computer literacy, languages, and careers. *School Library Journal,* 1982, 28(8), 19–22.

MAYER, RICHARD E. Contributions of cognitive science and related research on learning to the design of computer literacy curricula. Report No. 81-1. Series in learning and cognition. Santa Barbara, Calif.: University of California, Department of Psychology, 1980. (ERIC Document Reproduction Service No. ED 207 551)

MILNER, STUART D. Teaching teachers about computers: A necessity for education. *Phi Delta Kappan,* 1980, 61, 544–546.

MOURSUND, DAVID. *Teacher's guide to computers in the elementary school.* LaGrande, Oreg.: International Council for Computers in Education, 1980.

MOURSUND, DAVID. *Precollege computer literacy: A personal computing approach.* Eugene, Oreg.: International Council for Computers in Education, 1982.

O'BRIAN, LINDA. Computers—A first book. New York: Franklin Watts, 1978.

O'DONNELL, HOLLY. Computer literacy, part I: An overview. *Reading Teacher,* 1982, 35, 490–494.

PARKHURST, PERRIN E. Computer awareness programs don't have to fail. *Audiovisual Instruction,* 1979, 24(7), 43–44.

RICE, JEAN. *My friend the computer.* Minneapolis, Minn.: T. S. Denison & Co., 1976.

ROGERS, JEAN B. An introduction to computers and computing: A high school course outline. *The Computing Teacher,* 1980–1981, 8(7), 30–33.

ROSEN, ELIZABETH, AND HICKS, BRUCE. *Computer literacy.* Urbana, Ill.: University of Illinois, 1977. (ERIC Document Reproduction Service No. ED 142 200)

SPENCER, DONALD D. *Computer dictionary for everyone.* New York: Scribner's, 1979.

SPENCER, DONALD. *Exploring the world of computers.* Ormond Beach, Fla.: Camelot Publishing Co., 1982.

SPENCER, DONALD. *Microcomputer coloring book.* Ormond Beach, Fla.: Camelot Publishing Co., 1983.

SPENCER, DONALD, AND BEATTY, JOHN R. *Computer awareness book.* Ormond Beach, Fla.: Camelot Publishing Company, 1978.

STEVENS, DOROTHY JO. How educators perceive computers in the classroom. *AEDS Journal,* 1980, 13, 221–232.

TAYLOR, R. Computerless computing for young children or what to do till the computer comes. In O. Lecarme and R. Lewis (eds.), *Computers in education: Proceedings of the IFIP 2nd World Conference.* New York: American Elsevier Publishing Company, 1975.

WALL, ELIZABETH S. *Computer alphabet book.* Nokomis, Fla.: Bayshore Books, 1979.

WATT, DANIEL. Computer literacy: What should schools do about it? *Instructor,* October 1981, pp. 85–87.

WILSON, K. G. English teachers: Keys to computer literacy. *English Journal,* 1981, 70(5), 50–53.

Computer-Assisted Instruction

Computer-assisted instruction has been in use for over two decades. CAI is defined as "a teaching process directly involving the computer in the presentation of instructional material in an interactive mode to provide and control the individualized learning environment for each individualized student. These interactive modes are usually subdivided into drill and practice, tutorial, simulation and gaming, and problem solving."

There have been many studies to test the effectiveness of CAI. Evaluation of CAI suffers from the same problem as the evaluation of a particular teaching method. Just as the teacher in the teaching methods study makes a great deal of difference, the programming of the CAI lesson matters a great deal. With limitations of this sort in mind, we still can say with some confidence that

1. The use of CAI either improves learning or indicates no difference when compared to traditional instruction.
2. Achievement occurs with CAI regardless of the age level of children, the type of computer, or the type of CAI (drill and practice, tutorial, simulation).
3. CAI speeds up learning when compared to conventional methods.
4. Students typically have a positive attitude toward CAI.

5. Tutorial CAI seems to be more effective for low-level students than for middle-or high-ability students.
6. A positive teacher attitude increases CAI effectiveness.
7. Foreign languages and science are particularly good areas of CAI instruction.
8. CAI is helpful in review.
9. Pupils may not remember CAI-presented material as long as material presented via traditional instruction.
10. The cost effectiveness of CAI is improving.

CAI is one portion of an instructional program. Studies must be conducted to develop a time, learning style, teacher, and subject mix for the use of CAI. That CAI is here to stay seems likely. Tables 6-1 and 6-2 summarize two studies on use and projected use. Close to a thousand schools were involved in the studies. Below we look at several modes of materials and give an example of each in classroom use.

DRILL AND PRACTICE

As the name implies, drill-and-practice programs help children to remember and use information they have previously been taught. A drill-and-practice program replaces worksheets, flash cards, and oral drill. If the

TABLE 6-1   Trends (U.S. Experience)

	PERCENT OF SCHOOL DISTRICTS SAMPLED
1. Districts Using Computers	1980—90% 1985—94%
2. Instructional Usage	1970—13% 1980—74% 1985—87%
3. CAL	1980—54% 1985—74%
4. Application Priority	1. Math 2. Science 3. Language Arts 4. Business
5. Emphasis Shift Drill and Practice→Tutorial→Simulation	

(Courtesy of Centre for Information Processing, California State University.)

TABLE 6-2   Levels of Acceptance and Utilization Areas for CAI

	HOME PRESCHOOL	SECONDARY SCHOOLS	HIGHER EDUCATION	INDUSTRY	COMMUNITY INST.
1977 ACCEPTANCE	Zero	Widely dispersed emerging	Widespread	High level limited implementation	On the horizon
1977 UTILIZATION	None	Basic skills (heavy)	Skill and survey type instruction (moderate)	Testing and training drills (light) Basic skills and conditioning programs(light)	Vocabulary and procedural info in health areas
1990 ACCEPTANCE	Widespread	Widespread	Universal	Heavy	Broad by social and health institutions
1990 UTILIZATION	Heavy use in concept development	Universal for skill development and high level concept development	Extensive for entry level courses and high level professional development and continuing education	Heavy in specific training skills and management development	Heavy use by health industry for upgrading diagnostic skill. Heavy use for rehabilitation and deterrent programs in criminal justice.

(From Chambers and Bork, undated, 1978.)

(Courtesy of Centre for Information Processing, California State University.)

74

program is well designed, it can often do an extremely good job with this phase of an instructional program.

One fifth-grade teacher noticed that her children didn't remember the locations of the states in the United States (the fifth-grade social studies program usually focuses on the United States). The teacher found that there were several computer-assisted-instruction programs that could be used to aid their memory. One program, called State Capitols, simply presents the name of a state and asks the student to type in the name of the capital. Students who respond correctly are congratulated and then given the name of another state. If a typical error—such as indicating New York City rather than Albany as the capital of New York—is made, the student is given a comment such as "New York City is a very important city in New York, but not the capital. Try again." If an unexpected answer is given, the program directs the student to try again. After three tries the correct name of the state capital is given.

Another program involves a map of the United States in which the states are numbered. Students are asked to match the name of the state with the number on the map; and they are given hints if an error is made. Each of the programs gives the children a score indicating the number correct for the number of tries.

The teacher used these practice programs in several ways. If an individual child had free time and the computer was free, individual practice was given. A duplicated sheet was provided for all children so that they could keep a record of improvement. Thus, Claudia was able to see that she was right on forty-five out of fifty states, and that a week before she had only answered thirty-five correctly.

If between two and six children wanted to practice, they used a game sheet one of the children had "invented." To use the game sheet, the children divided into teams and then took turns answering the questions. Three points were given to a team if they were right on the first response, one point if they were right on the second try, and no points if they had to be given the answer. The children were challenged to figure out other ways of using the program.

Drill-and-practice programs are available in a variety of modes and a variety of subject matter areas. Care must be taken to carefully evaluate the program, for there are many poor programs that confuse the children and/or reward low-level thinking. Several computational mathematics drill-and-practice programs require a specific sequence of steps in recording the answer, and actually call a correct answer incorrect if it was developed by using a level of thinking higher than the program requires.

For example, in a division practice program, one child was given the computation

3)$\overline{684}$

The student knew that the answer was 228 but was required by the program to respond in the following steps:

$$
\begin{array}{r}
2 \\
1.\ 3\overline{)684}
\end{array}
\qquad
\begin{array}{r}
2 \\
2.\ 3\overline{)684} \\
\underline{6}
\end{array}
$$

$$
\begin{array}{r}
2 \\
3.\ 3\overline{)684} \\
\underline{6} \\
0
\end{array}
\qquad
\begin{array}{r}
22 \\
4.\ 3\overline{)684} \\
\underline{6} \\
08
\end{array}
$$

$$
\begin{array}{r}
22 \\
5.\ 3\overline{)684} \\
\underline{6} \\
08 \\
\underline{6}
\end{array}
\qquad
\begin{array}{r}
22 \\
6.\ 3\overline{)684} \\
\underline{6} \\
8 \\
\underline{6} \\
2
\end{array}
$$

$$
\begin{array}{r}
22 \\
7.\ 3\overline{)684} \\
\underline{6} \\
8 \\
\underline{6} \\
24
\end{array}
\qquad
\begin{array}{r}
228 \\
8.\ 3\overline{)684} \\
\underline{6} \\
8 \\
\underline{6} \\
24 \\
\underline{24}
\end{array}
$$

$$
\begin{array}{r}
228 \\
9.\ 3\overline{)684} \\
\underline{6} \\
8 \\
\underline{6} \\
24 \\
\underline{24} \\
00
\end{array}
$$

While these steps are logical and representative of a step-by-step approach to division, it is easy for anyone who has had experience teaching to recognize that there is a great chance of procedural error in following these steps. Such programs frustrate almost all children and are harmful to many. Such programs reward low-level thinking and penalize high-level thinking.

Before buying or using a drill-and-practice CAI program, it is suggested that you consider the following points. The program should provide

1. Practice on topics that lend themselves to the best use of the computer.
2. Topics that require immediate feedback, such as spelling practice, math facts, and typing practice.
3. Topics that lend themselves to using the computer to randomize and generate a variety of problems.
4. Programs that use sound when appropriate and use the keyboard in such a way that a child will have no difficulty operating it.
5. Topics that require spaced practice, such as state capitals, multiplication facts, and spelling words.

Drill-and-practice materials often lend themselves to instructional games; such use is discussed in the game section that follows. CAI offers a fine opportunity for practice, but the material is only as good as the author's skill in understanding teaching strategies, children, the subject matter, and the potential of the computer.

TUTORIAL

Programs designated as tutorial are typically associated with learning objectives at a higher level than drill-and-practice materials. In general, the goal of these programs is to systematically teach a topic. Because these programs usually teach new material, they require a great deal of effort to develop as well as great skill on the part of the author—both in knowledge of teaching strategy and knowledge of the computer's potential. At the present time the quality of tutorial programs is very mixed.

A good example of an effective tutorial program is a program on critical reading developed at the University of Pennsylvania and distributed by Borg Warner. This program presents interesting reading passages and then asks questions concerning the material that require a high level of comprehension.

On the other hand, there is a program listed as tutorial which is designed to teach the number of quarts in a gallon, pints in a quart, and pints in a gallon. The student is asked, "How many quarts in a gallon?" If the student responds correctly, a positive statement is made, and a gallon jug appears on the screen and then pours milk into four quart bottles. The child then goes on to the next problem. If, however, the child gives the answer as 2 rather than 4, the jug is shown spilling out milk, and the program states that the correct answer is 4 quarts. Next the program states, "There are 4 quarts in a gallon. To change quarts to gallons, multiply by 4."

This is a good use of computer graphics but a poor teaching strategy. First, the child does not get an idea of the size of quarts and gallons; second, the rule is given before the student has an opportunity to experiment with the ideas and understand them.

Before purchasing or using a tutorial CAI program, we suggested that you

1. Decide if the topic is one you should develop by using the computer or by personal teaching. (Note: You may find that a tutorial program designed for teaching a topic makes a better review or reteaching vehicle.)
2. Be sure there are effective means of handling logical errors. For example, if 25 + 18 is presented for the first time, the program should take into consideration the common error of answering 313 rather than 43. Students answering 313 should be "branched" into some material that helps them see the mistake in thinking involved in the response.
3. Be sure the tutorial makes use of the unique capabilities of the computer: movement, branching on the basis of error, keeping track of errors, pacing accordingly, moving children along rapidly when it is evident they learn well with few examples, and slowing the pace on the basis of student errors.
4. Consider using tutorial CAI programs to teach about the computer.
5. Consider mixed media tutorials which use the computer and other media. For example, there is an excellent introduction to the use of the Apple computer which makes use of audio tapes to instruct the learner on how to use the computer. In this case a sound tape works much better than a book, because learners have their eyes busy watching the monitor screen and possibly the keyboard.

GAMES

The use of games generated by the computer is one of the most effective aspects of computer-assisted instruction. By the term *games* we do not mean the typical arcade and home computer games which at best develop some thinking strategies and hand-eye coordination. Rather, we are referring to games designed to help teach or reinforce an instructional objective. A good instructional game requires active physical and/or mental involvement of the players. It involves an element of chance, so that a child with a greater amount of knowledge, ability, and/or skill would win a game more often than one who did not have these attributes. However, chance should play enough of a part so that the interest of the less-successful child is maintained.

One teacher at the upper middle school level was trying to help the students learn prime factors as a help in division, and to further better understanding of number relations. The instructional game Factors was chosen. This game involves choosing a set of numbers to be used in the game—for example, 1 to 81—and then playing against the program in the machine. The instructions are as follows:

FACTOR GAME:

THIS IS THE FACTOR GAME. YOU PLAY AGAINST THE COMPUTER. WHEN IT IS YOUR TURN, YOU CHOOSE A NUMBER FROM THE NUMBERS DISPLAYED. AFTER YOU HAVE CHOSEN A NUMBER, I CAN THEN CLAIM ALL THE NUMBERS REMAINING

IN THE LIST WHICH ARE FACTORS OF YOUR CHOICE. FOR EX-
AMPLE, IF YOU CHOOSE 18, THEN I CAN CLAIM 2,3,6, AND 9 IF
THEY ARE STILL ON THE POINT LIST. YOU WOULD RECEIVE
18 POINTS, AND I WOULD RECEIVE 20. THEN IT WOULD BE MY
TURN TO CHOOSE, AFTER WHICH YOU CLAIM FACTORS. THE
WINNER HAS THE MOST POINTS AFTER ALL THE FACTORS
ARE GONE.

To introduce the game, the teacher had the whole class play against
the program. After playing the game with the entire class twice, she
allowed groups of three students to play the game in their spare time
before or after school and during a portion of math time.

When selecting games, it is suggested that the following questions
and comments be used:

1. Do the games develop or reinforce important instructional objectives? A
   game that does not fit in with the current program is not worth school
   time. Inappropriate use of games can hurt proper development of learning
   sequences.

2. Is a great deal of the interest in the game created by the material to be
   studied, as opposed to outside motivation? The factors game described
   above makes use of mathematics itself to create interest in the game.

   Sometimes it is necessary to bring in outside interests with a game such as
   football or with arcade-type topics. However, if the motivation from the
   outside idea is too great, it can cause active participation without learning.
   For example, some teachers have observed that children playing a typing
   game that causes them to score by good typing make the number of words
   per minute and lack of errors the key motivation. These children improve
   more rapidly in their typing than those playing a game in which they are
   typing rapidly to shoot down spaceships or to avoid being shot down by
   another spaceship.

3. Are the instructions easy for the children to use? In computer terms, is the
   program friendly? That is, can someone with no knowledge of computers or
   of the game play the game?

4. Is the format interesting? Does the game seem like a "game" rather than a
   practice page? Too often games have little intrinsic interest—they are just
   disguised drill.

5. Does the game "stand on its own"? That is, is there enough in the game
   itself so that children will find it interesting as well as helpful in learning the
   subject taught?

6. Does the game accomplish one or more of the following objectives?
   a. Create a learning situation in which the fundamental concept or skill is
      being practiced in the process of participating in the game
   b. Reward players on a team for cooperative effort
   c. Provide an opportunity for the students themselves to serve as models
      for other children
   d. Require a playing strategy that forces the players to learn and/or under-
      stand a particular curriculum concept
   e. Provide a concrete frame of reference for dealing with the subject matter
   f. Cause the players to be active participants

     g.   Require very little waiting time between turns for the players

7.   Does the game produce measurable effects on those participating in the game?

There are many excellent games for children. In some cases children should be encouraged to use some of the games at home. Teachers can often help children choose computer games that are educational as well as fun. This benefits both the child and the teacher.

SIMULATION

A number of instructional programs are classified as simulations and are sometimes called simulation games. Simulations are used by the space program to test out ideas when a given environment is developed. Simulations are used to pretest cars. The game Monopoly is a board game simulation. We can be reasonably sure that children and adults like to work with simulations. In fact, Monopoly is the most widely sold specific game of all time.

One of the oldest computer simulations is an economic education program in which the students are to act as the rulers of a make-believe country and make economic decisions on the basis of data presented. If they apply good economic principles, the country prospers—if not, the country goes broke and the ruler loses the throne.

Another well-known simulation that can be used effectively in the fifth grade is called Oregon Trail. Oregon Trail is a public domain program which you can obtain from SOFTSWAP (see appendix). The simulation begins in Missouri, where the players make choices of how to spend their money outfitting themselves to go on the Oregon Trail. They need to balance outlays among food, ammunition, medical supplies, and the like. As they move along the trail, they decide how well to eat, what to do as a group approaches in the distance, and whether or not to hunt. They hunt with the game paddles. As the children use the simulation, they become familiar with the relationship between how they spend their money and the outcome of the simulation.

PROBLEM SOLVING

Microcomputers can be used for a variety of problem-solving activities. Some of them involve the development of computer programs by the children. There are a number of other problem-solving uses of microcomputers. For example, one teacher developed a program in which the children were given a display of grocery store food on the screen, similar to that shown below. They were to insert the cost for each item taken from the ads in the newspaper and then determine a grocery list. As they progressed, they used the computer to help them decide upon the best buys.

ITEM	TOPS	BELLS	SUPER
One-Half			
Gallon 2% Milk			
One lb. Hamburger	(each week new data is used)		
10 lb. Potatoes			
Etc.			

INFORMATION RETRIEVAL

Some teachers make use of computer programs such as Personal Filing System to help the children learn about computers and also learn organizational skills. A filing program lets the user set up files about one topic that may be used to keep track of information in a systematic way.

For example, writers might categorize their notes under headings that would fit with the basic chapters in a book that was being written. At a later time they might wish to obtain only the notes dealing with a particular individual. By loading the file on the computer and requesting the given name, the writers would cause all the material that included that name to be displayed.

One of the demonstration parts of most master disks for a microcomputer includes a program for keeping track of telephone numbers. While this is not a particularly productive use of a microcomputer, it demonstrates how a file system might be used. For example, the user makes up files on the persons that he or she might call. This file can include names—first and last—addresses, added information, and phone numbers.

To obtain the information, the user asks for any of the categories and is given the one or more names in that category. Consider a salesperson who wants to call all of the customers that live in a particular area. A request is made for all numbers with 661-xxxx, and a list is provided. Another person wants to call a company in Detroit but cannot remember the exact name. He or she asks for all Detroit numbers. Upon receiving the Detroit numbers and names, the person is able to make the call. What applications of such a system do you think you could use with sixth graders?

ANALYSIS

It is strongly suggested that after reading Chapter 8 you take time to study a number of individual CAI disks.

Self-Test

1. Research shows that CAI clearly is more effective than conventional instruction.
2. Slow learners work better on drill and practice than on tutorial.
3. Simulations work better for mathematics than for science.
4. Tutorials are harder to develop than drill-and-practice games.
5. If there is only one computer in a classroom, simulations are a better use of the computer than drill and practice.
6. CAI will probably never be used in the home.
7. Games should emphasize outside interests such as space war games.
8. It is important for a teacher to be involved in CAI instruction.
9. While they bring structure to material, rigid sequences can also confuse children.

Think About

1. On what topic would you like to have a CAI lesson for your use?
2. Which of the modes do you think will prove most productive?
3. What questions need to be answered concerning CAI?
4. About how much time per day do you think a child should spend on computer-assisted instruction?
5. What teacher skills are necessary for developing CAI programs?
6. How do you believe CAI will be used for home instruction?
7. Develop a CAI instructional strategy for teaching a topic of your choice.

Selected References:

Aiken, R.M., and Braun, L. **Into the 80's with microcomputer-based learning.** *Computer,* 1980, 13 (7).
What do Aiken and Braun project for CAI?

Atkinson, R.C. **Futures: Where will computer-assisted instruction be in 1990?** *Educational Technology,* 1978, 18(4).

Bitzer, D. **Futures: Where will computer-assisted instruction be in 1990?** *Educational Technology,* 1978, 18(4).
Compare Atkinson and Bitzer in their approach to CAI for the next decade.

Coburn, Peter, Kelman, Peter, Roberts, Nancy, Snyder, Thomas, Watt, Daniel, and Weinter, Cheryl. *Practical guide to computers in education.* Reading, Mass.: Addison-Wesley, 1982.

Doerr, Christine. *Microcomputers and the 3r's.* Rochelle Park, N. J.: Hayden Book Co. 1979.
Coburn et al. and Doerr are good sources. Use them to supplement this book.

Hirschbuhl, J.J. **Considerations for computer-based education in the 1980's.** *Journal of Research and Development in Education,* 1980, 14(1).

Gundlach presents an example of how one whole district implemented CMI with microcomputers. What do you think the advantages and disadvantages are of districtwide CMI? He stresses the importance of administration and teachers being completely trained in the use of the system. What do you believe you would want to know about a CMI program before you used it?

Hedges, William D. Lightening the load with Computer Managed Instruction. *Classroom Computer News,* July/August 1981, pp. 34–35.
Hedges provides an easy-to-read description of and checklist for evaluating CMI programs.

Bibliography

BAKER, FRANK B. Computer-based instruction management systems: A first look. *Review of Educational Research,* 1971, 41, 51–70.

BAKER, FRANK B. *Computer managed instruction: Theory and practice.* Englewood Cliffs, N.J.: Educational Technology Publ., 1978.

BAKER, FRANK B. Computer-managed instruction: A context for computer-based instruction. In H. F. O'Neil, Jr. (ed.), *Computer-based instruction: A state-of-the-art assessment.* New York: Academic Press, 1981.

BARRETT, BRADLEY K., AND HANNAFIN, MICHAEL J. Computer in educational management: Merging accountability with technology. *Educational Technology,* 1982, 22(3), 9–12.

BOZEMAN, WILLIAM C. Human factors considerations in the design of systems of computer managed instruction. *AEDS Journal,* 1978, 11, 89–96.

BOZEMAN, WILLIAM C. Computer-managed instruction: State of the art. *AEDS Journal,* 1979, 12, 117–137.

BREBNER, ANN, HALLWORTH, H. J., MCINTOSH, E., AND WONTNER, C. *Teaching elementary reading by CMI and CAI.* Columbus, Ohio: ERIC, 1980. (ERIC Document Reproduction Service No. ED 198 793).

CARTWRIGHT, GLENN F., AND DEREVENSKY, JEFFERY L. An attitudinal research study of computer-assisted testing as a learning method. *Psychology in the Schools,* 1976, 13, 317–321.

CAVIN, CLAUDIA S. Microcomputer generation of interactive quizzes. *Educational Technology,* 1982, 22(2), 31–32.

CHANOINE, J. R. Learning of elementary students in an individualized mathematics program with a computer assisted management system. *Dissertation Abstracts International,* 1977, 38, 2626A.

CROUSE, DAVID B. The computerized gradebook as a component of a computer-managed curriculum. *Educational Technology,* 1981, 21(5), 16–20.

DAYTON, DEANE K. Computer-assisted graphics. *Instructional Innovator,* 1981, 26, 16–18.

DOERR, CHRISTINE, *Microcomputers and the 3 R's.* Rochelle Park, N.J.: Hayden Book Co., 1979.

EISENBERG, BERNARD. Final exams—Let the computer write them. *Creative Computing,* November/December 1977, pp. 103–106.

ELLIS, J. A. A comparative evaluation of computer-managed instruction and instructor-managed instruction. Proceedings of the Association for the Development of Computer-Based Instructional Systems, 1978.

GUNDLACH, A. Managing instruction with a micro—The first steps. In N. R. Watson (ed.), Microcomputers in education: Uses for the '80's. Publication No. 3. Proceedings of the Second Annual Microcomputer Conference, Arizona State University, July 15 and 16, 1982.

HART, D. G. Computer Managed Instruction: An approach. *International Journal of Instructional Media,* 1981/1982, 9(1), 11–12.

HASSELBRING, TED, AND OWENS, SHERYL. Microcomputer-based analysis of spelling errors. *Computers, Reading and Language Arts,* 1983, 1(1), 26–31.

HAUGO, JOHN E. Management applications of the microcomputer: Promises and pitfalls. *AEDS Journal*, 1981, 14, 182–188.

HEDDEN, ROGER. Calling all teachers. *Kilobaud Microcomputing*, November 1981, pp. 306–310.

HEDGES, WILLIAM D. Lightening the load with Computer Managed Instruction. *Classroom Computer News*, July/August 1981, pp. 34–35.

INGRAM, JAMES A. Tame that blackboard jungle. *Kilobaud Microcomputing*, September 1981, pp. 91–92.

JOHNSON, DALE. A Grade Assignment Program—AGAP. *The Computing Teacher*, 1981, 9(2), 29–34.

JOOS, L. W. SING—A computer program for grouping students for instruction. *AEDS Journal*, 1980, 13, 214–220.

KIEREN, THOMAS E. *The use of computers in mathematics education resource series: Research on computers in mathematics education.* Columbus, Ohio: ERIC, 1973. (ERIC Document Reproduction Service No. ED 077 734)

KNIGHT, C. W., 2ND, AND DUNKLEBERGER, G. E. The influence of computer-managed self-paced instruction on science attitudes of students. *Journal of Research in Science Teaching*, 1977, 14, 551–555.

KOELEWYN, ARIE C. TESTSCORER: A computer program for grading tests. *Educational Technology*, 1983, 23(5), 31.

LECARME, O., AND LEWIS, R. (eds.). *Computers in Education: Proceedings of the IFIP 2nd World Conference.* New York: American Elsevier Publishing Company, 1975.

LUTZ, JOHN E., AND TAYLOR, PATRICIA A. A computerized home-based curriculum for high-risk preschoolers. *AEDS Journal*, 1981, 15(1), 1–9.

McIAAC, DONALD N., AND BAKER, FRANK B. Computer-managed instruction system implementation on a microcomputer. *Educational Technology*, 1981, 22(10), 40–46.

McKINLEY, R. L., AND RECKASE, M. D. Computer applications to ability testing. *AEDS Journal*, 1980, 13, 193–203.

OVERTON, VICTORIA. Research in instructional computing in mathematics education. *Viewpoints in Teaching and Learning*, Spring 1981, pp. 23–36.

SPUCK, DENNIS W., AND BOZEMAN, WILLIAM C. Pilot test and evaluation of a system of computer-managed instruction. *AEDS Journal*, 1978, 12, 31–41.

SPUCK, DENNIS W., AND BOZEMAN, WILLIAM C. A design for the evaluation of management information systems. *AEDS Journal*, 1980, 14, 30–44.

SPUCK, DENNIS W., AND OWEN, STEPHEN P. Computer managed instruction: A model. *AEDS Journal*, 1974, 8, 17–23.

TEOH, W. Grades: A class record updating system. *Creative Computing*, October 1981, pp. 166–168; 170; 172–177.

WILKINS, P. W. The effects of computer assisted classroom management on the achievement and attitudes of eighth grade mathematics students. Dissertation Abstracts International, 1975, 36, 3379A.

Software Selection

Locating good software programs is a major undertaking. While there is some similarity between the search for a good textbook and a good disk, there are a number of other factors that must be considered when selecting software. Teachers and administrators have had high hopes when they purchased a program, only to find that at best it is an electronic page turner or at worst goes against the teaching content and philosophy of the district. A large state is presently suggesting that its major cities spend almost $100,000 on material that was developed from a poor quality cut-and-paste individualized mathematics program. The material was professionally evaluated as being of poor quality, and there has been no evaluation of student progress. This group has forgotten the old computer saying, "Garbage in—garbage out."

How can this type of waste be avoided? Hopefully, the material that follows will help you to become an educated software buyer. A discount clothing store has the motto, "An educated consumer is our best customer." It is hoped that many of the software developers and distributors will develop products that are in keeping with that statement.

A few guiding principles of software selection will be identified below, and then suggestions for following them will be given.

1. Preview the software before you buy it.
   a. Preview all major software.
   b. Study reviews of software you are considering.
   c. Use an evaluation scale that fits your needs.
   d. Know why you want particular software—for what purpose is it to be purchased?
2. Find the answers to these critical questions about software:
   a. How are the students motivated? How is interest developed and maintained? Is the interest created through the use of an absorbing approach to the material itself—or does it come from some outside source?
   b. What is the teaching method? Does it involve the child in the thinking? Is it explanatory or discovery oriented?
   c. For what audience is the material appropriate?
   d. What background is required to use the material? What does the student need to know before starting?
   e. How does the program use the students' time—that is—is it time effective? How much time does it take to use the program in relation to the number of students that are to use the program?
   f. Is the program user friendly? Can a first-time user rapidly learn to use the material?
   g. Is the program well conceived? (Problems concerned with this issue are listed in a later section.)
   h. Is it well documented? Is the printed material that accompanies the disk or other medium very helpful in using the program? Does it give all the information needed in a well-organized fashion? Does it provide goals, entry skills, and design?
   i. Is the sequence of topics in keeping with the curriculum of the school?
   j. Can the materials be easily worked into the regular program?
   k. What portion of the teaching load does the material contain?
   l. Is the main thrust supplemental or basic?
   m. Is the material free from content (subject matter) errors?
   n. Does it provide good graphics?
   o. Is the program a good use of the computer? Does it make use of the unique strength of the computer?
   p. Does the material make good use of situations appropriate for the background of the children?
   q. If wanted, does the material provide for a variation in content to meet individual needs?
   r. Are back-up copies provided?
   s. Is the program cost effective in terms of use? Does the program have "unlimited" use—or is it locked into one time use—that is, will it only teach or practice one or a few days' lessons?
3. Involve those who are experts in working with children and in instruction in the selection of programs.
4. Test the material with the children who are to use it.
5. Think of particular individual needs of your classroom or of your district.

6. Check on the possibility of home use of some of the materials.
7. Be sure to consider materials for teacher use, such as grade books, worksheet developers, test-construction programs, and so on.
8. Be open in your selection. Give manufacturers the reason for rejecting their materials.
9. Send suggestions to manufacturers.
10. Do not place as much emphasis upon the size and longevity of the company as you would in adopting a textbook series.
11. Know the philosophy of the authors of the material.
12. Does the model of teaching match the content of the materials? For example, a simple drill program may give so many graphics that it requires a child to spend twice as much time as necessary on the program.
13. Soon on-line data bases which teachers can access with a computer will be available in many schools. They will allow for searching (as in a file system) for reviews and evaluations of educational software. A number of agencies that will be providing such services are listed in the appendix. We will now look at some of the above suggestions in depth.

IDENTIFY THE SOFTWARE BEFORE YOU BUY IT

The late E.F. Lindquist was one of the pioneers in developing standardized tests for elementary and secondary students. When asked how a school district should decide whether or not to use his test or another test, he usually said, "Have the teachers who teach the way the district thinks appropriate take each of the tests. Buy the one that these teachers think best presents the content and objectives of their program." Such advice is equally good in purchasing educational software.

As a first step in obtaining software, we would suggest that you locate as many reviews as possible of the type of software you need. Either find a software evaluation center near you that has a wide variety of reviews, or urge the school district to purchase journals and books on software. A partial listing of sources of software evaluations is given at the end of the chapter.

Be sure that you find out something about the review source and about the writers of the review. You would get quite a different review from someone who is interested in computer graphics more than in teaching methods than from a teacher with a great concern for motivating children. If possible, know about your reviewers and read a wide variety of reviews.

After you have read a number of reviews concerning the type of software you are after, order those that seem most appropriate for preview. Have the teacher and children who will be using the materials preview them along with the subject area supervisors, principals, and others responsible for software purchase. If the program is one that requires in-service before use, the faculty or others who would need to give the in-service should be involved in the selection. We have seen instances where a district has spent a good deal of money on programs that knowledgeable teachers and administrators feel to be "bad news."

To get a good idea of how the various reviewers feel about the programs, make use of an evaluation sheet. You may need to write to a company to obtain catalogs and other information. In most cases, since there is such a great interest in microcomputer programs, we would suggest that you write a very short letter indicating the information you want. Include the make and any special features of your computer, the drive used, and the subject matter areas of interest to your school.

When you order the program for preview, fill in a *software documentation sheet* such as the one included here.

When the evaluation sheets are completed, those disks that meet the standard of the district can be ordered. For those disks that prove less than satisfactory, a copy of the evaluation sheet should be sent to the publishers to aid them in improving their product.

HOW IS THE MOTIVATION DEVELOPED?

Motivation is, to a certain extent, an individual matter. However, for long-lasting motivation, the interest has to come from the material being studied—not from an external source. One practice typing program has the format of an arcade game in which the children shoot down a spacecraft before it shoots them down. The children get so involved in the game that they don't increase their interest in typing. On the other hand, a typing practice in which the motivation centers on playing against their previous typing score might increase their interest in typing.

WHAT IS THE TEACHING METHOD?

Some computer-assisted-instruction programs are modeled on earlier ideas of "programmed instruction." Many of these were a "fill in the correct word" approach. The computer allows for real interaction with the learner. CAI allows for methods of instruction that develop thinking skills and pupil discovery. Some of the formats using this approach include

1. Directing children's discovery through a series of leading questions. If the student makes a mistake, an easier question is asked. This approach is particularly helpful in remedial work and with the slow learner. The student pays careful attention because of the constant asking of questions and feels rewarded because he or she is able to answer the questions.
2. Presenting a pattern and asking the learner to find the pattern. This involves a higher-level skill than a step-by-step questioning and is a good technique for enrichment and for use with the able students.
3. Presenting a problem in which the child is to use past experience to discover the new idea. This method can be used well when two or three children are working together on the computer.

SOFTWARE EVALUATION CHECKLIST

PROGRAM NAME: _____ SOURCE: _____ COST: _____
SUBJECT AREA: _____ REVIEWER'S NAME: _____ DATE: _____

1. INSTRUCTIONAL RANGE
   _____ grade level(s)
   _____ ability level(s)

2. INSTRUCTIONAL GROUPING FOR PROGRAM USE
   _____ individual
   _____ small group (size: _____)
   _____ large group (size: _____)

3. EXECUTION TIME
   _____ minutes (estimated) for average use

4. PROGRAM USE(S)
   _____ drill or practice
   _____ tutorial
   _____ simulation
   _____ instructional gaming
   _____ problem solving
   _____ informational
   _____ other (_____)

5. USER ORIENTATION: INSTRUCTOR'S POINT OF VIEW

	low				high	
flexibility	·	·	·	·	·	
freedom from need to intervene or assist	·	·	·	·	·	

6. USER ORIENTATION: STUDENT'S POINT OF VIEW

	low				high	
quality of directions (clarity)	·	·	·	·	·	
quality of output (content and tone)	·	·	·	·	·	
quality of screen formatting	·	·	·	·	·	
freedom from need for external information	·	·	·	·	·	
freedom from disruption by system errors	·	·	·	·	·	
simplicity of user input	·	·	·	·	·	

7. CONTENT

	low				high
instructional focus	·	·	·	·	·
instructional significance	·	·	·	·	·
soundness or validity	·	·	·	·	·
compatibility with other materials used	·	·	·	·	·

8. MOTIVATION AND INSTRUCTIONAL STYLE

	passive				active
type of student involvement	·	·	·	·	·

	low				high
degree of student control	·	·	·	·	·

	none	poor			good
use of game format	·	·	·	·	·
use of still graphics	·	·	·	·	·
use of animation	·	·	·	·	·
use of color	·	·	·	·	·
use of voice input and output	·	·	·	·	·
use of nonvoice audio	·	·	·	·	·
use of light pen	·	·	·	·	·
use of ancillary materials	·	·	·	·	·
use of _____	·	·	·	·	·

9. SOCIAL CHARACTERISTICS

	present and negative	not present	present and positive
competition			
cooperation			
humanizing of computer			
moral issues or value judgments			
summary of student performance			

(Courtesy of the National Council of Teachers of Mathematics.)

1. The grade levels and ability levels for a particular program are primarily determined by the concepts involved. Other important factors are reading level, prerequisite skills, degree of student control, and intended instructional use. It is possible for a program to be flexible enough to be used across a wide range of grade levels and ability levels.

2. Some programs are designed for use by individuals. Others have been or can be modified for participation by two or three persons at a time. Simulations or demonstrations often pose opportunities for large-group interaction. A given program may be used in more than one grouping, depending on the instructor.

3. The time required for the use of a program will vary considerably. Include loading time for cassettes. A time range is the appropriate response here.

4. Instructional programs can be categorized according to their uses. Some programs may have more than one use, thus falling into more than one of the following categories:

Drill or practice: Assumes that the concept or skill has been taught previously.

Tutorial: Directs the full cycle of the instructional process; a dialogue between the student and the computer.

Simulation: Models selected, alterable aspects of an environment.

Instructional gaming: Involves random events and the pursuit of a winning strategy.

Problem solving: Uses general algorithms common to one or more problems.

Informational: Generates information (data).

5. These are factors relevant to the actual use of the program from the point of view of an instructor.

Flexibility: A program may allow the user or the instructor to adjust the program to different ability levels, degrees of difficulty, or concepts.

Intervention or assistance: A rating of "low" means considerable teacher intervention or assistance is required.

6. These are factors relevant to the actual use of the program from the point of view of a student.

Directions: The directions should be complete, readable, under the user's control (e.g., should not scroll off the screen until understood), and use appropriate examples.

Output: Program responses should be readable, understandable, and complete. If in response to student input, the output should be of an acceptable tone and consistent with the input request.

Screen formatting: The formats during a program run should not be distracting or cluttered. Labels and symbols should be meaningful in the given context.

External information: A program may require the user to have access to information other than that provided within it. This may include prerequisite content knowledge or knowledge of conventions used by the program designer as well as maps, books, models, and so on.

System errors: System errors result in the involuntary termination of the program.

Input: A program should ensure that a user knows when and in what form input is needed. It should avoid using characters with special meanings, restrict input locations to particular screen areas, and require minimal typing.

7. These are matters relevant to the subject-matter content of the program.

Focus: The program topic should be clearly defined and of a scope that permits thorough treatment.

Significance: The instructional objectives of the program must be viewed as important by the instructor. Also, the program should represent a valid use of the computer's capabilities while improving the instructional process.

Soundness or validity: The concepts and terms employed should be correct, clear, and precise. Other important factors are the rate of presentation, degree of difficulty, and internal consistency.

Compatibility: The content, terminology, teaching style, and educational philosophy of the program should be consistent with those generally encountered by the student.

9. Competition, cooperation, and values are concerns that may be a function of the way a program expresses them. (War gaming and the "hangman" format are sample issues.) Also, the "humanizing" of the computer may serve for motivation or to reduce anxiety, but it also may become tedious, misleading, and counterproductive.

The summary of student performance can be dichotomous (win or lose), statistical (time expended or percent of items correct), or subjective (as in the evaluation of a simulation). It may be for student, teacher, or both.

(Courtesy of the NCTM.)

🆖🆃🅼 SAMPLE SOFTWARE DOCUMENTATION SHEET

PROGRAM NAME: _____

SUBJECT AREA: _____

PROGRAM CLASS

_____ isolated program

_____ part of a _____ program cluster

INTENDED AUDIENCE(S)

_____ teachers

_____ students in grade(s) _____

_____ other _____
_____

PROGRAM USES: (1 = primary, 2 = secondary)

_____ drill or practice

_____ tutorial

_____ simulation

_____ instructional gaming

_____ problem solving

_____ informational

_____ other _____
_____

CRITICAL PREREQUISITE SKILLS

_____
_____

NAME(S) OF PREREQUISITE PROGRAM(S)

_____
_____
_____

NAME(S) OF FOLLOW-UP PROGRAM(S)

_____
_____
_____

DATE OF THIS DOCUMENTATION

_____

(Courtesy of the NCTM.)

PROGRAM SOURCE

name: _____

address: _____
_____
_____

phone: _____

program cost: _____

SYSTEM REQUIREMENTS

computer: _____

language: _____

memory needed: _____ bytes

input mode: cassette

              _____-inch diskette

              cartridge

              other _____
              _____

output mode: color monitor

              B/W monitor

              printer

              plotter

              other _____
              _____

CLASSROOM VALIDATION (describe)

_____
_____
_____

TIME FOR AVERAGE
EXECUTION   _____ minutes

OVER ➡

GENERAL DESCRIPTION OF THE PROGRAM (i.e., purpose of the program)

SPECIAL PROGRAM CHARACTERISTICS (e.g., use of graphics or sound, designed for use by groups of two or more persons at a time, level of difficulty can be modified by teacher (only) or student, exit from program is controlled by the teacher (only) or student, etc.)

DIRECTIONS FOR USE OF THE PROGRAM (e.g., directions not presented in the program itself but needed for program execution, directions regarding the use of the program within the total instructional process, notes regarding program options, etc.)

ANCILLARY MATERIALS REQUIRED (e.g., books, worksheets, charts, data lists, dice, geometric shapes, lab equipment, etc.)

ADDITIONAL DOCUMENTATION AVAILABLE (check box for each type)

☐ sample run (location _____)

☐ program listing (location _____)

(Courtesy of the NCTM.)

Software Evaluation Form

Reviewer's Name: _____ Date of Review: _____

Address/Phone: _____( ) _____

Program Title _____ Medium: ___ 5" disk; ___ 8" disk;

___ cartridge; ___ tape

Package Title _____ Copyright Date (if any) _____

Microcomputer (brand, model, memory) _____

Necessary Hardware _____ Necessary Software _____

Producer _____ Author(s) _____

Back-up Copy Policy _____ Cost _____

PART 1
Program Overview and Description

1. Subject area and specific topic _____
2. Prerequisite skills necessary _____
3. Appropriate grade level (circle) 1 2 3 4 5 6 7 8 9 10 11 12 college
4. Type of program (check one or more)

   ___ Simulation   ___ Testing
   ___ Educational Game   ___ Classroom Management
   ___ Drill and Practice   ___ Other (specify) _____
   ___ Tutorial
   ___ Problem Solving   ___ Remediation
   ___ Authoring System   ___ Enrichment
5. Appropriate group instructional size: ___ individual ___ small group ___ class
6. Is this program an appropriate instructional use of the computer? _____

7. Briefly list the program's objectives. Are they clearly stated in the program or in the documentation? Are they educationally valuable? Are they achieved?

   _____
   _____
   _____

8. Briefly describe the program. Mention any special strengths or weaknesses.

   _____
   _____
   _____

(Electronic Learning.)

4. Simulating a problem and having the children probe to find answers. This is very good for science, social studies, and general problem solving. One of the Minnesota (MECC) programs involves a simulation at Odell Lake. The children are to decide what fish they wish to represent, and then they are asked a number of questions concerning their action when another fish approaches. Through this simulation game they discover that certain fish eat other fish, while some fish eat only insects, worms, and so on.

FOR WHAT AUDIENCE IS THE MATERIAL APPROPRIATE?

Several things need to be taken into consideration in determining the audience. Type of motivation is important. Level of reading and previous skill levels need to be considered. Here is a place where the teacher who knows the children can decide. One program may be great for a certain fourth grade in the school district but not for another fourth grade in the same district.

Several teachers in a school district can make use of their children to aid in determining the appropriateness of the program. In one school the teachers identified one of their best students, a student they had identified as average, and a student that was experiencing difficulty in the area covered by the program. Then the teachers interviewed each of the children individually.

HOW DOES THE PROGRAM USE THE STUDENTS' TIME?

This question may not be as important when there are more computers available in the school. But while there is one or two computers per building, it is important to have the majority of programs accomplish something in a short time. A simulation game may be very good if used by the entire class working in teams, but it may require too much time if only two individuals are going to work with it at a time.

A reading lesson that requires the reading of several pages from the screen and then develops reading skills with comprehension questions may be excellent. However, if it requires twenty to thirty minutes per person, it is probably not a wise investment for a classroom that has use of a computer only two afternoons a week. It would be better used for a reading lab that has six children per hour and has four computers.

IS THE PROGRAM USER FRIENDLY?

"User friendly" is computerese for "You don't have to know much about the program to use it." User friendliness can be accomplished in a variety of ways. The program may give the user choices as to what he or she wants to do. It should allow the user to go back to the beginning of the program without turning off the computer (there are a number of programs in which the only way to stop is to turn off the computer). It should have easy response. For example, some older programs suggest that the user answer (1) for yes and (2) for no. The user will often type *yes* or *Y* and *no* or *N* and be told to try again. This is not user friendly. Some friendly programs allow a typing of *help* or *H* if there is a need to get directions. The word processing program we're using allows us to type Q (for question) with the control key held down in order to get a screen of helps.

IS THE PROGRAM WELL CONCEIVED?

Just as we all like different TV programs and movies, we may like particular CAI programs. There are, however, a number of programming procedures that detract from a program's effectiveness. Usually the following are best avoided:

1. A program that gives audible feedback that cannot be turned off. Some drill-and-practice programs have a loud noise when an error is made. Children should not have to advertise their errors.
2. A program that runs inconsistently. Some programs stop for no discernible reason, and the computer has to be turned off and started again. Or sometimes the program runs, and sometimes it doesn't. For a knowledgeable user, this is annoying. For a beginner, it is fear provoking. The latter is afraid the disk has been destroyed or—even worse—that the computer has broken.
3. A program that rewards failure. This makes it more interesting to make a mistake than to get the correct answer. Some Hangman programs do this.
4. A program that makes errors in factual material. This should not be allowed.
5. A screen advance that cannot be controlled. There are programs that give a paragraph of instructions and then pause for a predetermined time for their reading. This causes the person who reads rapidly or who already knows the instructions to be bored. At the same time, it may be too fast for a poor reader. The user should have control over the screen advance by hitting the space bar or another key.
6. A program that does not allow a user to skip the instructions. A game should not require everyone to read the instructions but should ask a question at the beginning—Would you like instructions?

After you have worked with programs for a time, you will no doubt find other reasons for rejecting programs (Lathrop, 1982).

IS THE PROGRAM WELL DOCUMENTED?

Documentation is a computer term for directions, manuals, and teachers' manuals. There are many good-to-excellent programs which do not have good documentation. One of the best word processing programs for the

Apple computer had very poor documentation in the early editions. It was almost impossible to learn to use the program without having help from someone who had used it already and had called the factory to ask several questions. As more educators have become involved in the development of materials, the documentation has improved. Some of the best documentation gives a long form for detailed study and a short form on a piece of heavy paper which can be covered with contact for ready reference. If the program does not fill up the majority of the disk, it is good enough to have documentation on the disk as well as on paper. Then the directions are always available.

IS THE PROGRAM COST EFFECTIVE?

Again, this is an individual decision. In general, programs that allow for multiple use are more cost effective than those that focus on a single lesson. Thus, addition games in which the numbers are randomly generated (at a determined level of difficulty) are usually better than addition games with a fixed set of problems. In the same manner, a word processing program is probably a better investment for eighth-grade language arts than a program on adjectives.

IS THE SEQUENCE OF TOPICS IN KEEPING WITH THE CURRICULUM OF THE SCHOOL?

Many of the reading and mathematics programs are based on a particular teaching order or set of materials. In reviewing materials it is important to consider how closely they match the other materials used in the classroom. If you are just beginning to use computer-assisted instruction and do not have many computers available, it is suggested that you make major use of supplemental materials for a time. This greatly helps in managing the system. Also, most teachers and school systems prefer to have the major teaching of a topic rest with the teacher, and use CAI for both remediation and enrichment.

IS THE MATERIAL FREE FROM SUBJECT MATTER ERRORS?

This criterion is always important, no matter what types of instructional material are being purchased. It is tremendously important in the case of CAI materials, for often the students may use the material without class or teacher discussion. If a few members of a sixth-grade class were using some physics CAI disks as a supplement to a unit on energy, they would probably accept errors without question.

DOES IT PROVIDE GOOD GRAPHICS?

The majority of reviews of CAI materials will be reasonably critical of the graphic presentation in terms of animation and general appearance. Another area to check carefully is the accuracy with which the material is presented graphically. One very good simulation that develops concepts concerning differences in animals has graphics that present each member of a given class of animals as all looking alike. Even though this is mentioned in the program, a child could go away with the idea that a camel and a horse look exactly alike.

IS THE PROGRAM A GOOD USE OF THE COMPUTER?

This question is of major importance at the present time. When most class members can have only very limited use of the computer in the classroom, the computer should do something that makes use of its unique possibilities. Thus, a straight drill-and-practice program on addition facts is not as productive a use of the computer as a program that keeps track of the students' errors and recycles through the program the addition facts the child has missed. A spelling program on the 200 spelling demons would not make as good a use of the computer as a program in which pupils could input a list of the words on which they needed further help.

Remember, it is not always important to have a "flashy" program; rather, the program must be effective and use children's time to the best advantage.

DOES THE MATERIAL PROVIDE
FOR INDIVIDUAL DIFFERENCES?

A program that moves students to easier or harder materials based on their performance makes good use of the computer. There are programs in word recognition and mathematics facts that speed up or slow down based upon pupil performance. This encourages rather than discourages, for the pupil who speeds up feels a sense of accomplishment, while the student who slows down begins to get correct answers. The computer can be very effectively used in this manner. Many college students enjoy speeding up their use of multiplication facts, using a program that keeps increasing the speed as the correct response is given. The authors enjoy periodically trying this type of speed drill with a typing tutor program which provides letters, words, and phrases based on the errors made and the typing speed.

ARE BACK-UP COPIES PROVIDED?

It is essential to have back-up copies of disks that are copy protected (cannot be legally and easily duplicated). If a disk is damaged during instruction, it may take several weeks to get another copy. If you have a back-up disk, you can send in the damaged disk while using the back-up.

THE FOLLOWING SUGGESTIONS MAY PROVE HELPFUL.

Involve experts on children and teaching in picking programs. Often the computer teacher or mathematics teacher alone is consulted by the administration concerning the purchase of CAI programs. While it is necessary to have technological know-how used in selection, it is much more important to consult teachers who know the needs, likes, and abilities of the children. Given the choice of someone who knows computers but not teaching, and someone who knows teaching but not computers, the writers feel that the knowledgeable teacher should be the key person in the selection of CAI software.

Be open in your selection. Let salespeople know upon what basis you are selecting CAI material. Tell them the type of programs you wish to see. Be critical of their materials in a constructive way.

There is no reason why computer-assisted-instruction materials can't be interesting and discovery oriented, provide for individual differences, and run smoothly. The only thing preventing this is the widespread sale of materials that are not this good. Many textbook series were written for the average to low-average student. It was too hard for many students and too easy for others. CAI material can and should be very much like having a personal discussion with a really good teacher. If it isn't, then it is not programmed well.

Evaluate the program on its own merit rather than on the reputation of the company. When one of the authors was an elementary principal, he found that about 85 percent of the textbooks used in the county were produced by one textbook publisher. When he asked the other principals the reason, they said, "We know we can depend upon (name company), they have a good salesman, and their material is always above average." While this may certainly be true for some computer software companies, there is a good chance that a small company will produce superior software. For example, one individual programmer has produced two of the best word processing programs and a number of the best-selling games. Individuals with their own computer and a program such as Super Pilot can produce a superior CAI program—graphics and all—if they know how to teach a particular bit of material better than 99 percent of the people teaching the material.

Use all the resources you can. The references that follow should give you a good start in reviewing educational software. Use the appendix to find other sources of information. Once you get started, you will find still more sources to help you.

Carefully sort out the essential from the less important criteria. The criteria for choosing software should vary from school to school and from teacher to teacher. However, it is essential that the user not get bogged down in nonessential criteria. As a brief summary, a short table is presented below (from Roblyer, 1981).

Software Evaluation

Essential
a. clear statement of purpose
b. the entry skills necessary for the program
c. good design
d. viable content
e. a sound teaching approach

Not Essential
a. sound (with the possible exception of a spelling program)
b. graphics
c. color

Depends upon Purpose
a. how much student control
b. quantity of feedback
c. graphics
d. amount of text on the screen

Self-Test

1. Only computer experts should be involved in the selection of school computer-assisted-instruction software.
2. It is not possible to develop discovery-oriented CAI programs.
3. In general, it is better to buy programs that have multiple uses than to buy those with a very specific use.
4. Small manufacturers cannot produce a good CAI product, for they will not have the necessary computer equipment.
5. The CAI materials should not follow the same instructional sequences as the other classroom materials.
6. Evaluation of CAI material is even more important than evaluation of textbook materials.
7. There are many sources of reviews of educational software.
8. Many educational software manufacturers allow a thirty-day review.
9. Children should be a part of the review team.
10. Sound is always a positive attribute of a CAI program.

Think About

1. What things do *you* think are most important in considering educational software for purchase?
2. Study the evaluation checklist. How are the items alike? How are they different? What could be usefully added? What items do you feel could be dropped?
3. Obtain two or three CAI disks and use one of the software evaluation sheets. Have a elementary/middle school student go through the material and use the same evaluation. How do your evaluations compare?

4. Would it be best to develop different evaluation forms for each subject matter area? What would be the advantages and disadvantages?
5. How long does it take to effectively evaluate a piece of instructional software?
6. Imagine you have been asked by a parent-teacher group to help the parents learn to evaluate software. Develop a hand-out and an outline for your presentation.
7. Select two or three disks you think would be good for teaching educational software evaluation (examples of good and poor practice).

Suggested References

Garner, Dave. Educational microcomputer software: Nine questions to ask. *Science and Children,* March 1982, pp. 24–25.
Study Garner's nine questions. Which are of greatest importance? What other questions would you add?

Holznagel, Donald C. Which courseware for you? *Microcomputing,* October 1981, pp. 138–140.
Which courseware does Holznagel say is "right for you"?

Lathrop, Ann, and Goodson, Bobby. *Courseware in the Classroom,* Menlo Park, Calif. Addison-Wesley, 1983.
Lathrop and Goodson provide a great deal of information on courseware in the classroom. Use it as a valuable reference source.

Riordan, Tim. How to select software you can trust. *Classroom Computer News,* March 1983, pp. 56–61.
How do Riordan's suggestions compare with the other suggestions you have studied?

Bibliography

LATHROP, ANN. The terrible ten of educational programming. *Educational Computer Magazine,* September/October 1982, p. 34.
ROBYLER, M.D. When is it 'good courseware'? Problems in developing standards for microcomputer courseware. *Educational Technology,* October 1981, pp. 47–54.

The Microkids: Early
Experiences with Computers

A visitor to Lamplighter School overheard a conversation between two young students. A five-year-old was speaking disparagingly of a peer, "Jonathan is already four, and he can't do the computer" (Fisk, 1982).

Whatever the views of young children, teachers may feel that computer technology belongs much later in the curriculum (or program). Let's take a look at applications of computer technology in early childhood to see if these beliefs are valid.

HELPING YOUNG CHILDREN LEARN

When discussing the use of computer technology with preschool children, we often overlook the fact that "dedicated" or special-purpose computers are commonly employed with this age group. Touch and Spell, and Speak and Math (by Texas Instruments) utilize microcoprocessors to combine sight, sound, and touch in introducing children to basic vocabulary and number concepts. However, more and more programs are being written for young children which will run on an all-purpose microcomputer. Obviously, a microcomputer with a variety of programs covering many different subject areas and ability levels is a much more powerful tool. We will briefly examine some of these programs, recognizing that new (and hopefully, even better) ones are being written every day. The teacher would greatly benefit from trying to keep abreast of these developments. First, however, consider the characteristics of preschoolers which make them unique computer users (Kimmel, 1981; Kleiman and Humphrey, 1982):

1. Most preschoolers can't read. Therefore, the programs should have limited written prompts, if any. This has been the standard form of communication for computers. However, different methods of feedback have been designed for the prereading child, including simple (but effective) smiling faces, faces or robots that shake their heads yes or no, "firework" displays, and sound effects. The teacher should ensure that this feedback is correctly understood by the children.

2. Most preschoolers have limited appreciation for games in the competitive sense. They do understand direct cause and effect. Beginning programs should be simple and provide for almost immediate action.

3. Fine motor skills are not well developed. This tends to eliminate typical arcade-game formats and programs that require complex typing skills. The child's responses, rather than a preset timer, should determine the pace of the program. It should be easy for the child to enter responses.

4. Young children do not seem to be able to learn through verbal rehearsal. We may not be able to train this, but we can provide needed (and patient) repetition with good computer programs (Cleary, Mayes, and Packham, 1976).

5. Preschoolers have limited ability and interest in complicated "set-up." Programs should be easy to get underway.

6. Preschool children are forming cause-and-effect concepts. Programs should facilitate this growth and avoid frustrating the learner, by clearly relating the child's action to the effects.

7. Young children are easily distracted. Programs for them should avoid irrelevant graphics, color, sound, or the like that do not direct attention to what is to be learned.

Several instructional computer programs (discussed below) deal with early readiness concepts. (Note that not every one complies perfectly with the above guidelines—every program can always be improved!)

1. Children select shapes that are different, match shapes, and make comparisons. They move a "line" which serves as a pointer across the screen by repeatedly pressing a key. Feedback is given only for a correct response (Match The Shapes, public domain).

2. Children are required only to push any key that is above, below, to the right of, or to the left of a simple line marker that is placed on the keyboard. Children create various colored visual displays with voice prompts and musical notes. Colored rectangles appear and are filled with color, and rainbows with dancing, multicolored rain adorn the television screen. Simple songs accompany the appearance of butterflies. Jugglers exhibit their skill (Juggle's Rainbow, from The Learning Company).

3. The child presses a few keys to move a shape onto an interconnecting one (Complete the Square, public domain).

4. Children type any key. A line is drawn in that direction (for example, keys located in the upper-right portion of the keyboard, when pushed, draw a line heading toward the upper-right section of the monitor (Early Games, from Counterpoint Software).

5. In series of programs based on the Muppets, children can guess words one letter at a time and play "layer cake," a version of the Tower of Hanoi game (Mix and Match, from Apple).

In one school two kindergarten classes shared a microcomputer and the above computer programs. One teacher "loaded" a different program into the computer every day, just before "free play" time (in which children chose activities from the many interest centers around the room). "Playing" with this program was one of the activities children could choose. Since this activity was always popular, the teacher challenged the children to invent a fair way to take turns. They decided to make a list every day, with those interested in working with the computer signing the list in order. It was each child's responsibility to cross off his or her name and then, when finished, figure out who was next and tell that child. Computer literacy, socialization, writing, and reading . . . all in one! As children became more accustomed to the microcomputer, it lost a bit of its power to provoke arguments, but never its attraction as a place to play and learn. In the open-minded manner typical of this age, the children came quickly to view the computer as one more exciting opportunity—but still a special and fascinating one—to try out and discover new things. In this way the computer was integrated into their lives and learning at school.

The second teacher established a creative computer center, slightly walled off from the rest of the classroom and next to another booth, where volunteer parents and her "one hour a day" teacher's aide worked with children individually. The parent or aide checked whose turn it was to work with the computer (a fairly complicated combination of children's requests, equal turns, and the teacher's assignment). Signaling unobtrusively to that child, the parent or aide helped the child select the program (sometimes self-chosen, sometimes designated by the teacher) and made sure that the child was off to a good start. The child's questions or problems were dealt with as they arose. With this system the teacher utilized the computer every minute it was in her classroom and also kept track of which students were working on what programs. We shall now look at some of the available software these teachers used.

Alphabet

Several programs have been written which provide practice with letters.

1. The child can press any key: letters corresponding to that key appear, march, bounce off walls, and explode.

2. Typing in a letter yields a song, picture, and/or animated picture related to that letter. Children are free to explore and are always rewarded as they simultaneously learn alphabet names, words, animals, musical scales, songs, and numbers (Hodge Podge, from Dynacomp).

3. An alphabet with a missing letter is displayed. If the child types in that letter, the child is reinforced—an additional part of a caterpillar walks across the screen to join the rest of the insect (Primary Math/Prereading, from MECC).

4. At a higher level, children can respond directly by touching the screen with a light pen to find the correct word; for example,

at	an
r/rat	?

rare
rat   ran

5. Children pick a picture from several displayed, and see and hear (!) a story that goes with that picture (from Texas Instruments).

6. In one extensively developed and tested program, Writing to Read (from IBM), children are provided with up to fifteen minutes of intense individualized instruction every day. The program teaches the child the forty-four (note—phonetic spelling) phonemes they will need to write everything they can say. Children are to recognize that they can recombine these to write down any word (although the program is based on thirty key words). Consistent use of phonetic spelling allows children to write more easily than if they were faced with all the inconsistencies of the English spelling system. Each cycle contains lessons on three words and the phonemes that make up the words, a mastery test, and a "make words" section giving practice on recombining sounds to make new words. Then, as children learn to write, they learn to read. The two interdependent processes help each other. The computer is only one part of this program. Children move from the computer to work journals and cassettes that correspond with the lesson they just completed. Cassette/book packages constitute the third part of the program. Finally, children write the words they have learned on typewriters, combine them into sentences, and compose simple stories.

7. Faces smile when the correct letter is pressed, and shake their heads in response to errors (remember to watch out for programs in which the wrong answer makes interesting things happen).

8. A large letter is displayed. If children type the same letter at the keyboard, they are rewarded with music and graphics; other keys produce no response (Early Games, from Counterpoint Software).

9. Upon the pressing of any key, a corresponding letter is "shot" up into a row (Letter Shooter, by Dave Stark).

Numbers

Simple math games are available for preschoolers.

1. A random number (between 1 and 10) of counting blocks are displayed. Children count them and type in the number (Early Games, from Counterpoint Software).

2. Bars of increasing height are labeled 1 to 10 for the child, accompanied by musical tones which climb up the scale. Then the child labels the bars. Directions are given in verbal speech (similar to Touch and Spell, but with the sound coming from the television set monitor); if a mistake is made, the child hears, "Uh-oh!" (from Texas Instuments).

3. Balls fall down, bounce off several walls, and finally pile up in a "tube." The child counts them and enters that number. If it is correct, a large face smiles; if incorrect, the face frowns. The child's score is kept by adding numbers under a pair of smaller but similar faces—one smiling, one frowning (Counting Bee, from Edu-Ware).

4. A train chugs onto the screen, containing a different number of cars each time. The child counts them and enters the number. If correct, a new train chugs on; if incorrect, the train falls apart. (Note: Which would *you* rather see?)

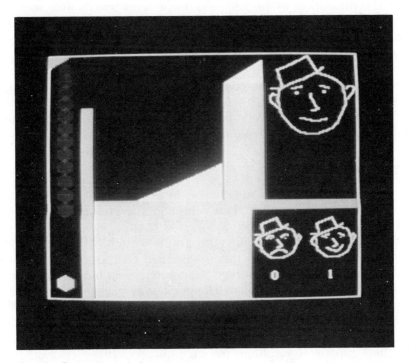

Counting Bee, courtesy of Edu-Ware.

5. Large numerals are displayed below a corresponding number of figures. Students must type the correct numeral. If the student's choice is incorrect, that numeral is crossed out (Primary Math/Prereading, from MECC).

Games

Games for exploratory fun are also available.

1. You type in a song (randomly, if you're young! Teachers can type in familiar tunes) and a speed. Demons dance wildly to your composition (Dancing Demons, from Radio Shack).

2. Children mix the legs, bodies, and heads of different Muppets and read the name of the new character. For example, "Erscar Bird" has Ernie's head, Oscar's body, and Big Bird's legs and feet (Mix and Match, from Apple Computer and CTW).

Does using such activities benefit children? Evidence is only starting to accumulate, but one teacher—using some of the programs described above (and ones that asked children to type in their names and telephone numbers)—found that kindergarteners who used them performed at least as well on all tasks and appreciably better on some tasks as they entered first grade (Hungate, 1982). The author of the above/below, left/ right program has shown that children improved on test scores in these concepts using the computer (Piestrup, 1981). Programs designed to build visual discrimination in preschoolers have been tested, with successful results (Smithy-Willis, Riley, and Smith, 1982). Others report that preschoolers love using the computers (Lewis, 1981; Swigger, 1982; Swigger and Campbell, 1981) and that they themselves integrate it easily into their day; while some work on the computers, others play house, paint, and build with blocks. For them, computers merely represent another way to explore their world. But the benefits are evident. Typing skills of young children are impressive. Peer interaction is cooperative and extensive. Peer teaching is common (from the Lamplighter project, Watt, 1982).

A COMPUTER ENVIRONMENT

One look at Sesame Place usually convinces people that microkids and microcomputers go together. This computer playground in Langhorne, Pennsylvania, features microcomputers with large, modified (and protected!) keyboards and computer programs written with kids in mind. With large keys to push and the *Sesame Street* characters on the screen, children are immediately absorbed. Computer programs include mirror-reflection activities, a nonviolent Hangman-type game, and experiences with space and gravity, motion, sound, illusions, art, patterns, reading, music, and creative writing. The founders of Sesame Place believe that computers can provide personalized educational experiences, especially with their capacity for infinite patience (Staples, 1981; Tekawa, 1980).

This is exciting. Yet we teachers must think carefully about when computer-assisted instruction should be used. It may seem amazing to us and to children that three-dimensional representations of blocks appear on the screen to be counted. While feedback is given quickly, and computer games are fun, we know that many people, like Piaget, believe that children must be *active*, counting real, movable objects. Traditional activities such as these may constitute a more complete and educationally meaningful experience for young children, whose mathematical and logical growth depend heavily on bodily action sequences. Similarly, simulations of real-world events may be impressive, but are they better than real-world experiences? As with most questions, the best answers are probably not a simple yes or no. This is all the more reason to give thought to the essential point: What experiences should and should not be computerized? What kinds of computer experiences benefit young children? Which may supplant other important experiences?

CAN EVEN YOUNG CHILDREN LEARN PROGRAMMING—AND WHY SHOULD THEY?

As a teacher, the computer represents a powerful tool; yet its real impact may be on children who *teach the computer*. Convincing arguments have been advanced that this approach will facilitate the child's learning and development. By programming the computer to do what they want it to do, children must reflect on how they might do on the task themselves. "In teaching the computer how to think, children embark on an exploration about how they themselves think" (Papert, 1980). Computers may serve as intellectual amplifiers for very young children. Marvin Minsky of MIT has said, "Eventually, programming itself will become more important even than mathematics in early education" (cited in Milner, 1980).

That young children can in fact learn, and learn from, programming in Logo has been substantiated in exploratory studies (Howe and O'Shea, 1979; Papert, 1980; Papert, DiSessa, Watt, and Weir, 1979). However, experienced teachers recognize that it is necessary to guard against uncritical acceptance of ideas and promises such as these. For instance, a leading exponent of the use of computer programming to expand chidren's intellectual power, Seymour Papert, based his ideas on the theories of Piaget, with whom he studied. However, Papert has not addressed certain Piagetian hypotheses which would tend to argue against the notion of the revolutionary potential of computer programming—for example, that no environmental conditions can allow young children to deal with abstract concepts before they reach the period of formal operations. Similarly, the claim that computer programming will restructure the way children think is not supported by the Piagetian notion that thinking progresses according to fixed biological laws, in conjunction with—but never determined by—interactions with the environment. Also ignored are the lessons from history, notably those of the Progressive Education Movement, which demonstrated that children in complete control of their own learning may limit themselves to a narrow range of interests. Such issues and controversies must be studied and discussed if teachers are to use computer technology wisely.

With these caveats in mind, we can explore just how much truth the (admittedly exciting) claims might have—how helping children program the computer might make us more effective in our jobs of facilitating learning and development.

In order to accomplish these aims, Papert worked with others to develop the computer language LOGO. LOGO is a "natural" language in that it uses words and ways of communicating that are similar to English. When you use it, you can "converse" with the computer. Children (and teachers) can teach the computer new words and new ways of doing things—new commands. LOGO is user friendly in that if something should not work out quite right, the program tells the user how the problem can be "fixed." Since LOGO is important for all teachers of children, an entire section of this book is devoted to it. You may wish to consult the chapter for several special activities and applications that are designed especially for very young children.

Self-Test

1. Studies have proven that computers are of benefit to young children.
2. Preschool children are too young to solve problems with a computer but can benefit from drill-and-practice programs.
3. Programs are available which not only teach letter recognition but also teach children to recognize words, read sentences, and compose sentences.
4. Dedicated machines are so named because they can remember what children learned in the previous lesson.
5. Young children require a lot of fancy graphics and music to remain interested.
6. Most CAI software designed for elementary school is appropriate for use with young children if its content is simple enough.
7. While not conclusive, research results hint that young children benefit from working with computers.
8. Repetition is not a good educational practice with the very young.
9. Children will probably learn to count better now that computer programs exist which can display blocks and trains on the screen to be counted.
10. Unfortunately, since the majority of young children cannot read, they cannot benefit from computer programs unless an older person helps them.
11. Young children can program a computer.

Think About

1. Do you see more potential in the near future for early childhood computing in the creation of more "dedicated" or special-purpose machines like Touch and Spell, or in the application of general-purpose microcomputers with CAI and LOGO programs as described in this chapter?
2. Of the characteristics of young children listed in this chapter, which do you believe are most important? Which are unimportant (or not even valid)? Which have been omitted from our list?
3. Do you believe young children need extra experience with cause-and-effect relationships before using a computer meaningfully? Should this experience be embedded within CAI programs themselves?

4. What should the role of color, graphics, and sound be in computer programs for young children?

5. What kind of programs are most suitable for young children: practice, tutorial, problem-solving and programming, or some combination of these?

6. Different ways to manage computer use in an early childhood setting were discussed. Which appealed to you? Can you think of a better way?

7. A program was described that responds to an incorrect response by voicing, "Uh-oh!" What would a young child's response to this be? Should programs tell a child he or she is wrong? How?

8. After rereading the chapter and thinking about the issue, defend one of the following two statements: (a) Computer programming is too abstract to be of much use to children in the stage of preoperational thought. (b) Computer programming can help children think abstractly sooner than was ever thought possible.

9. Do you think computer experiences in preschool will be one more step toward turning our children into machines?

Suggested References

Geisert, Gene, and Seegull, Eileen. Today's computers . . . At your service. *Early Years,* April 1982, pp. 35–36; 56.
Geisert and Seegull provide a description of various uses of microcomputers, and guidelines for these uses in early childhood.

Hastings, Donald. Pre-school math. *80 Microcomputing,* April 1980, pp. 77–78.

Keen, D. Kidstuff. *80 Microcomputing,* September 1980, pp. 124–126; 128–129.
If you would like to learn a bit about programming by entering other people's programs into your computer while at the same time getting a "free" preschool activity, obtain a copy of the articles by Hastings or Keen. There will undoubtedly be more available all the time.

Kimmel, S. Programs for preschoolers: Starting out young. *Creative Computing,* October 1981, pp. 44–46; 50–51.

Kleiman, Glenn, and Humphrey, Mary. Learning with computers. *Compute!,* May 1982, pp. 105–108.

Swigger, K. Computer-based materials for kids. *Educational Computer,* September/October 1982, pp. 48–50.
Other descriptions of programs suitable for young children can be found in these sources.

Staples, B. A visit to Sesame Place. *Creative Computing,* January 1981, pp. 56; 58–59.

Tekawa, K. Computers in the playground. *Interface Age,* October 1980, pp. 14–15; 120.
Descriptions of young children using computers are provided in Staples and Tekawa.

Taylor, R. Computerless computing for young children, or what to do till the computer comes. In O. Lecarme and R. Lewis (eds.), *Computers in education: Proceeding of the IFIP 2nd World Conference.* New York: American Elsevier Publishing Co., 1975.
Taylor describes activities designed to get children ready for computing.

Bibliography

CLEARY, A., MAYES, T., AND PACKHAM, D. *Educational technology: Implications for early and special education.* London: John Wiley, 1976.

FISK, EDWARD B. Grammar school use of computers isn't elementary. *Buffalo Courier-Express,* April 18, 1982, pp. c-1; c-4.

GEISERT, GENE, AND SEEGULL, EILEEN. Today's computers . . . At your service. *Early Years,* April 1982, pp. 35–36; 56.

HASTINGS, DONALD. Pre-school math. *80 Microcomputing,* April 1980, pp. 77–78.

HOWE, J. A. M., AND O'SHEA, T. Learning mathematics through LOGO. *ACM SIGCUE Bulletin,* 1978, 12(1).

HUNGATE, H. Computers in the kindergarten. *Computing Teacher,* January 1982, pp. 15–18.

KEEN, D. *80 Microcomputing,* September 1980, pp. 124–126; 128–129.

KIMMEL, S. Programs for preschoolers: Starting out young. *Creative Computing,* October 1981, pp. 44–46; 50–51.

KLEIMAN, GLENN, AND HUMPHREY, MARY. Learning with computers. *Compute!* May 1982, pp. 105–108.

LEWIS, C. *A study of preschool children's use of computer programs.* Proceedings of the National Educational Computing Conference. Iowa City, Iowa: National Educational Computing Conference, 1981.

MILNER, S. Teaching teachers about computers: A necessity for education. *Phi Delta Kappan,* 1980, 61, 544–546.

PAPERT, S. *Mindstorms: Children, computers, and powerful ideas.* New York: Basic Books, 1980.

PAPERT, S., DISESSA, A., WATT, D., AND WEIR, S. Final report of the Brookline LOGO Project: Project summary and data analysis. LOGO Memo 53, MIT LOGO Group, 1979.

PIESTRUP, A. M. *Preschool children use Apple II to test reading skills programs.* Advanced Learning Technology, Portolay Valley, California, 28 January 1981. (ERIC Document Reproduction Service No. ED 202 476).

SMITHY-WILLIS, D., RILEY, M., AND SMITH, D. Visual discrimination and preschoolers. *Educational Computer Magazine,* November/December 1982, pp. 19; 45.

STAPLES, B. A visit to Sesame Place. *Creative Computing,* January 1981, pp. 56; 58–59.

SWIGGER, K. Computer-based materials for kids. *Educational Computer,* September/October 1982, pp. 48–50.

SWIGGER, K., AND CAMPBELL, J. *Computers and the nursery school.* Proceedings of the National Educational Computing Conference. Iowa City, Iowa: National Educational Computing Conference, 1981.

TAYLOR, R. Computerless computing for young children, or what to do till the computer comes. In O. Lecarme and R. Lewis (eds.), *Computers in education: Proceedings of the IFIP 2nd World Conference.* New York: American Elsevier Publishing Co., 1975.

TEKAWA, K. Computers in the playground. *Interface Age,* October 1980, pp. 14–15; 120.

WATT, D. LOGO in the schools. *BYTE,* August 1982, pp. 116–188; 120; 122; 126; 128; 130; 132–134.

10

Typing, Science, and Social Studies

At first glance the chapter title may seem strange. In fact, these three topics were combined for purely practical reasons. First, typing is an important skill that is helpful in all areas of the curriculum and in almost any computer activity. Second, science and social studies use many of the same types of teaching approaches with simulation. Third, the material makes up about a chapter's worth of material.

TYPING

Two of the best-selling books on computers in education do not even list typing in the index. Often, when asked if it is necessary to be able to type to use the computer, the computer scientist indicates that typing is not a necessary skill. Why then begin a look at computers in the subject matter areas by studying typing? Here are some of the reasons.

1. Word processing in the language arts has been successfully accomplished by teachers from the first-grade level through the elementary/middle school. When the authors talked with over thirty teachers concerning typing and word processing, all indicated that touch typing was an important skill.
2. One of the authors taught typing to a club group of eighth graders several years ago. At the beginning of the one-semester/one-hour-a-week program,

several of the students could "hunt and peck" about fifteen words a minute. At the end of the semester, all the students could type over twenty-five words a minute. However, it took the hunt-and-peck group much longer to get into the thirty-plus-word-a-minute group than those without any experience. As with any motor skill, it is important to learn the correct techniques from the beginning.

3. With the number of home computers on the rise, many elementary/middle school students are using the keyboard every day at home. It is important to start them out right.

4. Studies in the 1960s using an expensive talking typewriter with preschool children found that by color coding the children's fingers, the pre-first graders learned the typewriter keyboard rather easily. Studies also found that those who learned to touch type were more creative in experimenting with words and in learning new words.

5. Typing is easy to teach using a microcomputer. There are programs that do the majority of the work for the teacher and are interesting to the children.

6. Several teachers have found that very young children pick up typing skills as fast as their brothers and sisters in junior high. They also found that the five-year-olds did not have much trouble with motor skills and that the fingers of these children were not too small for the keyboard.

Teaching Typing

There are a number of strategies that can be used to develop typing with children. How soon should schools begin? Preferably, when the students start to use the keyboard. If only a one-key response is necessary for computer use, then don't teach typing. When it is necessary to use several keys or type in words, start teaching the children typing skills.

One third-grade teacher color coded the keys and the children's fingers using washable paint. It was necessary to color code only the middle finger, the ring finger, and the appropriate keys, because it is easy to see that the outside keys are handled by the little finger and the inside keys by the index finger.

The teacher made use of an arcade-game typing program called TypeAttack to give the children practice using the proper keys. Type-Attack presents letters that are to be "shot down." The format is more of a target shooting than a shoot-to-kill format. When the children had developed some skill, the teacher began to use Typing Tutor, which presented the students with either letters, words, or paragraphs, at a level established by their typing. The program keeps track of the errors made, gives more practice on letters missed, and gives an analysis of the words per minute and percentage of accurate words.

A Note

Typing is a skill that is useful to every adult. As computers become more a part of our everyday life, typing will increase in usefulness. The elementary/middle school teacher should feel free to try a variety of approaches in order to interest children in typing and help them learn it. On occasion it gives the child who is not doing well academically a chance to feel a sense of achievement.

SCIENCE AND SOCIAL STUDIES

Professionals in all aspects of the sciences and social sciences are finding that a large part of their effort involves computers. For example, someone who is studying earthquakes finds that as much time is spent on computer use in analysis and projection as is spent on field work and instrument development and use. The economist has become data dependent, and the data filter through computers. The historian writes "history" with the aid of computers. Thousands of birth records, rent receipts, tax records, and grocery orders are analyzed. Census data provide the basis for many historical insights, such as the changing mix of rural-urban population, and the way people live—for example, renting or owning their place of residence. Computers help to answer such questions as, How do we travel? How do we spend our money? What is the typical use of leisure time?

What should be done concerning computers as we teach science and social studies? Time, equipment, know how, and goals will greatly affect how we use them. However, with these factors in mind, there are a number of questions that can be considered and a number of instructional supplements that can be used. In this chapter we are going to explore only a small number of possible uses. You are challenged to think of others.

We will look at computers in science and social studies in the following sections: Understanding the effect of computers on science and social science; and Computer-assisted instruction in science and social studies.

Understanding the Effect of Computers on Science and Social Studies

The general approach a teacher takes to the teaching of science and social studies can make a fundamental difference in the ease with which awareness can be developed concerning the use of computers in various fields. In general, the "problems approach" proves very beneficial. This approach involves the following teaching sequence:

1. Motivate—get the interest of the children.
2. Under teacher guidance develop a set of significant questions that need to be explored and answered concerning the topic.
3. Gather the answers to the questions by reading, surveys, experimentation, and so on.
4. Summarize the information in a usable form.

One fourth-grade teacher was teaching a science unit on the earth and the solar system. After getting the children's interest using a film about the Voyager space probe, she directed the "question raising" portion of the unit. One of the children asked, "How do they keep track of the information?" Another asked, "How are the pictures sent back?" A third said, "I think computers have something to do with each of those questions. Let's ask 'How are computers used in space exploration?' " As the questioning progressed, it became evident that an important part of the study could be focused on the role of the computer.

The next day the class organized the questions for study. One cluster of questions involved the computer and the unit. Some of the questions concerning the computer are recorded below. In all, the children asked ten questions concerning computer use.

Computer Questions

1. How are computers used in space exploration?
2. What special computers are needed?
3. What kinds of computers are used?
4. What does the computer do?
5. What kinds of scientists work with the computers?
6. What do you have to know to work with the computers?
7. What are the computers on the small satellites like?
8. How can they use computers in photography?
9. What kinds of computer programs are used?
10. Could any of the space work be done with the kind of computer we have in our school?

The teacher helped the children find books and magazines that contained information concerning the computers. Much of the material was too difficult for the children to understand, so the teacher suggested that several children arrange to interview the high school computer science teacher to see if they could get some less-complex answers to their questions. Also, one of the junior high school science teachers consented to spend a period discussing the questions with the class. As part of their project, the committee members on computers made a bulletin board entitled "How Are Computers Used in Space?"

Both science and social studies provide almost endless opportunities for studying the role of computers in society. There are several points to consider in teaching this material:

1. Because the information is so new, there have been few studies concerning the ability of children to understand the material. However, previous work with the "problems approach" to teaching science and social studies indicates that the questions children ask are very indicative of their level.
2. Don't feel that a question is too complex or too simple to be tackled by the children. Almost every question can be developed at many levels. At one

level the question, What kinds of computers are used? can be simply informational—the children can see pictures of the computers, find out the amount of storage space they have, and get an idea of what they do. At another level the children might explore the nature of the computer system and compare it with both similar and dissimilar systems.

3. The teacher should not feel that he or she must be able to answer all, or even most, of the questions children raise. In any class there will be children who are very interested and will spend a great deal of time on specific topics. Thus, at the fifth-grade level there will probably be one or more children who know more about some aspects of particular computers than does the teacher, in the same way that some children will know more about specific football statistics than does the teacher.

4. Don't develop more complexity than is necessary. There will be some children who want to go into a topic at a level that will bore and confuse many others in the class. The teacher should encourage this exploration but should ensure that the class discussions are at a level that is both interesting and understandable to the majority of the class.

5. Be sure to use the resource people available in the community. Often parents or other community members are more than willing to share with the children how they use computers in their occupations.

Computer-Assisted Instruction in Science and Social Studies

There are dozens of computer-assisted-instruction disks and tapes for use in science and social studies. As in the other areas discussed, they vary in quality. What are some valid uses of CAI in these areas? The following material will give some examples of educationally sound uses of CAI in science and social studies.

Simulation

Many of the better CAI programs involve the use of simulation. As we previously noted, simulation has the advantage of being reusable and of being able to be used with a large number of students. Note the following examples.

Grade Five. One fifth-grade teacher began the study of geology with a program called Geology Search. The program involved the entire class in working toward the search goals. The students were challenged to imagine that they were exploring for oil. The computer "performed" geological tests, helping the children to learn about rocks, fossils, and underground stuctures in order to make decisions about where to drill.

After the class had worked with the program to get maximum benefit without losing interest, the teacher conducted a "chalk-talk" discussion. One of the class members was asked to be chalkboard recorder. With the teacher's help, this student encouraged the class to make a record of their work on the program. The board material was written in two columns, headed What did we find out? What do we need to explore?

Grade Seven. As part of a study of factors affecting the American economy, the teacher made use of a simulation called Hamurabi, which was developed years ago on mainframe computers. In Hamurabi the students become the rulers of a make-believe country and are asked to make decisions concerning buying land, planting crops, selling crops, storing food, and so on.

This particular teacher used the simulation with the entire class and then allowed the children to use it in groups of two or four. The students were challenged to develop a chart of the relationships used in the simulation and to check out the likelihood of specific occurrences.

Grade Three. As part of a study of communities, the teacher made use of a simulation called Lemonade Stand. This simulation sets up competing lemonade stands on a street in Lemonsville. The entire class can split up into two teams to play, or it can be played in smaller teams or with up to four individual players. To introduce the game, the teacher divided the class into two groups.

The program tells the children the amount it costs them to make a glass of lemonade (this varies depending upon whether or not a mother furnishes sugar), the cost of signs to advertise their product, and how much money they start with. It also tells the weather and whether or not there is construction on the street. The children decide how many glasses of lemonade to make, how many advertising signs to buy, and how much to charge for a glass of lemonade. When this information is given, the computer calculates the number of glasses sold and the profit.

The teacher allowed the children to use the Lemonade Stand program in free time and determined the teams on the basis of student availability. It was decided to do more with the simulation at this level. Teachers in later grades also used Lemonade Stand but asked the students to try to determine the relationship between the various factors programmed into the simulation.

Grade Six. The teacher here used Odell Lake (from MECC) as part of a study of ecology. Odell Lake has the students imagine that they are one of several varieties of fish. It then asks them to decide what to do when another variety approaches them. They have the choice of trying to eat the other fish, hiding at the surface, hiding deep, or ignoring the other animal. When their time was up, the teacher asked the children to work in pairs and chart the relationships among the animals. A portion of one chart is shown below.

Otter—eats all the fish
Chub—is eaten by fish that eat other fish

Dolyvarden—eats all fish but . . .

Muskie—eats rainbow trout and chub but is eaten by Dolyvarden and . . .

A chart listing a number of MECC simulations is provided in this chapter to indicate the extent to which simulations are available.

Drill and Practice. A variety of drill activities can be effective in science and social studies. Among the types of practice programs teachers find effective are the following:

> *States.* A map on which children have to match the name of the state with drawing of the map. Such programs can also be used for other continents. Students are told immediately if they are right or wrong.
>
> *Stars.* A program in which students have choice among identifying constellations, indicating a constellation and then seeing it on the screen, or taking a quiz in which the constellation is shown on the screen and the student has to indicate which of four constellations it pictures.
>
> *Map reading.* The program provides practice on a number of specific map-reading skills.
>
> *Human body.* These are programs on each of the systems of the body, in whch the student has to indicate the part shown.
>
> *Insects.* The student identifies various insects by their characteristics.
>
> *Weather.* The student works with various weather instruments and conditions that produce weather.
>
> *Questions.* There are a number of programs which are basically review tests on specific subject matter areas, such as World War II, Colonial America, The Revolutionary War, and so on.

Suggestions

The fields of science and social studies lend themselves to a variety of computer uses. There is almost unlimited potential in simulations and the simulation games. It is hoped that in the future, a great deal of the game situations available for computers and video outfits will have both educational and entertainment objectives. At the present time great care should be taken in selecting commercial simulations in game format. Many of the adventure games that are take-offs on the Dungeon and Dragons idea have questionable aspects of the occult associated with them. Care must be taken not to have such adventure games available in the school.

The drill-and-practice aspect of science and social studies is limited only by time, interest, and funds. As more such materials become available, it is hoped that the majority of exclusively drill-and-practice programs will be found in game formats in which the interest of the game centers in the material to be learned.

TABLE 10-1 Comparison of Computer Programs by MECC*

NAME	GRADE	CONTENT	SKILL	CURRICULUM INTEGRATION	VALUES EMPHASIZED	COMMENTS
Biology FISH	7–8	circulation of blood in two-chambered heart	understanding blood circulation; associating simple pictures with actual circulatory system	supplements a lab dissection		mechanical model could serve the purpose as well or better
TAG	7–11	tagging fish as biological research method	estimating; simple math skills; applying samples to whole population	supplements population studies		could be effectively used in group discussion
WHALES	5–9	migration of gray whale	observing; investigating	none provided; many teaching possibilities		limited in scope; does not stress importance of preserving this endangered species
ODELL WOODS	2–6	food web among 4 forest animals	simple decision making; drawing conclusions about the food web from information	introduces ecological concepts in the food web	interdependence of all organisms	additional pictures could add much to programs since existing illustrations are not detailed
ODELL LAKE	4–6	food web among 6 lake fish				

*The table summarizes the results of the author's study of 40 educational computer programs. All the programs named in the chart are available through Minnesota Educational Computing Consortium (MECC) though some of them originated with other developers. MECC was used because the author found it to offer a larger selection of simulation programs for precollege students than any other source.

134

TABLE 10-1 Comparison of Computer Programs by MECC (cont.)

Earth Science QUAKES	5–9	location of epicenter of earthquake on U.S. map	map reading; applying basic math; estimating epicenter location	introduces the purpose of seismographic records and earthquake research	importance of early scientific investigation in avoiding disaster, emphasis on prevention	good background information; additional film available
Earth Science MINERALS	5–7	identification of 29 minerals through simulated tests	testing; classifying	supplements laboratory experience		only valuable as an addition to laboratory
URSA	5–6	names of 5 constellations; telling time by stars	memorizing associating simplified pictures with names	supplies legendary background for names of constellations		illustrations are over-simplified; unlikely to enable children to identify stars in night sky
SOLAR DISTANCE	3–6	distance in solar system; concepts of speed	memorizing; applying basic math	role playing of solar system		accompanying manual could be nicely integrated into curriculum

TABLE 10-1 Comparison of Computer Programs by MECC (cont.)

Ecology/Economics					
MALARIA 6–8	malaria control through hospitalization, drugs, preventive medicines, and insecticides	integrating economic and ecological goals; compromising, planning, and decision making	excellent ecology curriculum enrichment if the teacher presents additional scientific background material	impact of budget on decisions about method used to control malaria	every mistake in calculations makes it necessary to begin the whole exercise again; it would be much better to be able to correct after each single year
RATS 6–12	pest control through poisons of varying strengths and through hygiene			emphasis on hygiene rather than the need to use poisons	
POLUT 7–12	control of water pollution through various kinds of sewage treatment in varying settings			awareness of water pollution problems and possibilities of avoiding them	
Energy					
FUTURE 9–12	energy decisions and energy-related issues facing the U.S.	decision making and role playing; hypothesizing; interpreting and analyzing data in tables and graphs; interrelating data	could be used in conjunction with unit on energy or social decision making	energy conservation	requires a good deal of preparation on the teacher's part
ENERGY 9–12	managing energy crisis according to demand and environmental limitations	hypothesizing, interpreting, and analyzing data in tables and graphs; interrelating data			
Data Retrieval					
POP 10–12	information in tables and graphs about world population growth models	hypothesizing, interpreting, and analyzing data in tables and graphs; interrelating data	introduces concepts of data interpretation		graphs difficult to use on black-and-white screen

TABLE 10-1 Comparison of Computer Programs by MECC (cont.)

US POP	9–12	studies on U.S. population growth and key variables				
LIMITS	9–12	based on book, Limits to Growth; 5 variable parameters				
MINNAG	11–12	data and information about agricultural development, soil, water in Minnesota				good background; too many random events interfere with exercise
Geography NOMAD	4–6	following simplified street map to Grandmother's house	basic map reading; following traffic instructions	provides opportunities for creative writing		
History OREGON TRAIL	3–6	emigration West around 1800 based on actual trip diaries	analyzing; simple economic planning; fast hand/eye coordination; problem solving; simple decision making	supplements history class; provides good bibliography	spirit of pioneering	hazards based on actual trip diaries and historical sources; fun
FURS	5–6	French fur trading on Lake Ontario in 1770s	analyzing; simple economic planning	illustrates the interaction of geography and history		
VOYAGEUR	5–6	canoe trip and trading in Canada				

TABLE 10-1 Comparison of Computer Programs by MECC (cont.)

SUMER (HAMURABI)	5–8	simple agrarian planning in ancient Sumer over a 10-year period	planning; performing basic math	program could add to units on government, economics, geography, and anthropology	the importance of population management could be stressed	oversimplified model
Nutrition DIET	6–8	balanced diets; proper eating habits	planning; analyzing diet components; performing basic math	could be adapted to include wider food choices as part of nutrition curriculum	improvement of eating habits	limited food choices
NUTRITION	4–6	balanced diets; proper eating habits; nutritious food compared with junk food				
Politics ELECT 1, 2, 3	8–12	historical and contemporary elections	analyzing political situations; drawing conclusions and decision making; role playing; negotiations; problem solving	simulates social decision making; could be adapted to involve a whole class	aspects of political and social processes of the West	require thorough preparation and well-informed activity leader, would add much to curriculum if adapted for group interaction
HAIL TO THE CHIEF	5–12	presidential elections; 4 graded levels				
FAIL SAFE	8–12	based on book *Fail Safe*; emergency arising when nuclear-armed Air Force nears Russia by mistake				

TABLE 10-1 Comparison of Computer Programs by MECC *(cont.)*

CRISIS	11–12	decision making during international conflict in West Berlin			
POLICY	9–12	policy formation in U.S.; socio-economic choices	analyzing; drawing conclusions; decision making; role playing; negotiating; group interaction	possibilities for group interaction would add to economics unit	could be adapted to lower age level
BARGAIN	10–12	collective bargaining in labor management			
Populations BUFFALO	6–12	population management of a buffalo herd, beginning in 1870	analyzing; planning; manipulating simple statistics; managing herd numbers; problem solving	introduces general principles of population management	ecological significance of population management	good handbook and worksheets exist; difficult; many repeats necessary
STERL	7–12	biological population control through sterilization of male fly	planning; manipulating simple statistics; managing populations; problem solving	illustrates biological control versus pesticides	avoidance of pesticides	technical short-comings; every time a player encounters difficulty, the game must be restarted.

Reprinted with permission from *Science and Children*, May, 1983. Copyright NSTA, 1983. From Orah Elron, "Teaching with Computer Simulations," pp. 13–17.

FURTHER STUDY

Video tape and video disk technology have a great deal of potential for CAI. Use of video disks under computer direction allows for the student to directly interact with a variety of realistic situations. For example, a video disk of a variety of birds and their calls would provide matchless experience in identifying birds by sight and sound.

Self-Test

1. Children below grade six cannot be taught touch typing.
2. Typing skill is not necessary for word processing.
3. Simulations require teacher creativity for maximum effect.
4. Children's questions cannot be used as the basis for a CAI science unit.
5. Children cannot deal with questions concerning computers in society.
6. In general, science and social studies are excellent subjects in which to use simulations.
7. There are few places in science or social studies where drill-and-practice programs can be used.
8. Video disk technology will be of little use in elementary/middle school CAI programs in science and social studies.
9. The teacher must be prepared to answer any questions students have concerning CAI science and social studies material.

Suggested References

Anderson, Ronald E., Klassen, Daniel L., Hansen, Thomas P., and Johnson, David C. **The affective and cognitive effects of microcomputer based science instruction.** *Journal of Educational Technology Systems,* 1980/1981, 9(4).
What impact did Anderson et al. find that computers have on science instruction?
Grier, Jamesa W. **Ecology: A simulation model for small populations of animals.** *Creative Computing,* 1980, 6(7), 116–121.
Grier gives many good ideas for uses of simulation. Think of others.
Harvey, Michael R. **The computer in science education: Defining the role of technology.** *The Computing Teacher,* April 1982, pp. 32–35.
How does Harvey think the microcomputer will affect science education?
Jackson, Robert W. **Teaching where children are.** *Teaching and Computers.* Spring 1983, p. 6.
What is Jackson's view of typing and computer education?
Sparks, R. A. **Microcomputers in science teaching?** *The School Science Review,* 1982, 63(224), 442–452.
What are the types of computer uses Sparks sees for science education?

11

Reading and Language Arts

There are many facets of a reading and language arts program that can make unique use of the microcomputer. Programs have been written, or are being designed, which

1. Provide dynamic contextual situations for reading and writing instruction.
2. Meet the needs of diverse populations—gifted, average, and handicapped.
3. Provide interaction with students with regard to their reading and writing.
4. Support a variety of approaches to reading instruction.
5. Help students develop a variety of skills and abilities—from letter recognition, to vocabulary development, to critical reading skills.
6. Help good reading teachers do even more effectively what they have already been doing.
7. Improve the creative, expository, and analytical writing skills of children.
8. Improve the spelling of elementary/middle school pupils.

Several examples of reading programs will be given below, and a number of classroom descriptions of written communication skills in the language arts will be presented.

EXAMPLES OF READING PROGRAMS

The following are some examples of reading programs that are currently being produced and suggestions as to how they may be used.

1. The Magic Wand Speaking Reader is a hand-held device which translates specially coded texts into a humanlike voice for beginning readers. The child slides the wand along tracks printed beneath the text (of the books that accompany the wand). An optical scanner converts bar codes into synthetic speech. Words, phrases, sentences, songs, and sound effects are produced. Each book also contains exercises designed to build grammar, vocabulary, phonics, and comprehension skills. Teachers can use such material with beginning readers or with children who have had early reading difficulties. The teacher must ensure that some human discussion and interaction is provided along with the materials.

2. One extensive package attempts to diagnose the cause of reading problems and provide the appropriate remediation, targeted at those problems. Teachers can use such programs as an added means of diagnosis and treatment. There are several programs which use this format. Care must be taken that the teacher develop the interest of the students in the material and that the students understand each error.

3. Other series attack specific skills. One phonics series delivers instruction primarily through audio tapes which provide directions and examples. The corresponding letters and words are shown on the screen. (Note that while this is obviously valuable, it restricts the program to a "forward only" linear sequence.) A single, simple presentation is used. All letters to be included in the lesson are introduced. Each is shown in turn in several example words. The audio says the words and asks the students to repeat them. Finally, the audio pronounces each word and asks the students to type the letter whose sound is present in the word. Words are sometimes put into sentences, sometimes illustrated, and sometimes animated. Skilled teachers must integrate this material with their ongoing reading program for maximum effect.

4. Games are available in which children find hidden words and construct puzzles similar to crossword puzzles. While such puzzles may provide interest, there is little reason to believe that they will greatly affect the vocabulary development of the students. (See the MECC material for one reading-language arts crossword puzzle program in which the teacher determines the words to be used.)

5. A computerized version of Concentration reinforces children's vocabulary and language arts skills. Such programs work well with two to four children playing the game. The Concentration format provides a chance for the child who remembers the format of the game but is not as good as the other children with vocabulary development.

6. CAI materials are available which reinforce grammatical skills, including parts of speech, sentence patterns, spelling, paragraph usage, and English usage.

7. Cloze-type exercise programs exist which will provide cues or hints if the student requests them. The individual teacher can develop games which can be used with this type of disk.

8. Language arts games have students unscramble whole sentences or present sentences in code, allowing students to work with grammar and syntax without the traditional linguistic terminology.

9. One series has programs for children on each of several levels. Beginning readers may pick a picture, whereupon a corresponding story is displayed and read to them. In another program they pick a word which correctly completes a sentence. Later they make a story by selecting words which determine how the story develops. More advanced readers are asked to be

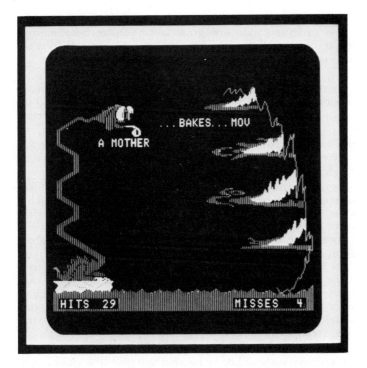

The *Verb Viper* is an elastic-necked creature that helps students master subject agreement with regular and irregular verbs. *Courtesy of DLM.*

"story solvers." Three skills are involved—determining what the problem is, why something happened, and how characters feel. After reading stories, the children are asked to respond. For example, they may be asked to choose a possible solution. They are then shown how events might have progressed if the characters had followed that path.

10. While not widely available at the time of this writing, programs are being written that help users understand the structures of language while simultaneously exploring writing, reading, and language in a "language workshop" (Sharples, 1981). In one of the series, the user is prompted by the computer to type in words which are then combined randomly in (usually nonsense) phrases. In the next program the user defines the parts of speech of the words he or she types in, which are then added to the program's vocabulary. The user then specifies the sentence pattern desired. For instance, if "article/adjective/noun/verb/noun" were picked, the computer might generate, "The bad boy ate the candy." By defining more extensive rules for titles, lines, paragraphs, and the like, sophisticated grammars and compositions can be created. This is an example of a context-free grammar.

Such programs can also generate music, arithmetic algorithms, foreign languages, computer programs—anything that follows sets of rules. However, note that no meaning is yet involved; the computer could just as well have generated "The bad candy ate the boy." Other programs associate meaning descriptors with each word (for example, *candy* might be associated with *food* and *good*). Text thus generated contains words that agree in meaning. Finally, other programs transform grammatical constructions, improving the grammar of computer-generated sentences, or allow children to apply to their own text prewritten rules for sentence combining.

11. Sentence-combining programs are also available. For example, one allows the child to select the correct "describing" word from one sentence, and the proper location in which to place it within a kernel sentence, so as to combine the two.

12. One program asks students to select words so as to make changes in traditional nursery rhymes. The words must fit computer-generated grammatical functions. The rhyme is then printed out with the student's choices.

13. Story Maker has three parts. In the first the child is presented with a "story tree"—a branching story designed with choices to pick from at each level. A path starts at the top. The child then chooses one of several choices for the next "line" of the story. This choice branches him or her to another set of choices, and so on. A child learns about the structure of stories and about the consequences of certain choices while engaging in meaningful, purposeful reading. The child can also work toward a goal generated by the computer; that is, the computer specifies in a general way what the story should entail. To achieve this end, the child must continually read for meaning, apply knowledge of story structure, infer, evaluate, and make predictions. In variations, children must make up their own branching story tree. Here reading, writing, creative thinking, and planning are integrated.

14. In an adaptation of Hangman, children choose which sentences go together to make up paragraphs. It should be recognized that while this game can be effective, it has a reasonably short life span in terms of holding children's interest.

15. Several programs exist which calculate the readability level of any text. The teacher need only type in a few hundred word samples of the material. Teachers using such programs have found that they need to consider the reading material from several standpoints, since they find that each of the several readability formulas gives a different level.

One teacher had her sixth-grade children develop stories for use with the second-grade children. When they had written their stories, they used the readability program to help them edit the stories so that they might in fact be read by the second-grade children.

A readability disk such as that in the MECC materials usually sells for less than forty dollars and is one of the most useful disks available. Many teachers analyze the reading level of the worksheets and directions which they develop for the materials they use with children. Other teachers check the readability of mathematics problems, science books, and social studies books.

16. Reports on the use of computers to help children develop abilities in reading and other related language arts are promising (Mason, 1981). One project used the computer to print out dictated language experience stories. The computer recorded "new" words not previously used by the student and generated word recognition tests based on the student's emerging reading vocabulary. One study reported remarkable gains in remediation of spelling problems of learning-handicapped students (Hasslebring, 1982).

17. Computers have been used both to teach students reading and to record their progress. Findings from these uses have aided research efforts in reading.
18. There are speed-reading programs which allow the students to set their own pace on the material and take comprehension tests following the reading. Some allow for the teacher to insert the reading passages and the comprehension questions that he or she has developed.
19. Several series have been designed for students having difficulty in reading and/or other language arts. Frequently these present stories with accompanying exercises on literal and inferential comprehension; interpretation; analysis; synonyms, antonyms, or homonyms; composition; punctuation; vocabulary; spelling; structure; and dictionary use. Many contain a built-in management component.

LANGUAGE ARTS

Language arts have always been one of the most challenging areas for elementary/middle school teachers. Along with mathematics, the language arts have usually been taught by having the children learn a rule and then apply it. Such a procedure provides little motivation. No wonder a majority of adults would rather do almost anything than write. At the same time, we are finding today a generation of young people who are willing to sit at a computer keyboard and work for hours on a computer program.

The computer can be used to help make children as enthusiastic about writing as they are about using the computer in other areas. Along with the improvement of writing will come an interest—and therefore an improvement—in spelling. The improvement of oral communication can also be enhanced.

Improving Written Communication/
Word Processing

If the authors could use the computer in the elementary/middle school for only one purpose, it would be word processing. This is because written communication has been very difficult to teach, and teachers find that children change their attitude about writing when they use word processing. (If you are quite familiar with the use of word processing, move on to the heading "Teaching Writing." If not, follow along.)

What is word processing? It is simply using the power of a computer to allow you to write on the screen, make changes, and then print out your manuscript with a printer. This does not seem like much of an advantage over a typewriter. However, there are many things you can do with a word processor that you can't do with a typewriter.

There are many different types of word processors. Therefore, it is important to choose the system that gives you the most of what you want for the money that is available. Most teachers, however, will be locked into the system that is selected by school officials. However, if you do have a chance to choose a system for yourself or to help choose a system for your school, you do need to consider the ways in which the equipment will be used.

For most school uses you need a computer with a moderate amount of memory, a tape or disk drive, a screen, and a printer. Many schools will place the printer in a central location which allows individuals to bring in their disks or tapes and print out their copy. If at all possible, a disk drive should be used, for it will speed up the operation greatly. With a disk drive, a child will have to wait only a second or two for the computer to locate a portion of his or her writing.

A description of the word processor that is being used to write this material will be given below, and then several of its features will be discussed. The computer is an Apple II with 64K of memory, two-disk drive, a green screen monitor, and an Epson printer. The total cost was about $2,400 in 1981, but it would be less today. The word processing program is Screenwriter II, which costs $100.

With the word processing program, you can do the following:

1. Correct typing or spelling errors merely by typing over the incorrect word.
2. Easily insert letters, words, phrases, or sentences any place in the manuscript.
3. Replace all occurrences of one word with another word. For example, if a sixth-grade student had written a theme on Mississippi and had spelled it Missisippi, he or she could have all of the incorrect spellings changed at one time to the correct spelling. This certainly makes correction much more to the child's liking.
4. Get a word count by hitting two keys. For example, I'm now going to check the number of words I've written in this version of the chapter—wait, I'll be right back—it's 756 words. This function is helpful if you want to keep your writing within a certain number of pages.

   For example, a newspaper writer can write her daily column at home with her word processor. Since she is able to keep track of the number of words she writes, she can send in the manuscript over telephone lines ready to be printed—without its needing to be edited for length.
5. Use a tab in the same way as you would on a typewriter. But it is possible to move material around after it has been written.
6. Delete individual letters or individual lines by hitting one key.
7. Move paragraphs, lines, or pages from one part of a manuscript to another.
8. Find any word in the manuscript.
9. Save one version of a letter or other written material and then make changes in the material—but still have the original for later use.
10. Make up form letters in which only certain words or phrases are changed in each one. One teacher used this feature to write letters to parents. She used several paragraphs in all the letters which gave general information about the class. Then she added personal information about each child to the appropriate letters.
11. Insert material in the middle of any portion of already-written material. One word, a sentence, or many pages can be inserted.
12. Center any line without doing any counting.

13. Print the material single spaced, double spaced, and so on. It is often handy when you are first using a word processor and don't feel too comfortable doing your editing on the screen to print the material in with triple spacing, which makes it easy to edit. Later the material can be printed with single or double spacing. Children can do the same when working on a first draft.

14. Automatically develop an index. (Note: Not all word processing programs can do this.)

15. Print the page numbers in either Hindu-Arabic or Roman numerals, or omit page numbers.

16. Have "invisible lines" which only show up when you look at the material on the video screen, but which do not appear in the printed material. One teacher had the children put their themes on floppy disks and then corrected the paper by using the same word processor as the children. She made comments they could use in editing that appeared on the screen as the children worked; but these comments did not appear in the printed material.

17. Change margins at will. You can change margins from one printing to the next.

18. Check all the words for spelling. There is a program that checks the words in a manuscript against the words in the Random House Dictionary (90,000 words). It goes through ten pages in under a minute (if there aren't many words that aren't in the dictionary). The spelling program shows you the word that doesn't match, and you decide what you want to do. If it is a technical term that is spelled correctly, you can hit a key and indicate that it is to be included in the dictionary. If it is a plural, you can hit a key which indicates that you want it left as is. If it is an incorrect spelling, you can change the spelling both there and in the remainder of the manuscript. The spelling program doesn't catch "their and there" errors, nor does it notice when the writer types *the* for *they*. Children using a spelling program become much more conscious of spelling errors and are very willing to make changes. Research is needed to ascertain the effect of such a program on their general spelling.

19. Print the material in a particular order.

Using the Word Processor in Teaching

Here is an example of how a teacher used word processing to improve language arts instruction. It is just representative. There are actually hundreds of other ways in which word processing could be used.

Example. Ms. Smith, a fifth-grade teacher, was given the use of a computer with word processing for three afternoons a week. Her principal suggested that she try using it for language arts instruction for three months.

She obtained the manual for the word processing program and took the computer home over the weekend to learn to use it. She got some help from a ninth-grade girl who was familiar with that type of computer.

After working over the weekend, Ms. Smith decided to limit the number of word processing commands she would use with the children. She later found that those who were interested in using the full power of the word processor were more than willing to work in groups of two or three before school, after school, and during the noon hour. One student read the manual while the other student tried out the commands.

Ms. Smith began her lesson in the following manner: "We've been given the use of this computer for the next few Monday, Wednesday, and Friday afternoons, to see what we can do with it to improve our writing. Do you have any ideas of how we might best use it?"

Several suggestions were made. They included the following:

1. Have the committee that was developing social studies reports use it to develop and print their reports.
2. Use it for writing and editing the class paper.
3. Use it for writing letters. (One class member suggested that as a group they develop several paragraphs that would be of general interest to relatives of the class members and then have each class member write one or two paragraphs to complete and personalize their letter.
4. Write poems.
5. Write stories.

Ms. Smith and a mechanically oriented teacher attached a large video monitor to the computer so that the class would be able to work out some of the basics of word processing together. She decided that the first day the children (who had not worked with computers at school—although several had computers at their homes) would learn to turn on and off the computer, load the word processing program, and learn how to start a file (computer talk for starting a story, theme, and so forth).

She first made use of an audio tape called How to Operate the Apple (FlipTrack Training Tapes, A Division of Mosaic Media, Inc., 526 N. Main St., Box 711, Glen Ellyn, Ill. 60137). The tape gave simple instructions for getting started and "booting" (loading) disks.

The next step was to use one of the inexpensive typing programs and over a period of time help the children become familiar with the keyboard. (Techniques for teaching typing were considered in Chapter 9.)

The class then instructed Ms. Smith on what to do to load the word processing program disk. She followed their directions and a display appeared on the video screen. The screen directed that a choice was to be made between

1. EDITOR
2. RUN OFF
3. EXIT
4. ENTER CUSTOMIZE

The children figured out that the editor probably was what they wanted. They correctly decided that RUN OFF was probably printing and that the other two choices probably had to do with specific things with which they were unfamiliar (also correct). The teacher explained that it would be possible to do all their work without using option 4. She mentioned that later some might want to study the manual and see what option 4 involved.

One of the children was chosen to operate the keyboard. He touched the 1 (L would not have worked) and the return key. The disk whirred and OUTPUT FILE? appeared on the screen. Ms. Smith asked the class to think of a name for their first file. They chose Smith's Fifth, which was typed in.

The lesson continued as the the children learned how to begin to write. At this time they were given a single page that contained information about the movement of the cursor (the lighted box) on the screen.

Word Processing

1. BOOT WORD PROCESSING DISK
2. GO TO EDITOR
3. NAME YOUR FILE
4. FROM COMMAND LINE : TYPE C AND 5. RETURN TO WRITING MODE.

+COMMANDS+		
+Command Level+	+Writing Level+	+Direction+
A	control A	advance one line
→	→	move right
←	←	move left
space bar	space bar	remove letters by typing over them
	not use	save your writing

The first few times the children used the word processor they worked in teams of two or three. (It has been found that this greatly relieves pressure and aids the children in figuring out the proper procedure.) For the first project the team had a choice as to the content they would write. When they were finished writing and had saved the material, the next group took over. As individual children became proficient in the use of the machine, they helped the new teams.

All the beginning paragraphs (about five per team) easily fit on one disk which the teacher took to the office at the end of the day and printed out. (In some situations it may be possible to have a printer in a classroom; however, it is most likely that a building will have a single printer, which will be kept in the office.)

Over the next few weeks, the children used the word processor on each of the projects they had suggested. On some occasions the children composed at the word processor; on other occasions they wrote the material out and then typed it on the processor. It is probably easier for the children to write the first draft by hand until their typing skills have matured. If there is time, it is desirable that the children learn to compose at the keyboard. Writing in this manner allows the flow of thoughts and words to go along at almost the same pace. In fact, writers such as Isaac Asimov are able to write copy at a word processor at the rate of more than eighty words a minute.

Later in the year the children learned to use the companion spelling program.

Some Thoughts on the Word Processor

What is the advantage of word processing? Users have noted the following:

1. Children and adults are more willing to write. They feel free to make errors, knowing that mistakes can easily be corrected.
2. Since spelling can be corrected and checked later, the writer uses a larger vocabulary than when writing by hand or at the typewriter. Think about it. Haven't you often changed a word in order to be sure of your spelling? Actually, some children find the spelling program so much fun to use that they truly enjoy checking spelling errors.
3. Once typing is mastered, one's writing speed is greatly increased.
4. Writers state that it is easier to get down their ideas with a word processor.
5. Neat material is produced. The children have pride in their writing and therefore try harder. This is particularly true of children who have physical disabilities which hamper good writing. It is also true of the child who has a tendency to be like Pigpen in the Peanuts cartoon strip. This kind of child seems to make a mess of every paper that he or she works on. Parents in particular are pleased with the neat word-processed letters and reports.
6. Much of what is learned is carried over into adulthood. The learning going on in word processing can be used for a lifetime on a variety of tasks.

Other Suggested Uses of the Word Processor

In addition to instruction in writing, the teacher can use word processing equipment for a number of other tasks. These include the following:

Testing out vocabulary for example, substituting different words in paragraphs and discussing the effect upon the meaning and the style.

Example: Mr. Kim was not satisfied with the manner in which his textbook introduced adjectives. It merely defined them and then asked the children to underline the adjectives in paragraphs. He began his lesson by saying, "My father always liked to read *The Legend of Sleepy Hollow* each fall because of the way it described the fall foliage in the Catskill Mountains. Close your eyes and listen while I read it to you." He then read two descriptive paragraphs and asked, "Which words really help you picture the mountains?" Then he turned on the large video screen that was attached to his microcomputer. The two paragraphs were shown. Next, the individual children capitalized the words that caused them to picture the scene.

After a discussion, Mr. Kim asked the children to describe the kinds of words with which they had been working. Their description closely resembled the book definition of adjectives. He then said, "Words such as these can often help us to speak and write much more interestingly. What would you put in these?"

He then presented a series of paragraphs in which the children were to replace the adjectives with words that were more colorful. Later the word processor was used to change specific adjectives throughout a one- or two-page passage. The children discussed the advantages and disadvantages of each.

Developing worksheets. Many teachers have found that they can develop a format for worksheets that saves them a great deal of time. The basic layout is saved in the word processing program, and each new worksheet requires only some creative effort. This procedure can be used for all types of teacher hand-outs.

Spelling. There are commercially developed spelling programs available which help children learn the standard spelling lists and also allow for the insertion of words that are causing specific difficulty.

Several microcomputers come equipped with a speech synthesizer that can be effectively used in spelling. Others have moderately priced add-on devices. The speech synthesizer is excellent for use in spelling, for it allows a proper sequence of spelling instruction. Many of the textbook spelling programs available today use a study-test format in which the children spend one or two days studying the words and then have a pretest at midweek. Research indicates that children learn spelling better when they are given a pretest, since they can devote their attention to the words they do not know.

A well above average spelling program can be developed by a format in which the word is presented, used in a sentence, and then presented again. The child is then asked to spell the word. The program analyzes the spelling and puts on the screen the portion of the word the student has correctly spelled. If a child spelled *cat* as *kat,* the program would type out "+at."

Spelling games can also be used effectively to help those who need extra help with specific words. Programs can be used in which the game centers on the words that have been entered by the teacher or the pupil.

A Thought. There are countless ways in which microcomputers can be used to improve reading and language arts programs. There are also many poor ways to use microcomputers in teaching reading/language arts. The key is the manner in which the teacher uses the computer.

Self-Test

1. All CAI reading programs use sound.
2. Most CAI reading programs are limited to one approach.

3. Computerized reading instruction could individualize both the content and the testing of students.
4. An advantage of computerized reading instruction lies in its ability to require responses from children, as well as to integrate reading and writing.
5. Some computerized instruction in reading uses auditory (voice) output along with the printed word.
6. Word processing requires special machines.
7. A spelling program automatically corrects misspelled words.
8. Word processing is the only use for a word processing program in the classroom.
9. Spelling cannot be taught via CAI.
10. Word processing improves children's attitudes toward writing.

Think About

1. Of the uses described in this chapter, which do you believe are the soundest and most useful?
2. What are some disadvantages of word processing?
3. Will monitors replace books as the medium of reading in the future? If so, what will be gained? Lost?
4. Should computerized reading instruction be designed to measure and control a child's rate of reading?
5. Will computers cause us to read more or less? Why?
6. Will computers cause us to write more or less?
7. List ten possible language arts activities that can use the computer.
8. What do you think the best use of the computer is for language arts?

Suggested References

Badiali, Bernard J. Micros make time for readability. *Educational Computer Magazine,* September/October 1982, pp. 26–27.
What does Badiali suggest concerning micros and readability?

Blanchard, J.S. Computer assisted instruction in today's reading classrooms. *Journal of Reading,* 1980, pp. 430–434.
Study Blanchard's CAI reading suggestions.

Gula, Robert J. Beyond the typewriter: An English teacher looks at the word processor. *Classroom Computer News,* May/June 1982.

Rothman, Milton A. A writer's craft transformed: Word processing. *On Computing,* Winter 1980, p. 60.
How do the suggestions made by Gula and Rothman concerning word processing compare with those in this chapter?

Schuyler, M. R. Readability formula program for use on microcomputers. *Journal of Reading,* 1982, 25, 560–591.
How would you use Schuyler's readability program?

Shostak, Robert. Computers and teaching English: Bits and pieces. *The Computing Teacher,* 8, 7, 1981, pp. 56–57.
What suggestions on teaching English does Shostak make?

Bibliography

BADIALI, BERNARD J. Micros make time for readability. *Educational Computer Magazine*, September/October 1982, pp. 26–27.

BLANCHARD, J.S. Computer-assisted instruction in today's reading classrooms. *Journal of Reading*, 1980, 23, 430–434.

HASSELBRING, T. S. Remediating spelling problems of learning-handicapped students through the use of microcomputers. *Educational Technology*, 1982, 22(4), 31–32.

JUDD, DOROTHY H. Avoid readability formula drudgery: Use your school's microcomputer. *The Reading Teacher*, October 1981, pp. 7–8.

MASON, GEORGE E. Computerized Reading Instruction: A review. *Educational Technology*, October 1980, pp. 18–22.

MASON, GEORGE E. The computer as a teacher of the disabled reader. *Journal of Research and Developmental Education*, 1981, 14(4), 97–101.

MATUSIK, VALERIE. Computers: An aid to reading instruction. *Ohio Reading Teacher*, 1981, 16, 18–20.

SCHUYLER, M.R. Reability formula program for use on microcomputers. *Journal of Reading*, 1982, 25, 560–591.

SHARPLES, M. A computer written language lab. *Computer Education*, 1981, 37, 10–12.

SHOSTAK, ROBERT. Computers and teaching English: Bits and pieces. *The Computing Teacher*, 1982, 9(7).

ZACCHEI, D. The adventures and exploits of the dynamic storymaker and textman. *Classroom Computer News*, May/June 1981, pp. 28;29;76.

12

Mathematics, Art, and Music

There has been a greater amount of work done with computers in the field of mathematics education than in any other teaching field. This is natural, since the majority of persons in computer science have a strong mathematics background, and those in mathematics education have either worked with computers or at least feel more comfortable with computers than educators in other fields. There also exists the unfortunate belief that because mathematics is a structured field, it lends itself to easy programming of computer-assisted-instruction materials. Those who follow this view tend to perceive mathematics as narrowly as a person who considers the language arts to consist merely of spelling and rules of grammar.

MATHEMATICS

Before making suggestions on the use of computers in mathematics instruction for the elementary and middle grades, we would like to review a few principles of teaching mathematics that should be considered when planning the computer program. We will emphasize only those principles that directly affect computer usage.

1. Children should have an opportunity to explore and use an idea before analyzing the principle behind it. Thus, children should have an opportu-

nity to solve addition problems using counting and any other procedure with which they are comfortable before generalizing about the principles of addition.

2. Students should have an opportunity to explore several methods of finding the answer to a computation. Thus, if computer-assisted-instruction programs teaching a particular mathematical concept are developed, they should provide the student with the opportunity to branch out into a variety of ways of looking at the idea. This concept will be explored later in the chapter.

3. The learner should be provided with specific procedures for learning and remembering the facts and processes in mathematics.

4. Emphasis should be placed on estimation and on finding a reasonable answer. As the use of the hand-held calculator and the microcomputer increases, many of the procedural errors become those of place value. For example, if a child uses a calculator to find 21.56 × 41.67 and does not, by a quick estimation, know that the product is over 800, he or she will not correct the product 8984.052, which was produced by hitting the decimal point at the wrong time.

5. Provide a great deal of the drill and practice through games in which the major interest is provided by the mathematics involved.

6. Provide children with the opportunity to discover concepts, instead of teaching by a rule-application procedure.

7. Teach geometry with an emphasis on relationships and concepts rather than on vocabulary and rules.

There are four major uses of microcomputers in teaching elementary school mathematics: computer-assisted instruction; problem solving; using graphics such as those in LOGO to develop geometric concepts; and demonstrating the relationship between computers and mathematics. Suggestions for each use follow.

Computer-Assisted Instruction

The large majority of mathematics computer-assisted instruction available for the elementary and middle school are either drill-and-practice programs or step-by-step rules to teach a concept. However, more programs are becoming available which emphasize good teaching procedures. Here are a few examples of good uses of computer-assisted instruction in mathematics.

Grade One. A first-grade teacher found that while several of her pupils could count effectively to find the answers to addition and subtraction problems, they did not know the number symbols. She made use of a game in which the children scored points by correctly identifying numbers of objects. The game worked this way: A number of objects were displayed on the TV screen, and four numerals were displayed in large type at the bottom of the screen. The cursor paused at each numeral, and the child hit the space bar if it was wrong and the return key if it was correct. For each correct response, one point was scored.

Grade Two. The teacher made use of the Herkle game, developed by the Minnesota Educational Computing Consortium to help the children with the sequence of numbers. The portion of the game used here was the positive number line.

Problem Solving

There are a number of computer programs which provide opportunities for children to work with aspects of logic and may even provide a prelude to computer programming. For example, The Factory—sold by Sunburst Communications—is described as a microworld of problem solving. The computer houses industrial machines that rotate, punch, and stripe raw material. Problem-solving strategies (working backward, developing sequences, and applying creativity) are put to work as the students construct assembly lines on the screen that will turn a raw material into a finished product. One screen is shown below.

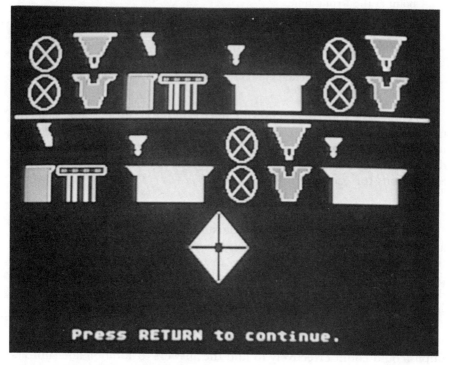

A factory assembly line. (Electronic Learning.)

Using Graphics

In addition to LOGO (see Chapter 15), there are LOGO-like programs which allow very young children to work with geometric shapes. For example, Delta Drawing (by Spinnaker) challenges young children to create a host of graphics material.

Mathematics and Computer Relationships

This topic is more thoroughly handled in the chapter dealing with programming. However, it should be stressed that working with computers may provide the first opportunity for a majority of children to see the results of logical thought.

The paragraphs that follow give a few examples of the types of situations teachers deal with in working with computers in the mathematics program.

Mr. Williams watched as the students in the computing lab worked with different drill-and-practice arithmetic programs. He and Deedee together saw her screen light up with

$$\begin{array}{r} 8 \\ \times 3 \\ \hline \end{array}$$

Deedee started to type 24, but after entering the 2, the machine erased her answer and presented the same problem again. Mr. Williams tried to restrain himself, but when he saw Deedee getting frustrated, he told her she had to enter the 4 first, just as if she were doing a longer problem like

$$\begin{array}{r} 88 \\ \times 3 \\ \hline \end{array}$$

"But that one's just 24," protested Deedee, "You can see that right away." Mr. Williams agreed but explained that the computer just had to have it that way. Deedee finally got the answer accepted by the computer and was rewarded with an attractive picture.

"At least that's nice," thought Mr. Williams, walking away. He didn't stay long enough to see that rather than thinking about arithmetic, Deedee first touched the picture on the screen, then got bored with it and began looking around the room.

In the microcomputer lab in the district's other building, Mrs. Helenbrook was also surveying a class working on programs. She had spent a considerable amount of time researching, previewing, and evaluating programs before purchasing any, and was pleased with the results. Many of the children were working with a comprehensive mathematics software program that kept track of where they had been at the end of the previous session, diagnosed the students' needs at the end of content sections, assigned appropriate work, and altered the pacing and difficulty of the arithmetic drill on the basis of the students' responses. Mrs. Helenbrook could instruct the computer to print out reports concerning individuals or groups at any time. Students could instruct the computer to go faster or slower, to use graphic rewards, or to just continue to the next problem.

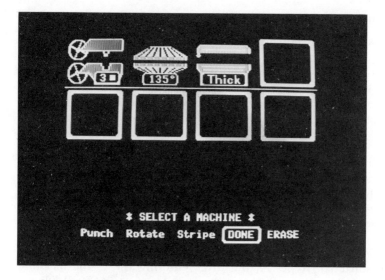

In *The Factory* children design a factory assembly line to create geometric "products." Sequencing, inductive thinking, spatial perception, logic, and problem-solving are developed. (Courtesy of Sunburst Communications, Inc.)

Some other fifth graders were working with a tutorial program that provided a choice of solution strategies that could be used to solve problems in mathematics. After picking a strategy, children could manipulate the words, numbers, and graphics to help them solve the word problem. For example, children might choose to use a number line and could then label points on it. At any time a single keystroke would branch the program into a tutorial illustrating the use of the chosen strategy in solving the particular problem. Furthermore, the tutorial itself could be cut off at any time, allowing students to finish the problem themselves.

When they finished these assignments, Mrs. Helenbrook's students had several choices. Ermine played a factoring game. She could pick any number from a series of numbers, and it would be added to her score—but the computer could (and would!) choose any factors of that number that were still available. This made the choice of, say, 12, early in the game unwise, as the computer could choose 1, 2, 3, 4, and 6—for a score of 16. (Later in the game, if 6 and 4 had been chosen and thus were no longer available, 12 would be a worthwhile pick.) On the other hand, 29 was a good choice. (Why?) Then the tables were turned, and the computer chose. The player then had to locate all the factors still available. Ermine was excited—after two weeks she had finally won a game! She was trying again. Two boys in the corner were writing their own program, which was designed to drill younger students on number facts.

Wide ranges in the quality of computer programs, such as the arithmetic programs used by these two teachers, are common. Educators must realize that time spent selecting good quality software yields considerable benefit to both the teacher and the students. It is important for the teacher to ask, "What do I want to accomplish by using microcomputer technology? What do I want my students to know, to learn, to experience? What are my goals?" With these goals in mind, the teacher can select programs which offer valuable educational experiences. Many good programs in mathematics are available. However—perhaps partially because so many programmers with moderate experience view the computer as an advanced calculator—there is a lot of simple drill with few redeeming factors. Should a costly machine be used to present worksheet pages? Should computers drill children endlessly in long division, when the very advent of computer technology has almost eliminated the actual use of that form of paper-and-pencil computation? Should other uses prevail? There are excellent programs being developed in geometry, problem solving, and logic.

One example is a program called SemCalc (Semantic Calculator), a combination of CAI and a calculator (Schwartz, 1982). Designed to help students solve arithmetic word problems, SemCalc provides electronic scratch paper set up in rows and columns (in a manner similar to the electronic spreadsheets that will be discussed in the chapter of utilities). The student fills in the numbers and corresponding units of measurement, as well as the mathematical operation to be used. For example:

	HOW MANY?	WHAT?
A)	116	MILES
B)	8	GAL
OPERATION	A/B	

The computer would then print:

```
THE UNITS TO THE ANSWER ARE MILES/GAL
DO YOU WISH TO CARRY OUT THE CALCULATION? (TYPE Y)
OR INDICATE A DIFFERENT OPERATION? (TYPE N)
```

If the student, deciding that the units are appropriate, types Y, the computer prints:

```
116 MILES/8 GAL = 14.5 MILES/GAL
```

The quantity 14.5 miles/gal is added to the scratch pad for possible future use.

If the student had chosen a different operation, say A times B, the computer would have responded:

THE UNITS TO THE ANSWER ARE MILES∗GAL.

The student must then decide if this is appropriate for the task. The computer will still carry out this computation at the student's request, leaving it to the student to discover if anything is wrong with the answer to the problem. Thus, SemCalc is a problem-solving tool, not an expert system instructing and correcting the student. Its purpose is to help students learn how to use what they know about the semantic properties of the referents of the numbers (miles, gallons) to help find a solution to the problem, avoiding inappropriate computations.

Another example illustrating this process concerns the classic problem of adding apples and oranges. Assume that a student had entered the following:

	HOW MANY?	WHAT?
A)	7	APPLES
B)	12	ORANGES
OPERATION	A+B	

The computer would respond:

CAN APPLES BE CONVERTED TO ORANGES

OR

CAN ORANGES BE CONVERTED TO APPLES? PRESS Y OR N.

If the student types N, the computer asks

APPLES AND ORANGES ARE BOTH WHAT?

If the student types FRUIT, the program displays

> 7 FRUIT + 12 FRUIT = 19 FRUIT

and the quantity 19 FRUIT is added to the scratch pad.

Could the student have answered PIZZAS instead of FRUIT? Of course. SemCalc is merely a tool; it is not designed to tell students the answers. In other cases, of course, conversion is possible. If the student had attempted to subtract grams from kilograms, the computer would ask

> CAN GRAMS BE CONVERTED TO KILOGRAMS?
>
> OR
>
> CAN KILOGRAMS BE CONVERTED TO GRAMS? PRESS Y OR N.

In order to proceed, you must specify

> A) HOW MANY KILOGRAMS IN ONE GRAM OR
> B) HOW MANY GRAMS IN ONE KILOGRAM. PRESS A OR B.

If the student chooses B, the program responds

> HOW MANY GRAMS IN ONE KILOGRAM?

Typing 100, the student then sees

> 2000 GRAMS − 500 GRAMS = 1500 GRAMS

Of course, option A would not have been incorrect—the student would respond that there are .001 kilograms in a gram, and the answer would be correctly calculated in kilograms.

SemCalc also allows students to calculate answers in a range of possibilities. For instance, if the thirteen steps in a stairway range between 28 and 30 centimeters in height, one might average the height of the steps and calculate the stairway to be 13 times 29, or 377 centimeters in height. However, a better answer is to calculate the range of possibilities—from

364 centimeters (28 times 13) to 390 centimeters (30 times 13). This becomes even more important when an answer implies a level of precision that is not warranted. For example, say that in the gas mileage problem, a car traveled 91 miles on 7 gallons of gas on one day, and 109 miles on 7 gallons the next day. Averaging these distances and dividing by 7 yields 14.2857143 miles per gallon. A level of precision is implied that is not appropriate. SemCalc allows the student to obtain the more reasonable result, a range of possibilities.

Programs are also available which will provide practice in solving equations. If the student wants help, the program illustrates, step by step, one method of solving the problem. The graphic capabilities of microcomputers, along with their ability to interact with the student, make them a "natural" for teaching geometry in ways that are active and discovery oriented. Instead of being static and laden with names and theorems, microcomputer geometry can be visually active, taking advantage of students' spatial imagination and intuition.

From preschool child to adult, people can learn by programming the computer to draw various shapes and designs (see the discussion on turtle geometry in the chapter on LOGO). CAI programs can lead students to move polygons in explorations of congruency, or illustrate and offer hints on the solutions of spatial problems. Other graphic programs display a line or curve representing an equation typed in by the student. Students can experiment freely within this environment, or the teacher might provide a sequence of equations to be graphed with the aid of the computer.

Graphics may assist the learner in understanding other areas, too, such as fractions. In one program an animated person pulls a rectangular region representing ½ over to another, representing ¾. After the two are congruent (lying directly on top of one another), he points to them and then points to the equality ½ = ¾.

Programs that are not too difficult can be written by teachers or students to illustrate probability concepts. For instance, one simple simulation continually graphs the result of consecutive tosses of a coin. If it comes up "heads," the next plotted point is one unit higher; if it lands on "tails," it is one unit lower. If the plotted line reaches the top or bottom border, the program ends. If your goal is to provide drill and practice for your students, many programs are available which avoid problems such as those described at the beginning of this chapter. Some provide minimal instruction.

Most worthwhile programs will keep student records, and some will diagnose and prescribe. The use of both tutorial and drill-and-practice CAI programs has been supported by several research studies (Bracey, 1982; Burns and Bozeman, 1981; Overton, 1981). The implications of one study are important to teachers (Alderman, Swinton, and Braswell, 1979). Children exposed to a drill-and-practice CAI program in mathe-

Thought-provoking programs like *Snooper Troops 1* from Spinnaker Software are helpful in developing problem-solving skills.

matics outperformed control group children; however, a close look revealed that the former made roughly the same type of errors. They merely omitted fewer items. Thus, they were more adept and efficient at answering questions without necessarily having a stronger grasp of the concepts. This suggests that teachers using drill-and-practice computer programs need to closely integrate use of these programs and classroom work on conceptual understandings. They need to make sure their students possess the prerequisite understandings necessary to work with the program correctly—in other words, practicing procedures that are both correct and meaningful to them.

ART AND MUSIC

The microcomputer provides a device that can greatly expand the opportunities for children to engage in art and music activities on several levels. The computer is of particular use in art and music to the child who does not think that he or she is at all artistic. Space does not permit a thorough study of all the ways in which a microcomputer can be used to improve the art and music programs, but enough classroom illustrations will be given so that you can develop music and art lessons on your own.

Music

If you were to ask a hundred persons on the street, "Do you think that computers and music go hand in hand?" you would get a variety of answers. People first saw computers and music mixed in the album "Switched on Bach," which makes use of a computer to develop the music. Today there are hundreds of electronic pianos and music synthesizers which are basically computers.

How can computers be used in the elementary/middle school to improve the music program? The following suggestions may be helpful.

1. Computers can be used to help teach factual material. Many teachers want the children to have some idea about composers, their works, and when they lived. One elementary music teacher challenged her sixth grade to develop a set of materials that could be put on the computer to teach and review the subjects of composers for the fourth and fifth graders. The children developed graphic pictures of the composers and a format for guessing names and dates. The children working on the material had the choice of identifying a composer after one hint, two hints, and so on. For most composers, four to six hints were given. For example:

Name this Composer

Hint one: Died in 1750.
Hint two: Most believe he was one of the greatest.
Hint three: During his life he was more famous as an organist.
Hint four: Many of his works were religious.
[etc.] . . . . . . Name: Johann Sebastian Bach

A group of high school computer students programmed the material for the school microcomputer.

2. Computers can also help in ear training. A seventh-grade music teacher used the MECC drill-and-practice program in music to increase the students' ability to detect correct notes. The program gives the user the opportunity to select the number of sharps or flats and the greatest interval distance between notes. The six notes are randomly generated within the parameters the user selects. Then the notes are played by the computer using its small speaker (both the Apple and the Atari can use this program without special music equipment). However, the notes are played with one error. The students then decide which note was wrong.

In the case above, the teacher began the lesson with the whole class. She had connected a large TV monitor to the computer, and she had the students move their chairs so that they could easily see. For the first few attempts, the teacher limited the selections to those with no sharps and flats and one interval. When the students were familiar with the program, she increased the difficulty and broke the class into two groups. She gave each class member a note "cube" which she had made of soft sponge rubber. Each note "cube" was about one and one-half inches on a side. The teacher had marked each of the sides of each "cube" with a note name—A, B, D, E, F, G. She directed them to hold their cube so that the name of the wrong note would appear between their thumb and index finger. If the wrong note was C, the students were directed to hold up a closed fist.

The game went as follows:

a. The computer showed the notes on the screen and then sounded the six notes.
b. The teacher directed the children to think about which one was incorrect and then place the cube in their hand so that the wrong note appeared between the thumb and index finger. When the teacher said, "Show," all the students held up their hands. Either the teacher or directors selected from each team counted the number of correct notes.
c. A team received one point for each correct note.
d. The first team to score 250 points won.

We have found that children really can improve their "ears." In fact, one of us found that for the first four or five times he used this program with a group of elementary teachers, he was wrong in his selection of the incorrect note the majority of the time. (He was one of those to whom the music teacher had suggested, "Just move your lips or sing very softly at the performance.") However, the more he used the program the more times he was right.

3. Another teacher used a "music generator" program disk costing about $30. The program provided a staff and allowed the children to place notes on the screen by typing in the name of the note. It also allowed for sharps, flats, and differences in tempo. After a series of notes was written, the students touched the appropriate key and the music was played on the computer "bell." Another teacher attached a speaker to the computer for better sound.

The first time this program was used, the class worked together under teacher direction to write a song. The class members were challenged to write another song in their spare time and drop it off at the teacher's office. The teacher then put all the songs into the computer, and they were played in class the next day. As the semester progressed, a number of the students became serious about writing better music. A parent-teacher group bought a music board to go with the computer, which allowed for the development of really excellent music which played through a stereo. (Note: A description of such a set-up can be obtained by writing to Micro Music Inc., P.O. Box 386, Normal, Ill. 61761.)

Later, several of the pieces the children had written were performed at a school open house using the computer and a stereo. Some of the better pieces were also played on the school intercom system during the lunch hour.

There is little doubt that this type of computer use in music will give a number of children who cannot perform on an instrument a chance to compose music and enjoy their creativity. For not a great deal of money, this type of material can be added to a home computer so that the children will have an opportunity to continue their musical experimentation. When the children become more sophisticated musically, they can try to write music of various periods and styles.

4. Still another teacher purchased two disks of computer music that were played through the computer bell. He used this procedure as a method of motivating the children to try their hand at developing similar music.

5. One class developed computer-generated music, tape recorded some at home, and then played their recorders with the composite music.

There is little doubt that only cost and teacher imagination limit the amount of learning and pleasure a computer can bring to the elementary/middle school.

Art

Computer-generated art is being recognized as true art in the same way that computer-directed instruments are recognized as producing true music. There are a number of art galleries today that display and market computer-generated art. When computer scientist-computer educator Steve Rogowski spoke at a meeting for elementary teachers several years ago, we found that his hobby was developing computer graphic art. As with music, the computer allows persons who think they cannot "draw" to engage in art.

In some ways the use of the microcomputer in art is easier than in music; in other ways it is harder. In most cases art requires one computer and one person—which is somewhat difficult to arrange. However, a number of the techniques of computer painting and drawing can be taught to a large group, and then to a small group, and finally individual sessions can be scheduled. We will see below how art can be developed using a microcomputer. Several examples are provided showing how teachers have used this technology to increase the artistic creativity of their students.

An exhibit called "Art by Computers," which featured a collection of computer-generated works of American and European artists toured nationally. The exhibit included an Apple II with an Apple Graphics Table (the Apple graphics sketch pad is a table on which the user can draw and have the graphics appear on the monitor screen; this can be printed out by a dot matrix printer with graphics capability). In addition to viewing the art produced by computer artists, the visitors were able to try their hand at using an electronic pen on the graphics sketch pad. The sketch pad makes developing computer graphic art very similar to drawing in another medium. Graphic art can be produced on almost all microcomputers by developing a program that produces it on the screen.

Another type of graphic art can be developed by using a program that breaks the screen into small portions that have a designation number. The "picture" is produced by indicating a color number and the location number.

1. One art teacher demonstrated a graphics tablet and then asked the students to give suggestions for color changes and shading suggestions.
2. A teacher used LOGO, which is explained in detail in Chapter 15, to develop children's thinking concerning art design. One of the first activities pupils could do after generating shapes was to try to develop a number of quilt or weaving patterns. (There are several computer programs for the home weaver who wishes to see ahead of time what a given design will be like. The only special requirement is a color TV.) When the pupils had developed several patterns as a class, the teacher had them develop individual patterns with pencil and paper and then change their work into LOGO language.
3. Another class read an article on how computers are used to develop animation. An Apple computer was used on the Disney movie *Dragonslayer* to save hours and hours of movement. After reading and discussing the article, student teams tried to simulate the means of animation. Instead of the method used by the Disney group, the class used LOGO.
4. One teacher developed a series of computer graphic exercises that the pupils could work with after school, at home, or during study time.
5. After over 1,750 school children had an opportunity to explore the Apple system and the Designer's Toolkit, the Palo Alto Unified School District's art coordinator suggested that the district might look into getting such equipment, so that all children would have an opportunity to explore art and the new technology.

Suggested program uses included using the paint program as an electronic blackboard to look at principles and elements of the visual arts; and using personalized art disks so that each child could develop and save pictures and so that a "computer slide show" could be presented.

Self-Test

1. The best use of the computer in mathematics is in drill-and-practice material.
2. LOGO is beyond the grasp of elementary school students.
3. LOGO can be used in both art and mathematics.
4. There is little that can be accomplished in music using CAI.
5. Art and mathematics may be combined on the computer.
6. Weavers often use the computer.
7. Electronic music began with the microcomputer.

8. There are problem-solving programs which help students develop logical thought.
9. SemiCalc locks the student into fixed responses.
10. Geometry is harder to teach with the computer than is arithmetic.

Suggested References

Burns, Patricia K., and Bozeman, William C. Computer-assisted instruction and mathematics achievement: Is there a relationship? *Educational Technology,* October 1981, pp. 32–39.
What effects on achievement in mathematics are reported by Burns and Bozeman?

Fleischer, Dave. Computer animation: The art of hyper-reality. *Science Digest,* February 1982, pp. 46–48.

Freidman, Batya. Art and the computer. *Creative Computing,* July 1982, pp. 97–99.
Fleischer and Friedman give suggestions for the use of microcomputers in art. What suggestions could you use?

Hatfield, Larry L. A case and techniques for computers: Using computers in middle school mathematics. *Arithmetic Teacher,* 1979, 26(6), 53–55.

Kantowski, Mary Grace. The microcomputer and instruction in geometry. *Viewpoints in Teaching and Learning.* 1981, 57, 71–81.

Kock, Helen, Inductive experiences using the Apple II microcomputer. *Monitor,* November 1979, pp. 10–13.

Piele, Donald. Digital didactices. *Creative Computing,* November 1981, pp. 238; 240–247.

Wright, Jim. Micro music for the TRS-80. *Creative Computing,* January 1980, p. 34.

Bibliography

ALDERMAN, D. L., SWINTON, S. S., and BRACEWELL, J. S. (1979). Assessing basic arithmetic skills and understanding across curricula: Computer-assisted instruction and compensatory education. *Journal of Children's Mathematical Behavior,* 2, 3–28.

BRACEY, G. (1982, November/December). What the research shows. *Electronic Learning,* pp. 51–54.

BURNS, PATRICIA K., and BOZEMAN, WILLIAM C. Computer assisted instruction and mathematics achievement: Is there a relationship? *Educational Technology,* October 1981, pp. 32–39.

OVERTON, VICTORIA. Research in instructional computing in mathematics education. *Viewpoints in Teaching and Learning.* Spring 1981, pp. 23–36.

SCHWARTZ, J. (1982, March/April). The semantic calculator. *Classroom Computer News,* pp. 22–24.

13

Computers and the Exceptional Child

Jerry has a mild handicap. Without some special help, he could not be educated utilizing traditional means; he could not be employed in the vast majority of jobs; he could not enjoy most kinds of entertainment, and he would be incapable of participating in most sports. What technology is provided for him which helps him live a normal life? Eyeglasses. Jerry is quite myopic; but being a bright popular teacher—who happens to wear glasses—no one really considers him handicapped at all. Without the technology of eyeglasses, many teachers would not now be teaching; many might not be reading. This is not to equate myopia with other severe handicaps. It does indicate that what is—and what is considered by others to be—a handicap is largely determined by society's ability or lack of ability to allow the individual to compensate for that handicap.

Who is the exceptional child? What do we mean by handicapped? What can we design—often with the help of computer technology—which will provide support for those we *now* consider handicapped? Can we enable them to do more for themselves? To live like Jerry—fully, with few constraints? To an ever-increasing extent, we can. There are many special children who are "exceptional" in a myriad of ways. While computer technology has been applied extensively to help some of these children, it has helped others relatively little. As professionals, it is our responsibility to ensure that each child is helped to achieve his or her potential. What of economic considerations, a cynic might ask? One reply: Lifetime support for a totally disabled person is over half a million dollars.

This chapter will deal with several "traditional" uses of the computer—for example, organizing and presenting instruction—because any computer application which will help children with special needs is important. However, other approaches and aids are being developed which will move us closer to reducing, and in some cases almost eliminating, the handicaps. This is the ultimate goal.

HELPING THE TEACHER OF THE SPECIAL CHILD

Computer technology can be an invaluable aid to those who work with special children. In some cases this involves appropriate modification of techniques described in other chapters. We will look at these capabilities and some unique applications as they apply specifically to the needs of special children.

Computers can be especially useful in creating mandated Individualized Education Programs (IEPs), reducing the time needed for construction from several days to a few hours. It is, of course, still a tool—people are the final decision makers concerning what should be included. But it can help by analyzing the results of multiple measures and compiling the information in a usable form. It might also have access to a data bank—a large collection of goals and short-term objectives—and allow the users to match any relevant goals to the assessment information. For example, the screen might show a list of goals and objectives alongside the assessment results that lead to their selection. Pushing one key might instruct the machine to include a particular objective. Another would direct it to pass to other objectives. The educational team might decide that an objective should be included which was not contained in the data base. They would merely type it in.

Software packages are available which perform many of these functions. Level I of IEP Management Systems (from Creative Educational Services) prepares the IEP document with modifiable data files. Level II, in addition, prepares progress reporting documents for teachers and parents. Level III prints IEPs in multiple foreign languages. Level IV combines all the features in the first three levels. SuperPlanner (from Learning Tools) is a three-part package: The Curriculum Management System serves as a resource bank for materials; the Individualized Planning System keeps records for students and interacts with the Curriculum Management System to plan goals; and the Administration Planning System updates student records for administrators automatically. Project I.E.P. (from Evans-Newton) helps educators meet government guidelines for special education students by issuing status reports. It also provides diagnostic and prescriptive reports, individual status progress reports, and student personal data reports.

Once goals are established, other data bases can be used, including a collection of instructional methods, resources, and activities that are keyed to these goals. With a modem and telephone, the teachers can tie into other special education organizations to find materials, activities, and ideas from huge data banks—compilations of thousands of entries that have been found to be effective around the country.

HELPING THE EXCEPTIONAL CHILD

Many of these resource materials are computer programs. A computer-managed-instruction program may test children in broad areas. Based on their answers, it asks them other questions specifically chosen to find out just what they need to learn. It automatically keeps a record of their responses. On the basis of this diagnosis, it informs the children and their teacher what materials they should work with next. It can also print out weekly progress reports from this information. The computer-generated instructional prescription might include CAI programs that are designed to help children develop certain concepts and abilities.

Special education has been one area that has welcomed and integrated technological innovations openly. Before the advent of micros, computers had been used for instruction of hearing and visually impaired, mentally retarded, emotionally disturbed, and disadvantaged students. Possibly, their early acceptance can be traced to their compatibility with accepted practices in special education, such as presentation of carefully sequenced activities, finely tuned task difficulties, controlled provision of feedback (usually immediate), elimination of as much stress as possible, patience, and provision of a large degree of structure. No wonder special educators like computer-assisted instruction!

There is evidence that children with special needs like this method of learning, too. Poorly motivated students have become more enthusiastic about their studies (Cartwright and Derevensky, 1976). They feel more "in control." They are taught in a context that is positive, patient, reinforcing, and nonthreatening. Experienced authorities report that positive effects like these are not fleeting but continue over long periods (Joiner et al., 1982). One study offered minimally brain-damaged children four individual tutorial sessions (Berthold and Sachs, 1974). For some children the lessons were presented entirely by teachers in one-to-one sessions. Others were presented the lessons by computer. The rest were presented half the lessons by computer and the other half by teachers. The computer-only group scored lower than the other two, but there was no difference between those taught entirely by teachers and those taught half by teachers, half by computer. It would seem that computers can effectively supply up to one-half of one-to-one tutorials, with the same resulting performance. In another study of CAI drill and practice, children made substantial gains in math (Fricke, 1976).

CHARACTERISTICS OF PROGRAMS FOR EXCEPTIONAL CHILDREN

Programs have often been designed or modified to meet the needs of exceptional children in the following ways:

1. They leave spaces between printed lines of text. Those that did not do this sufficiently were modified by the teachers, who sometimes added extra solitary PRINT statements to leave a blank line. For other wordy programs they merely added REM before the PRINT statement. This made a "remark" out of the line: The line was still there, but it was not printed on the screen.

2. Children with learning problems sometimes have attention difficulties. Appropriate software highlights important information through visual and sound displays—color cues, music, buzzers, flashing arrows, underlining, and so on—when that is appropriate.

3. Conversely, extraneous, distracting material should be removed. Presentation should be simple and clear, in "chunks" of appropriate size.

4. Exceptional children do not always recognize their mistakes. Good courseware gives feedback when an error is made.

5. These children sometimes are impulsive, jumping to answer too quickly. Rate of presentation can be controlled by the teacher. Signals to "slow down and think" can be offered if the student response time is too fast. For slow-responding pupils, programs should be acquired, or existing programs modified, which allow the student to control the speed of responding, possibly providing a prompt or hint after a certain time period.

6. Programs should provide that amount of "scaffolding" or help that will allow the student to respond successfully. For example, at first a student may only be required to choose a correct answer among three possibilities.

7. The level of difficulty should be altered frequently, if not constantly, so that the task set for the student is neither too easy nor too difficult—many small increases in difficulty are often most beneficial.

8. Programs should use a wide variety of materials and situations that are as concrete and "real-world" as possible, to help students generalize what they have learned.

9. Most important, programs should follow the principles of instructional design. Thus, they should possess: (a) specified objectives and entry skills; (b) activities that are designed to be matched to objectives and are carefully sequenced; (c) content integrity; and, usually, (d) a management component—testing, keeping records, constructing assignments, reporting progress, and so on.

10. Program characteristics should match the needs of the specific group of children for whom they are designed. For example, one study (Kleiman, Humphrey, and Lindsay, 1983) found that hyperactive and other attention-deficient children benefited from working with computer programs providing drill in arithmetic in which (a) the level of problem difficulty was individually tailored; (b) the display was easily readable; (c) the answer format was designed to be similar to the typical paper-and-pencil answer format (that is, answers for problems with three or more digit answers were entered right to left); (d) problem solving was self-paced; (e) motivational features in the form of graphic displays and praise statements were incorporated; and (f) there were messages specifically related to the children's problem of

hyperactivity—for example, when a child answered incorrectly, too quickly, or made too many inappropriate button presses, the computer would print STOP IT!. Compared to matched paper-and-pencil practice, children chose to spend more time on the computer drill, working out more problems. The percentages correct in the paper-and-pencil and the computer treatments were equivalent (Grimes, 1981).

PROGRAMS FOR THE EXCEPTIONAL CHILD: SOME EXAMPLES

MECC offers a spelling program for children with special needs. The Math Machine (from Southwest EdPysch) is a drill-and-practice program that has been shown to be effective with learning-disabled students in research investigations (Watkins and Webb, 1981). Excellent reviews of other programs which are appropriate for use with exceptional children are available on paper or computer disk from the Special Education Computer Technology On-line Resource (SECTOR Project, Exceptional Children Center, Logan, Utah 84322).

Five interesting programs are being produced by Laureate Learning Systems. First Words is a receptive language tutorial which will be discussed in the next section. Micro-LADS is aimed at remediating syntactic constructions frequently found to be problematic for language-learning-disabled children. It is a package of six disks which cover nouns, plurals, and noun-verb agreement; verb forms; prepositions, pronouns, negatives, and Wh-questions, and passive and deictic expressions. Speak Up allows teachers to build their own audible words and phrases. It can be used as a utility for facilitating the production of audible augmentative communication systems and programs, and as an instructional tool. Children can build words themselves, using the word processor to learn the relationship between written and spoken representations. Through building words and sentences, children can create a story which they can subsequently have read to them. A sample instructional program which comes with Speak Up is a tutorial program involving nouns and their categorizations. An expanded version of this—First Categories, which utilizes speech, text, and graphics—includes animals, clothing, food, vehicles, body parts, and utensils. The Story Teller shows a written story with pictures, reads it to the child, and requests that the child read it alone. The program provides help whenever necessary.

COMPUTERS AND THE HANDICAPPED CHILD

A victim of cerebral palsy speaks his first words through choosing words presented on the computer screen under his control. A speech synthesizer then pronounces the words. Deaf children learn to hear as speech vibrations are transformed into tactile patterns they can feel. An autistic child, assumed to be deaf and without speech, speaks her first words after manipulating the LOGO turtle.

These are the modern-day miracles of the microcomputer in the education of the handicapped. This technology is quickly becoming the most powerful prosthetic device.

The Deaf

The deaf are probably the largest group to benefit from this new technology. Microcomputers are excellent tutors for deaf children. For those who cannot be helped by hearing aids, computers have been connected to devices which present words as vibrations on the abdomen; thus, sound recognition is learned similarly to conventional language. This is especially advantageous as compared to lip reading, since the latter cannot be used when the speaker is not easily seen, or with devices such as tape recorders or audio records. However, video interactive devices to teach lip-reading skills are also available. With a modem, computers can replace telephones as communicative devices for the deaf.

Another exciting development along these lines is the use of computer-based writing laboratories. For instance, highly motivating interactive adventure games exist which provide remarkably intelligent responses to a small range of words and sentences. Players can initiate communication rather than just responding to the computer's questions. Often involving mythical lands and exciting situations, these games stimulate a great deal of involvement and exploratory and problem-solving behavior. Their benefits are increased as children share the adventure, possibly through computer networks.

Studies have demonstrated that many profoundly deaf students have poor linguistic competence in comparison with their hearing peers. One language manipulation program provides children with the opportunity to interact more fully with a language environment, formulating and testing linguistic hypotheses (Sewell, Clark, Phillips, and Rostron, 1980). Deaf children are presented with photographic slides of themselves in everyday activities. On the computer screen they see a rearranged sentence describing the slide being displayed, for example, IS KICKING JOHN THE FOOTBALL. The words are manipulated by pressing the key corresponding to the first letter of any word on the screen. That word then moves down the screen. In this way, new arrangements of words can be constructed by moving words with single key presses. When all the words have been rearranged, a smiling or frowning face provides feedback as to the correctness of the solution. After all the jumbled sentences have been rearranged, a paper printout listing all attempts is generated. If desired, entire phrases can be moved as single units. Teachers, of course, can easily add sentences to the program. For the deaf child, this provides experience rapidly manipulating whole units in constructing sentences, together with immediate feedback.

Communication between the deaf and the hearing world is difficult. But computers can convert normal speech into line configurations. The deaf can learn to talk by matching their own speech pattern to this pattern for a given sound. However, deaf children undoubtedly learn language best by actively operating on it, just as normal children do. Therefore, we should provide deaf children with computer-based opportunities to use and develop with their language in meaningful contexts.

The Mentally Retarded

Although the research is not extensive, it does support the use of computer-assisted instruction with the mentally retarded (see Williams, Thorkildsen, and Crossman, 1983, for a review). Because of the limited reading skills of these children, computer-controlled videotapes, and especially videodisks, will undoubtedly provide a powerful new tool for aiding and teaching this segment of the population, as well as other handicapped children. "Talking" computers have been successfully used to increase the reading vocabularies of retarded people (Lally, 1981). Students were presented with sixteen words at a time. These words were placed over a matrix of sixteen buttons. At first children were free to push any word. The computer would light up the word and simultaneously speak it. Whenever the child chose, he or she could go on to the second activity. Here the computer gave verbal instructions, directing the child to press a word. If correct, the word was flashed and spoken by the computer three times. If incorrect, the computer told the student what word was pressed, asking again for the correct word. If no response was made after five seconds, the word flashed. If the child then touched the word, the computer said, THAT WAS RIGHT, BUT TRY AGAIN. At the end of the trials, the computer told the student how many words were correct and asked if he or she wanted to try again. After just four weeks of instruction, twenty minutes a day for four days a week, children increased their sight vocabularies by 128 percent, as compared to the 38 percent increase of a control group.

First Words is a microcomputer tutorial program which teaches receptive vocabulary to very young and/or very handicapped children (Wilson and Fox, 1982). If can be useful for children with a cognitive functioning level of less than a year. Fifty referential nouns are organized into ten category sets. Pictures, animation, and synthesized speech are used to teach children these words and their categories. At one of several difficulty levels, children are presented with a stimulus picture and verbally told the word. Then two pictures are displayed, the word is spoken again, and the children are asked to identify the correct picture. Children can respond by pressing the space bar when an orange box encloses the correct response, or by using a game paddle to position the box directly. Cues are provided as needed. The training levels move from a single picture presentation with antecedent instruction, cueing, and feedback, to two pictures and feedback alone. Complete records are kept. Teachers can specify the content, level of difficulty, and parameters, including speed of scanning, length of time program waits before moving to next item, and criterion. This program can be used by a wide range of children with and without handicapping conditions; for example, the mentally retarded, language-learning disabled, motor impaired, autistic, and emotionally disturbed.

Other devices that have been constructed to aid handicapped learners include touch panel terminals and computer-controlled "button boxes" which aid coordination, memory, attention, and sequencing (Macleod and Overheu, 1977). Another panel displays lines and text and allows the student to "draw" by plotting points under the pressure of a pen. It can thus allow interaction with the pupil in a way that would be difficult with conventional methods. For example, children might attempt to copy a well-formed figure or line, receiving immediate feedback as to the accuracy of their effort. If they move off the line, the tracing stops and a blinking spot shows them where they should be. Thickness of line can be controlled, so graduated levels of difficulty are easily achieved. Their own tracing might also be displayed. Every tracing can be stored by the computer, to be displayed again at any time. Letters can be presented one stroke at a time so that students have to form the letters in the correct direction and order. Regardless of the number of attempts, only the well-formed example is reinforced and eventually displayed; therefore, a satisfying and accurate final product is reinforced. As a reward for work in handwriting, children are presented with "secret drawings." They trace lines—presented out of order—which eventually form a car, robot, or cartoon.

Another important advance is reliable voice input. Voice recognition systems will have tremendous implications in special education, for CAI/ CMI, for speech therapy, and for enabling special education students to control the computer for a myriad of purposes. The VBLS voice-based learning system (from Instruction Systems Group, Scott Instruments Corporation) can be trained to understand almost any utterance, allowing children with speech disabilities and other physical handicaps to control the computer without using a keyboard, mouthstick, or headstick. The package comes with a mini-authoring system to allow teachers to construct individualized drills, tutorials, and tests for students.

The Blind

Because the traditional output device for the computer has been the CRT, the blind have benefited very little from computer applications. However, technological advances should soon change this state of affairs. These include: (a) the use of terminals which allow traditional typewriting for input but which use voice synthesis for output; and (b) computerized devices which can quickly scan written material and provide either voice or tactile output. One device, the Optacon (OPtical to TActile CONverter), produces the shape of letters under its camera on an array of vibrating pins. The camera is held with one hand and passed over the printed page. The other hand is placed over the pins. This device is not easily used by everyone, however, and research is progressing to develop a similar device which produces spoken output. Thus, conversations with microcomputers and reading with the help of microcomputers will soon be more commonplace.

Talking microcomputers are already being used by the blind in some projects. A similar, simple example is the Speech+ talking calculator, with synthesized voice output. The near future will bring aids to help the handicapped person communicate with the computer itself: for example, foot controls, suck/blow switches, and specially designed keyboards, to name a few. One example, the Autocom, is an electronic communication board. Items are selected by pointing with a special hand control or headset. The display is a thirty-two-character LED array. It can be used to communicate with others or to control devices, including computers. Computer-based itself, it has a fully expandable vocabulary. There will be Braille printers and keyboards with Braille-regular print translators, and/or large screens for the visually impaired. Braille printout computer terminals and printers are already allowing many blind students to graduate from computer programming programs. A Braille computer terminal which also supplies a paper copy of what appears on the screen is available (from Maryland Computer Services).

These terminals are also being used to reproduce textbooks in Braille, allowing blind students to be mainstreamed more readily. Previously, less efficient methods of Brailling could not keep texts up-to-date. Of course, any material already stored on a computer, such as international news and other information and computer-aided instructional materials, could be produced rapidly in Braille. In using CAI, the student might type in information on a regular keyboard but receive responses from the computer in the form of paper embossed with Braille characters continually fed from the terminal. These advances are currently being used at the level of higher education, but their use in all grades is not far off.

In the future, publishers should produce machine-readable tapes of their books for Braille reproduction, and optical scanners which can translate printed language into Braille, as well as other forms, should be used more widely. One project uses a device which translates speech into tactile stimulation, enabling the blind to read by feeling the shape of the letter without Braille. Use of electronic mail by handicapped people, especially the deaf-blind, would greatly facilitate their ability to communicate with others.

SOME CURRENT DEVELOPMENTS

Technological advances are making it possible for computers to recognize human speech. This will enable all handicapped people to use computers to control appliances, telephones, lights, doors, typewriters, and other everyday devices. Bedridden people will be able to control any electrical device in the home from a central location. Using computer recognition of speech, those with severe mobility handicaps have been able to learn computer programming and have gotten jobs in industry. One disabled computer programmer, Geoff Busby, has created a terminal which allows severely disabled people to program without depressing more than one key at a time. It can store words which can be chosen from a list. In the near future it will be possible for many who cannot leave their homes to be gainfully employed with the aid of communications technology. Similarly, handicapped children will be able to learn and to communicate with others at home; and/or they will be able to control many devices at school. Even those without speech will use input systems utilizing EMG muscle potential to control computers. Given variations in the amplitude and duration of pulses and the intervals between these pulses, complex commands may be produced by a single muscle. Thus, even spastic children may be able to output commands to a computer as quickly as a typist. Those who can produce only a few vocalizations can control a computer with an inexpensive vocal input device. Often these children have little reason to practice these virtually nonfunctional vocal noises. With such a device, producing patterns of sounds can make a computer draw pictures, play a game, control a wheelchair, or say words the children are not yet capable of producing. The benefits include increased control of the world, meaningful activity, and incentive to learn more skills.

One particularly interesting development is MAVIS (Microprocessor-driven Audio-Visual Information System), a general system that offers several facilities for a range of widely differing disabilities (Schofield, 1981). It is a small suitcase that attaches to a standard television set as well as to other equipment, if desired. The case contains a microcomputer with a large memory and a removable keyboard. Its many uses include word processing, drawing, making music, game playing, and environmental control—controlling lights, heat, televisions, telephones, and so on. Input can be by keyboard or by special switch (anything from joysticks to simple hand or foot switches to suck/blow tubes). With the use of switches, arrays of items such as characters, words, and choices are usually displayed for selection. MAVIS has the ability to modify these arrays, including their content and speed of operation.

Those who are unable to use a pencil can now write their thoughts. Those who had to wait to have someone else perform actions for them and who had to be taught by someone else can now control their world and learn on their own. Computers can be designed to bridge communications gaps for all special children, even the autistic, by adapting to the child's ability to communicate rather than forcing the child to adapt to the ways of others. In allowing the handicapped to control their world and communicate with others, computers can hardly be seen as agents of dehumanization.

AN ACTIVITY APPROACH TO EDUCATING EXCEPTIONAL CHILDREN

Another valuable approach is providing exceptional children with activities in which they can explore, construct, and communicate. Previously discussed tools, such as word processors, serve this purpose. Other programs have been specifically designed for exceptional children.

For those with communication handicaps such as deafness, cerebral palsy, and autism, there is a need to approach language development through meaningful, purposeful communication. This approach taps the powerful motivating potential of communicative interaction and the effective teaching technique of integrating the language arts. Building on the work of O.K. Moore, some computer programs create a series of exploratory, interactive language activities. For instance, the computer might first pronounce the sound of any letter, and later word, typed by the child.

In CARIS (Computer Animated Reading Instruction System, now commercially available), children select a noun and a verb by touching the CRT with a light pen. The computer then generates a brief animated cartoon acting out the meaning of that sentence. Later, the children type in the whole words. Many combinations can be explored. With the child in control and the immediate, direct visual feedback, the "best of both worlds" is achieved in facilitating reading success.

LOGO has also been used successfully in this manner. Even children with severe handicaps have been able to explore the picture-drawing, problem-solving, and other general-purpose programming which the language offers. Reading-disabled children have created their own reading materials by programming in LOGO to generate random sentences, as illustrated in our chapter on LOGO. Cerebral-palsied nonverbal students have drawn pictures, directing the computer to draw what they imagined. Autistic children who balked at performing upon the requests of others enthusiastically explored the commands that instruct the turtle.

An advantage of LOGO is the ease with which the activity or learning environment can be simplified so that children can engage in self-directed learning. For instance, physically handicapped children have worked successfully with an implementation of LOGO using a scanning system. Children view a two-dimensional array of numbers and letters. A cursor, or moving "pointer," moves past the rows until the children make a response—hitting any key, or one large button, or the like. It then moves past the characters in that row, allowing the children to select precisely the character desired. Often, at first, whole commands were spelled out and selected, so that children could "get going" quickly. As this became too restrictive, the character-by-character selection process was substituted.

This illustrates a powerful method of working with the handicapped—letting them use their present capabilities to control a world, even if it is first the small world of computer graphics or the like, and gradually expanding the range of that control. Even the repetitive behavior of an autistic child might come to have meaning if a computer sensed it and gave interesting visual feedback. As the child becomes interested in this effect, the input device might be changed to allow a greater variety of responses and a greater degree of shared meaning. This technique is similar to behavioral shaping, with important differences. The rewards are not contingent upon the observation and approval of an adult. The adult knows what the child wants but does not give it until certain behaviors are produced by the child; the computer does not willfully withhold a reward, it merely responds to the child's commands. It may be that existing prostheses can be used to greater effect, and with a greater ability to motivate children, in a LOGO learning environment. With control via eye tracking, even severely cerebral-palsied children may be able to "do anything the computer can do"—draw, write, compose music, communicate with others, and so on—with ease and efficiency (Papert and Weir, 1978).

Impressive case studies of affective and cognitive gains resulting from LOGO programming have been reported by many authorities (for example, Geoffrion and Goldenberg, 1981; Goldenberg, 1979; Weir, 1981). LOGO demands that children try things out, be exacting, and respond to feedback—learning by doing by themselves. It emphasizes process more than product, along with the debugging of processes. Children obtain experience with geometry, algebra, and other mathematical ideas, as well as with reading, writing, spelling, and typing.

With this approach, children control a microworld. They can interact with it, and they or others can increase its capacity to do complex and interesting things. Other people can be involved in this interaction. Cause and effect, predictability, and availability are provided without placing demands on or control over the children. This approach shares the characteristics of most quality educational activities. Children learn by discovering rules and knowledge for themselves. Different environments can be tailored to the needs and interests of different children. The focus is on strengths and on building upon them, rather than on weaknesses.

THE GIFTED AND TALENTED

Altered appropriately, many of these approaches, such as constructing sentences, would be valuable activities for young gifted children. Programming in LOGO to explore microworlds and solve problems is an excellent activity for talented children of any age, in any area—music, art, mathematics, language arts, science, and so on.

Experiences for gifted children should include expectations of both convergent and divergent thinking and should contain subject matter that is so current that it is on the cutting edge of the discipline. Computer technology allows for this as well or better than any other vehicle. From the work that has been done to date, it appears that specially designed experiences are necessary. Gifted junior high school students, given a chance to work with a university's PLATO CAI facilities, quickly became bored. Students who were allowed access to terminals for learning programming did benefit—but without supervision, much of their time was spent playing games. Adequate guidance, expert advice and direction, and interesting, appropriate CAI material seem to be required.

Every child, but especially the gifted child, should learn to use the computer as a tool to extend his or her talents. Most of these types of applications have been described in previous chapters; the gifted child should be guided to use these programs—utility programs, programming, and other exploratory programs—in ways that are broader and deeper. It is especially beneficial to arrange for these children to interact with a "mentor" who uses computers in the areas in which the child is interested.

Self-Test

1. Many children with special needs benefit from a controlled, sequenced presentation of material, with lots of practice.
2. The use of computers has been accepted by special educators only slowly and reluctantly.
3. There is a good match between computer capabilities and the instructional needs of handicapped children.
4. Research evidence suggests that children with special needs resent learning from a computer.
5. In order for programs that exist for "average" children to be used with children with special needs, extensive (and expensive) modifications will have to be made.
6. Computer programs for special children need to provide plenty of help in the form of elaborate directions.
7. Hyperactive or impulsive children should not work with computers, as they will only learn to push buttons in a random, rushed manner.
8. The level of difficulty of good computer-based material should be altered frequently as the child works.
9. Computers can help deaf children learn because these children can read the displays; but computers cannot really help such children communicate with other people.
10. Unfortunately, it would appear that blind children will not benefit from computer technology for some time.
11. Computer activities for the handicapped have been limited to drill and practice.

12. Although they can learn from the computer, exceptional children should not usually be expected to learn to control the computer through programming.

13. Gifted children can profitably be allowed to learn from CAI material, or to experiment with programming, virtually on their own, so that they receive valuable experiences without the necessity of costly supervision.

Think About

1. Given limited computer facilities, what application (for example, CMI; CAI; IEP construction; prosthetics; record keeping; data base management; and so on) or combination of applications do you believe would be most valuable in aiding special children?

2. Since they do have special needs, do you think special children should receive top priority in terms of access to technological facilities?

3. Several of the CAI activities mentioned in this chapter utilized carefully sequenced activities, controlled difficulty levels, immediate feedback, a high degree of structure, and provision of a large amount of practice. Are there any other elements you would add to this list? Are these characteristics valuable for all handicapped children? If so, should CAI for *all* children be so characterized? Why or why not?

4. Would some children with special needs benefit more from interaction with a machine than with people? Are there dangers here? How can we decide on the best course?

5. How would you respond to the person who says, "The schools do a mediocre and inadequate job teaching the handicapped. It would be better to leave them in a good home with several hours a day of on-line computer time"? What role do you think the computer should play in the home and the school for these children?

6. Gather information and prepare a report on the programs discussed that are designed to help prepare IEPs. If this process is increasingly efficient, should IEPs be mandated for every child?

7. Will computers increase our ability to mainstream handicapped people? How?

8. Write to some of the people and organizations using computers to aid the handicapped. (Some are mentioned in the articles cited in this chapter. Also write to the IEEE Technical Committee on Computing and the Handicapped; to Dr. Paul Hazan at the John Hopkins University Applied Physics Lab; and to G. C. Vanderheitden at the Trace Research and Development Center for the Severely Handicapped, 1500 Highland Ave., Madison, Wis. 53706). You might also contact other sources of information:

   Closing the Gap
   P.O. Box 68
   Henderson, Minn. 56044

   ERIC Clearinghouse on Handicapped and Gifted Children
   CEC
   1920 Association Drive
   Reston, Va. 22091

   M. Mason, Project Micro-Ideas
   1335 N. Waukegan Road
   Glenview, Ill. 60025

HEX
Richard Barth
11523 Charlton Drive
Silver Spring, Md. 20902

Project CAISH
3450 Gocio Road
Sarasota, Fla. 33580

SpecialNet
c/o NASDSE
Suite 404E
1201 16th Street
NW, Washington, D.C. 20036

Trace Research and Development Center
University of Wisconsin-Madison
314 Waisman Center
1500 Highland Ave.
Madison, Wis. 53706

Western Center for Microcomputers in Special Education
Suite 275
1259 El Camino Real
Menlo Park, Calif. 94025

9. Defend or attack the following statements:

a. The overuse of computers in special education will undermine the humanism that is possibly more necessary in this field than in any other.

b. It is better for a handicapped person to live life honestly, even if that means he or she is incapacitated to a degree, than to live dependent on a machine—or worse, to virtually *be* part machine.

c. Computer activities are too abstract for many of these children. They need more concrete, "real" experiences.

d. Appropriate personal computer facilities should be provided for handicapped children at home and at school at public expense, from the time their handicap is identified.

e. Computers provide the perfect challenge for many gifted children.

f. Computer use will only encourage gifted children to become "computer eggheads," socially inept and detached from the "real world."

g. The communication-based "activity approach" to educating exceptional children is more humanistic and sound than the CAI approach and should be used instead.

h. Gifted children have a special need to be challenged; they should receive priority in access to computer facilities.

Suggested References

Brudner, Harvey J. Light on: Microcomputers, special education, and CMI. *Educational Technology*, 1982, 22(7), 25–26.
Brudner lists several publishers that are developing systems that can help write IEPs and CMI systems which test entire classes in reading and mathematics—spotting those areas where each child needs help and directing parents and teachers to appropriate activities. He argues that wider utilization of CMI in individualizing the education of every child is the single most

important need in the area of educational applications of computers. What do you think?

Dugdale, Sharon, and Vogel, Patty. Computer-based instruction for hearing impaired children in the classroom. *American Annals of the Deaf,* 1978, 123, 730–743.

Many of the currently available CAI materials can be adapted easily for use with the hearing impaired. Read Dugdale and Vogel for examples of PLATO materials which have been modified appropriately. What adaptations do you think could be made to use materials with special children that you teach?

Goldenberg, E. Paul. *Special technology for special children.* Baltimore, Md.: University Park Press, 1979.

Grimes, Lynn. Computers are for kids: Designing software programs to avoid problems of learning. *Teaching Exceptional Children,* November 1981, pp. 49–53.

Goldenberg describes many exciting projects involving LOGO programming and special children. He argues that teaching special children with CAI materials is the "hospital model" of educational intervention and as such is full of dangers, since it sees the child as a patient rather than as the agent. Do you agree? Read his descriptions of activities he believes will promote autonomy and initiative. Read Lynn Grimes to gather ideas for worthwhile computer programs for exceptional children.

Hasselbring, T. S., and Crossland, C. L. Using microcomputers for diagnosing spelling problems in learning-handicapped children. *Educational Technology,* April 1981, pp. 37–39.

Hughes, Karen. Adapting audio/video games for handicapped learners: Part 1. *Teaching Exceptional Children,* November 1981, pp. 80–86.

Hasselbring and Crossland describe a microcomputer program designed to diagnose spelling problems in learning-handicapped children. Would such a program help you in your teaching? How would you use it? In what other areas of the curriculum do you think similar programs would be beneficial? To gather other ideas about simple modifications of programs for the handicapped, read "Audio/Visual Games for Severely Handicapped Learners: Possibilities for Simple Adaptations," by Karen Hughes. What is described there that would benefit children you teach?

Macleod, Iain, and Overheu, Don. Computer aided assessment and development of basic skills. *Exceptional Children,* 1977, 24, 18–35.

Schofield, Julia M. *Microcomputer-based aides for the disabled.* London, Eng.: Heyden & Son, Ltd, 1981.

These sources also discuss interesting programs for mildly handicapped children, including some innovative pieces of equipment.

vonFeldt, James R. A national survey of the use of computer assisted instruction in schools for the deaf. *Journal of Educational Technology Systems,* 1978–1979, 7(1), 29–38.

The article by vonFeldt presents a survey of how CAI materials are being used in schools for the deaf.

Bibliography

BERTHOLD, HOWARD C., AND SACHS, ROBERT H. Education of the minimally brain damaged child by computer and by teacher. *Programmed Learning and Educational Technology,* 1974, 11(3), 121–124.

BRUDNER, HARVEY J. Light On: Microcomputers, special education, and CMI. *Educational Technology*, 1982, 22(7), 25–26.

CARTWRIGHT, P., AND DEREVENSKY, J. An attitudinal study of computer assisted testing as a learning method. *Psychology in the Schools*, 1976, 13(3), 317–321.

CLEARY, A., MAYES, T., AND PACKHAM, D. *Educational technology: Implications for early and special education.* London: John Wiley, 1976.

COMDEN, TIPPI. The many uses of Apple computers at the Western Pennsylvania School for the Deaf. *American Annals of the Deaf*, 1981, 126, 591–599.

DUGDALE, SHARON, AND VOGEL, PATTY. Computer-based instruction for hearing impaired children in the classroom. *American Annals of the Deaf*, 1978, 123, 730–743.

FRICKE, JAMES. *CAI in a school for the deaf: Expeded results and a serendipity or two.* Scranton, Pa.: Scranton State School for the Deaf, 1976.

GEOFFRION, LEO D., AND GOLDENBERG, E. PAUL. Computer-based exploratory learning systems for communication-handicapped children. *Journal of Special Education*, 1981, 15(3), 325–331.

GOLDENBERG, E. PAUL. *Special technology for special children.* Baltimore, Md.: University Park Press, 1979.

GRIMES, LYNN. Computers are for kids: Designing software programs to avoid problems of learning. *Teaching Exceptional Children*, November 1981, pp. 49–53.

HARPER, DENNIS, AND STEWART, JAMES (eds.). *Run: Computer Education.* Monterey, Calif.: Brooks/Cole, 1983.

HASSELBRING, T. S., AND CROSSLAND, C. L. Using microcomputers for diagnosing spelling problems in learning-handicapped children. *Educational Technology*, April 1981, pp. 37–39.

HUGHES, KAREN. Adapting audio/video games for handicapped learners: Part 1. *Teaching Exceptional Children*, November 1981, pp. 80–86.

JOINER, L., VENSEL, G., ROSS, J., AND SILVERSTEIN, B. *Microcomputers in education: A nontechnical guide to instructional and school management applications.* Holmes Beach, Fla.: Learning Publications, 1982.

KLEIMAN, GLENN, HUMPHREY, MARY, AND LINDSAY, PETER. Microcomputers and hyperactive children. In D. Harper & J. Stewart (eds.). *Run: Computer Education.* Monterey, Calif.: Brooks/Cole, 1983.

LALLY, M. Computer-assisted teaching of sight-word recognition for mentally retarded school children. *American Journal of Mental Deficiency*, 1981, 85, 383–388.

MACLEOD, IAIN, AND OVERHEU, DON. Computer aided assessment and development of basic skills. *Exceptional Children*, 1977, 24, 18–35.

PAPERT, SEYMOUR A., AND WEIR, SYLVIA. Information prosthetics for the handicapped (LOGO Memo No. 51). Boston: Massachusetts Institute of Technology A. I. Laboratory, 1978.

SCHOFIELD, JULIA M. *Microcomputer-based aides for the disabled.* London, England: Heyden & Son, Ltd, 1981.

SEWELL, D. F., CLARK, R. A., PHILLIPS, R. J., AND ROSTRON, A. B. Lanugage and the deaf: An interacive microcomputer-based approach. *British Journal of Educational Technology*, 1980, 1(11), 57–68.

WATKINS, MARLEY W., AND WEBB, CYNTHIA. Computer assisted instruction with learning disabled students. *Educational Computer Magazine*, September/October 1981, 1(3), 24–26.

WEIR, SYLVIA. LOGO and exceptional children. *Microcomputing*, September 1981, pp. 76–82; 84.

WEIR, SYLVIA, AND WATT, DANIEL. LOGO: A computer environment for learning-disabled students. In D. Harper and J. Stewart (eds.), *Run: Computer Education.* Monterey, Calif.: Brooks/Cole, 1983.

WILLIAMS, JOSEPH, THORKILDSEN, RON, AND CROSSMAN, EDWARD K. Application of computers to the needs of handicapped persons. In D. Harper and J. Stewart (eds.), *Run: Computer Education.* Monterey, Calif.: Brooks/Cole, 1983.

WILSON, MARY S., AND FOX, BERNARD J. *User's manual for First Words.* Burlington, Vt.: Laureate Learning Systems, 1982.

14

Programming in BASIC

BASIC is an acronym for Beginners All-purpose Symbolic Instruction Code. This computer language was developed by Professors Kemeny and Kurtz in 1963 to help college students write programs. As the name implies, it was intended that BASIC should be easily learned and used. There are actually many versions of BASIC—it is therefore a family of interactive languages which are widely used, especially by people who are not computer specialists. Because BASIC consists of a small number of English-oriented words, it is called a "high-level" language (low-level languages are closer to machine code and are more difficult to read and understand).

In recent years there has been much criticism of BASIC as a language for children. The chief complaint has concerned the language's lack of structure. Critics contend that individual procedures or parts of programs cannot be read easily, and there is too much jumping around within the program. It is not a structured language—it does not start with the general and work toward the specific in a "top-down" planning style. It is not standardized, and it is not necessarily easy to teach.

Why, then, a chapter about BASIC? One of the most important reasons is that it is the most widely available language on microcomputers. Usually it is the only language that is "built into" the machine; that is, it is present in the computer's ROM and is thus immediately usable when the computer is turned on (although other languages can be "loaded into" most microcomputers). Many programs are written in BASIC. Therefore, teachers who wish to modify programs for their use, or who wish to use one of the many published programs, would find knowledge of BASIC useful. Also, Luehrmann (1982) has made the point that the important thing is not using any particular computer language but rather teaching children to think carefully and write clearly for the computer in whatever language is available. With correct use of BASIC, several (but not all) of structured programming's powerful ideas can be taught. However, BASIC may not be the ideal language for children's use. Furthermore, no one chapter can fully teach a programming language (several references which do teach this material are listed at the end of the chapter). Therefore, this chapter will be limited to introducing fundamental programming commands and their functions and illustrating the use of computer programming languages in the classroom. These illustrations pertain to the teaching of any computer language.

TEACHING BASIC TO CHILDREN

An Overview: Fundamental BASIC Statements

There are only a few fundamental statements in BASIC. On one hand, this appears to be an obvious advantage. But some have said that this makes it easy to learn but hard to use; or easy to write simple programs but almost impossible to write complex programs.

Nevertheless, the few BASIC statements that do exist are English-oriented. They consist of English words but have very specific meanings. Table 14-1 lists some important "pointers" to remember about programming. Table 14-2 describes and illustrates some fundamental BASIC statements. These are intended to serve as guides. Teachers might present such information directly to students. Or, through discussions and hands-on computer activities, teachers could elicit similar pointers and descriptions from their students. They might then engage students in the construction of instructional handbooks for computer programming. If a computer is available, typing in the brief programs will aid your understanding of the commands. However, just reading the programs slowly should help you develop an idea of the way the commands work.

Making Statements Meaningful

After you have read the descriptions and illustrations of the commands, take a moment to think how you might explain them to students. One way is to present analogies and personifications. PRINT is relatively easy to understand. It instructs the computer to act like a typewriter and print something on the screen. The quotation marks mean "Don't mess with this; just print it on the screen."

TABLE 14-1 Programming Pointers for You and Your Students

Computers do not speak English; they "speak" BASIC (as well as other computer languages). Typing NEW clears any old programs out of the computer's memory.

Each statement is preceded by a number; the computer then performs the directions in order. A program is a set of numbered instructions.

You must push RETURN at the end of every line.

Remember that the blinking rectangle (■) is called the cursor. It shows you where your next letter will be typed. It also usually means the computer is waiting for you to type in something.

Programs almost never work right the first time! You have to fix them. Is this unfortunate? Not really. By seeing the mistakes in our programs and fixing them, we learn to correct errors and misconceptions in our thinking. Also, it's a relief for some children to see that it's OK to make mistakes—even adult programmers make mistakes. This is a bit of an antidote for the overemphasis we often place on "the right answer the first time." To fix mistakes, we use editing.

Editing
1. Fix mistakes by pushing the back arrow (←) key and typing over the mistake.
2. If you pushed RETURN, you cannot do this. Not to worry! Just retype the whole line, including the line number.
3. To erase a whole line, just type in the line number and then push RETURN. (Note that some computers have special editing features, including DELETE and INSERT keys and other methods. It is best to read the manuals that come with the computer for this specific kind of information.)
4. Similarly, insert lines by using an appropriate line number. In other words, if you want to add a line at the end, type in a line number that is higher than the last one you used. If you want to insert a line in between lines 20 and 30, merely use the line number 25 (that's why BASIC programs usually are numbered by tens or fives—so that other lines can be inserted if needed).
5. Different makes of microcomputers have different statements for letting you draw (graphics) or write (text) on the screen. It is best to check the computer manual.

RUN instructs the computer to execute the program.

Problems to Avoid . . . For You and Your Students.

Working the machine. Make sure students know how to start the computer, "boot up the disk" if that's necessary, turn the computer off, and so on. Direct, whole-class instruction, peer "experts," and signs posted near the computer will help avoid this problem with your students.

On a computer you must be very exacting. For example, zero (0) and the letter O are different. So are one (1) and lower case *l*. Even one little comma left out will stop the program and give you a message about a syntax error. Sometimes beginning programmers can become frustrated by the "nit-picky" computer. It may help to discuss work and professions that demand precision (art, sports, medicine, banking), pointing out that sloppiness is really not desirable in many areas.

Translating English to BASIC. This takes a lot of discussion, dramatization, and, mostly, direct experience. Use all these approaches to help students see how problems and solutions originally stated in English can be expressed in BASIC so that they can be "understood" by the computer. Experiencing several short problems being discussed, translated, and RUN will help greatly.

Different versions of BASIC. Remember that almost every microcomputer has some BASIC statements that differ from those of other computers. You (and your students, if they are able) must check the manuals that come with the computer or one specifically written for it to learn its unique statements.

TABLE 14-2 Fundamental Basic Statements

PRINT	Displays information.

NEW
10 PRINT "HEY, THIS ISN'T SO BAD!"
RUN
HEY, THIS ISN'T SO BAD!
PRINT 36 + 4
40 |
| *LET* | Assigns a value (a number or a "string" of alphabet, numerical, and punctuation characters) to a variable. (Values that are numbers are represented by letters or a letter and a number like Y3; values that include alphabet characters are called "strings"; their variable names are followed by a dollar sign, like B$.)

10 LET X = 25
20 LET A$ = "MY FAVORITE NUMBER IS"
30 PRINT A$; 2 × X
RUN
MY FAVORITE NUMBER IS 50

Note the difference between printing "X" (or anything inside quotations marks):

PRINT "X"
X

and printing "the thing that is named X" (i.e., the value of X):
PRINT X
25 |
| *REM* | REMark—used to explain parts of a program to people reading it. The computer does not do anything. |
| *INPUT* | Instructs computer to print a "?" and wait for the user to type in something.

10 REM Division by 4.
20 PRINT "TYPE ANY NUMBER TO HAVE IT DIVIDED BY 4."
30 INPUT N
40 PRINT N/4
RUN
TYPE ANY NUMBER TO HAVE IT DIVIDED BY 4.
?12
3 |
| *GOTO 90* | Instructs the computer to jump to line 90 (or any that is specified). This statement can create infinite loops in which the computer repeats something again and again (until you push "CTRL-C" or RESET). This is usually considered poor programming practice, but in its place it can be fun. For example, children can print their names again and again. Or try this simple approach to rocket ship animation: |

TABLE 14-2 Fundamental Basic Statements *(cont.)*

```
10 PRINT "   A    "
20 PRINT "   AAA   "
30 PRINT "  AAAAA  "
40 PRINT "AAAAAAA"
50 GOTO 40
```

Because line 50 always returns the program to line 40, an endless series of "AAAAAAA" is printed. This causes the program to "scroll" or move up the screen, and the "rocket" appears to blast off. Note that to be effective, some computers must be slowed down (the technique for this differs; please see the programming manuals).

END Ends program.

IF . . . THEN Instructs the computer to make a decision. If the first statement is true, the second statement is carried out.

```
10 REM A PROGRAM TO AVERAGE GRADES.
20 PRINT "TYPE IN FOUR GRADES SEPARATED BY COMMAS
   ONLY."
30 INPUT G1, G2, G3, G4
40 LET A = (G1 + G2 + G3 + G4)/4
50 PRINT "THE AVERAGE IS "; A
60 IF A < 75 THEN GOTO 90
70 PRINT "THIS IS PASSING."
80 GOTO 100
90 PRINT "THIS IS NOT PASSING."
100 END
RUN
TYPE IN FOUR GRADES SEPARATED BY COMMAS ONLY.
?80, 90, 100, 70
THE AVERAGE IS 85
THIS IS PASSING.
RUN
TYPE IN FOUR GRADES SEPARATED BY COMMAS ONLY.
?72, 76, 78, 72
THE AVERAGE IS 72.
THIS IS NOT PASSING.
```

FOR-NEXT Sets a "counter" and "loops," or repeats a part of the program a set number of times.

```
10 REM CREATES A MULTIPLICATION TABLE.
20 PRINT "MULTIPLICATION TABLE. FOR WHAT NUMBER?
   (PLEASE TYPE A NUMBER IN.)"
30 INPUT N
40 FOR M = 1 TO 10
50 PRINT M; "TIMES" N " = "; N × M
60 NEXT M
70 END
RUN
```

TABLE 14-2 Fundamental Basic Statements *(cont.)*

MULTIPLICATION TABLE. FOR WHAT NUMBER? (PLEASE TYPE
  A NUMBER IN.)
?8
1 TIMES 8 = 8
2 TIMES 8 = 16
3 TIMES 8 = 24
4 TIMES 8 = 32
5 TIMES 8 = 40

READ, DATA   DATA specifies information within the program, which is read by the READ
                statement.

GOSUB 1000, RETURN
                Instructs the computer to jump to line 1000 and then return to the starting
                place at the statement RETURN.
                10 REM A DEMONSTRATION OF GOSUB STATEMENTS AND
                    GRAMMATICAL DECISIONS
                20 PRINT "WHAT PET WOULD YOU LIKE TO OWN?"
                30 INPUT R$
                40 GOSUB 1000
                50 PRINT " WHAT WOULD YOU LIKE TO RIDE ON?"
                60 INPUT R$
                70 GOSUB 1000
                80 PRINT "WHAT IS YOUR FAVORITE TOY?"
                90 INPUT R$
                100 GOSUB 1000
                110 END
                1000 LET F$ = LEFT$(R$,1)
                1010 LET A$ = "A"
                1020 IF F$ = "A" or F$ = "E" OR
                    F$ = "1" OR F$ = "O" OR
                    F$ = "U" THEN A$ = "AN"
                1030 PRINT "YOU WOULD REALLY
                    LIKE"; A$; " "; R$
                1040 RETURN
                RUN
                WHAT PET WOULD YOU LIKE TO OWN?
                DOG
                YOU WOULD REALLY LIKE A DOG
                WHAT WOULD YOU LIKE TO RIDE ON?
                AIRPLANE
                YOU WOULD REALLY LIKE AN AIRPLANE
                WHAT IS YOUR FAVORITE TOY?
                COMPUTER
                YOU WOULD REALLY LIKE A COMPUTER

Other manipulations can be done on string variables (groups of letters, numbers, punctua-
tion marks, etc., that are grouped together and specified with a name like A$; e.g., A$ = "AN
APPLE"). PRINT LEN(A$) will fill the LENgth (number of characters in the string A$ (i.e., 8).
Strings can be "added" (referred to as concatenation). For example

TABLE 14-2 Fundamental Basic Statements *(cont.)*

```
10 LET A$ = "AN APPLE"
20 LET B$ = "IS RED"
30 PRINT A$ + B$
RUN
AN APPLE IS RED
```

Certain parts of strings can be selected; e.g., the right-most four characters. Notice the way the first letter of the word was selected in line 1000 of the program above. See your manual for details.

More efficient ways to store information (e.g., a lot of related variables) exist. ARRAYS are arrangements of information in a pattern which will help store and recall it easily. For example, the addition/subtraction table is an array. Again, if you are interested in pursuing programming further, please consult programming manuals for instruction on these type of processes.

BASIC SYSTEM COMMANDS
(instructing a computer what to do with the program):

NEW   Instructs the computer to clear its memory.

RUN   Instructs the computer to execute the program in its memory.

SAVE   Instructs the computer to record the program in its memory on the memory device such as a disk or tape.

LOAD   Instructs computer to retrieve a program from a disk or tape and place it in its memory.

LIST   Instructs computer to display all the numbered statement lines in the program.

Remember, the simplest way to edit a BASIC program is merely to retype the line, including its number, with the corrections. The computer will replace the old line with the new one.

We use the idea of a LET statement every day. "Who's the leader in line today?" "Jackie." (LET LEADER = "JACKIE"; another day, LET LEADER = "GERRY".) "Leader" is the *variable name*—the people who are the leaders vary day by day. Do you remember how we compared the computer's memory to a row of mailboxes? LET X = 25 tells the computer, "Find the mailbox with 'X' on it (if there is none, label one). If there is a number in it, throw it out. Put the number 25 in the mailbox." Later, PRINT X would instruct the computer to print whatever is in mailbox X—25, in this case.

INPUT allows the computer to ask the user for information. In a program, INPUT N instructs the computer to (a) print a "?" on the screen; (b) wait for a number to be typed on the screen, followed by the pressing of the RETURN key; and (c) put that number in the "mailbox" (memory location) named "N."

GOTO and the IF/THEN can be thought of as traffic police. GOTO 100 instructs the computer to "drive" immediately to line 100 and do what it says ("Do not pass GO, do not collect . . ."). IF A < 75 THEN GOTO 90 is a bit more involved. IF A is less than 75, then the program goes immediately to line 90; otherwise, it does not, and the program continues uninterrupted. Our police officer is now doing some checking: IF the man broke the law, THEN he must GOTO jail; otherwise, he does not. (Or as one sixth grader said, "I know that one. If you cleaned up your room, then you can go out. If not, keep working!") Create any analogies, personifications, and the like you believe will help the children in your classes. In this way, age-appropriate models and lists of rules or procedures for each command can be provided for students.

Graphics: A Good Place to Start

Perhaps the best way to introduce programming to children is to have them write graphics programs, creating pictures on the screen. However, the statements that generate graphics have not been included in the outline above. This is simply because different microcomputers use different statements. Therefore, rather than confusing readers, it is wiser to recommend reading the manuals that come with each particular type of computer. Some may instruct the user to type PLOT 20, 20 to light up a certain small rectangular region; others may use the statement SET 20, 20, 2 to light up that location in a certain color (the color corresponding to number 2). Still others may use the PRINT statement with special graphic characters (shapes, lines, and so on) or use a statement such as POKE 7910,162. This instructs the computer to place (POKE) a shape (number 162) into a memory location (number 7910) which corresponds to the location on the screen (about the center of the screen in this case). Regardless of the particular version of BASIC used, children enjoy and learn from copying, modifying, and finally writing and debugging graphics programs. As always with "hardware-specific" problems such as these, it is best for you to refer to the manuals that come with the computer, or books written specifically for your machine.

Students in a third-grade class wrote the programs which drew the pictures shown in Figure 14-1. They used only statements that place a rectangular region or a vertical or horizontal line on the screen. After their initial introduction to computer programming, they learned to color their intended design on a grid their teacher copied for them. They then translated this into a computer program which would reproduce the design on the screen. Finally they typed in and debugged their programs. Not only did this encourage thinking ahead, but it allowed computer access to more students, because only one part of the procedure had to be conducted on the computer. The teacher pointed out that the more time they spent planning and thinking beforehand, the less computer time they wasted.

FIGURE 14-1
Brian's picture of a house.

Active Learning: Dramatizing Computer Programs

There are many activities teachers can use to help students understand these BASIC statements. Here is how a fourth-grade teacher dramatized a FOR-NEXT loop.

"Bobby wrote an interesting program yesterday using a FOR-NEXT loop. Not all of us have used those statements before. Can you show it to us Bobby?"

Bobby LISTed his program:

```
10 REM  BOBBY'S ADDING PROGRAM
20 FOR N = 1 TO 10
30    PRINT N" + "N" = "N+N
40 NEXT N
50 END
```

Bobby said, "Now watch it run!"

```
RUN
 1 +  1 =  2
 2 +  2 =  4
 3 +  3 =  6
 4 +  4 =  8
 5 +  5 = 10
 6 +  6 = 12
 7 +  7 = 14
 8 +  8 = 16
 9 +  9 = 18
10 + 10 = 20
```

"Can it go higher?" Cheryl asked.

"As high as I want it to," answered Bobby. "Watch, I'll just change one line!"

Bobby typed in LIST and the screen showed:

```
10 REM  BOBBY'S ADDING PROGRAM
20 FOR N = 1 TO 10
30    PRINT N" + "N" = "N+N
40 NEXT N
50 END
```

He then typed:

```
20 FOR N = 1 TO 100
RUN
```

The class broke out in spontaneous squeals of delight and admiration as Bobby's program proceeded to add every number from 1 to 100 to itself.

"That's nothing," bragged the author, "I made it go to 1000 + 1000 already."

"Thanks for showing us, Bobby. Let's act out what our computer does when it's running Bobby's program, so that we'll understand it more clearly," suggested Mrs. Bruce. She asked several children to pull their oval rugs into the middle of the room. She placed the box on which the class had written *memory* for a previous computer dramatization near the edge of the rug. Several children drew a picture of the monitor on the chalkboard. Others, under Bobby's direction, wrote each statement (with the line number) on a separate strip of tagboard. An ordered deck of cards (1–10) was placed near the rug. The arrangement looked like Figure 14-2.

FIGURE 14-2 Dramatizing a computer program run.

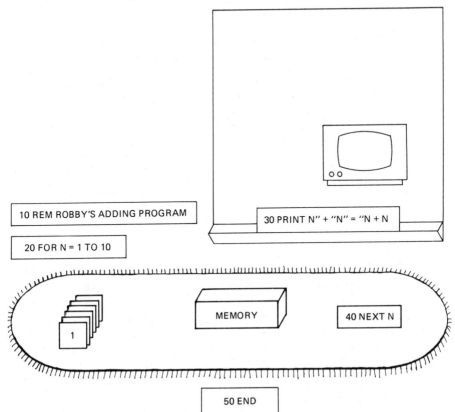

Children took turns taking the role of the computer. Ignoring line 10 ("That's just a remark") the students would go to line 20, pick up the next card from the pile, deposit it in the memory box, and print the correct number sentence on the board. Then, passing line 40, they would have to check if they had reached the last number. If not, they headed back to line 20. When card 10 had been processed, the loop was finished. They then went on to line 50, which told them to END. Everyone had a chance to participate, especially as the class experimented with changing several lines in Bobby's program. First they changed line 20 to read FOR N = 1 to 7. Then they changed line 30 to print x × x (multiplication or squaring a number), 2 × x, x + x + x, and so on. Each of these new programs were checked afterwards on the computer. In this way children also learned to use the computer to check on their intuitive and creative ideas. When the children decided to try x / x (division), some children were perturbed. "They're all the same!" protested Annie. "Of course," said Erik and Danny almost simultaneously, "Every number goes into itself just one time." (There used to be at least one mathematician in every class. For some reason, after the computer became a regularly used tool, there were more mathematicians than ever before.)

Active Learning: Other Simulations

Another classroom built their own "simulated computer"—a box with one student hidden inside, and input and output slots. Slips of paper with number lines of BASIC statements were placed in the input slot; for example:

```
10 PRINT "THIS IS JENNY"
20 PRINT "3 + 4"
30 PRINT 3 + 4
40 END
```

The child in the computer-box "output" on other slips of paper:

```
THIS IS JENNY
3 + 4
7
```

Mrs. McKillan taught older students and wished to present a more detailed and accurate picture of the workings of a computer. The first day she introduced the parts of the computer and their functions. The next day she set up her room as in Figure 14-3. Let's visit this classroom in progress:

"You all have a copy of the program we'll act out. What needs to happen first?"

"The user at the keyboard has to type in the first line."

"Right. Go ahead."

The student at the "keyboard" wrote out the first line of the pro-

```
10   REM THIS WILL AVERAGE FOUR NUMBERS
20   INPUT "GIVE ME A NUMBER"; N1
30   INPUT "GIVE ME A SECOND NUMBER"; N2
40   INPUT "GIVE ME A THIRD NUMBER"; N3
50   INPUT "GIVE ME A FOURTH NUMBER"; N4
60   LET A = (N1 + N2 + N3 + N4)/4
70   PRINT "THE AVERAGE IS"; A
80   END
```

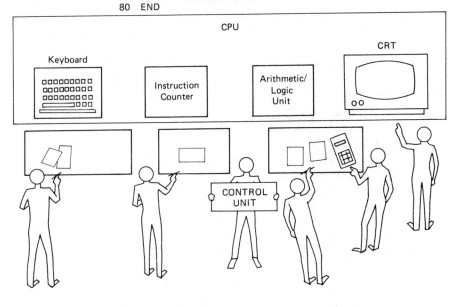

PROGRAM MEMORY BOXES   USER MEMORY BOXES

FIGURE 14-3   Another dramatization.

gram. The "control unit" student then took it, showed it to the CRT to display, and then walked over to the program memory boxes and gave it to the student who was holding the first box. These actions were repeated until each line was entered. (If any were entered out of order, the control unit had to put them in order by line number.)

"Now are we done?" Mrs. McKillan asked.

"We didn't do anything yet!" protested a student.

"The user has to type RUN," said another.

The student at the keyboard promptly typed RUN. The control unit student started to head toward the programming memory boxes.

"Wait," said the teacher, "you don't know which line to execute."

"The first one."

"You don't know which that is yet. Who does he need to ask?"

"Oh yeah, the instruction counter," someone volunteered.

The instruction counter student told the control unit to execute line 10, and then wrote 10 on a card. The control unit asked the student with program memory box 10 to read her line.

"10 REM THIS WILL AVERAGE FOUR NUMBERS"

"What should the control unit do?" inquired Mrs. McKillan.

"Nothing. That's just a remark."

The control unit returned to the instruction counter and asked for the next number. The instruction counter said "20 is next" and wrote that number down. After having that line read by the student with program memory box 20, the control unit told the CRT to write GIVE ME A NUMBER and then waited.

"Hey, wake up, user," said an impatient student. "You have to type in a number." Chastised, the user wrote 24 on a card. The control unit gave the card to the CRT to write on the chalkboard and walked over to the students holding the user memory boxes. He wrote N1 on the first one and put the card with 24 written on it in the box.

This process was repeated with the next three numbers. The set-up was now as pictured in Figure 14-4. When line 60 was reached, the control unit got the instruction from program box 60, looked at the number in user memory box N1, wrote this down on a card, and gave it to the arithmetic/logic unit. He then read the number in box N2, wrote this on a card, and gave it to the arithmetic/logic unit, saying "Add this to what you have already." The arithmetic/logic unit told the register (who was equipped with a calculator) to add the numbers. This was repeated for N3 and N4. Finally, he instructed the arithmetic/logic unit to divide the sum by 4 and give him the answer. The arithmetic/logic unit again told the register to do the calculations, then gave the answer to the control unit. The control unit then wrote this on a card and placed it in the next user memory box, which he labeled A.

After again checking with the instruction counter and reading the next instruction, PRINT "THE AVERAGE IS";A, the control unit copied

```
10  REM THIS WILL AVERAGE FOUR NUMBERS
20  INPUT "GIVE ME A NUMBER"; N1
30  INPUT "GIVE ME A SECOND NUMBER"; N2
40  INPUT "GIVE ME A THIRD NUMBER"; N3
50  INPUT "GIVE ME A FOURTH NUMBER"; N4
60  LET A = (N1 + N2 + N3 + N4)/4
70  PRINT "THE AVERAGE IS"; A
80  END
```

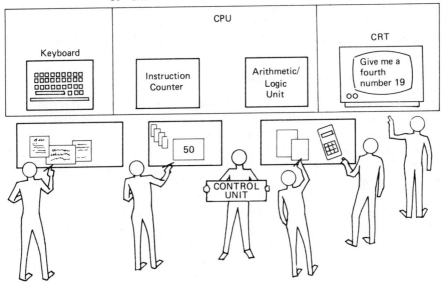

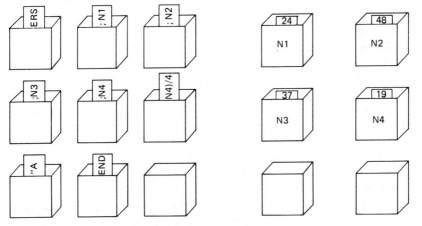

PROGRAM MEMORY BOXES

USER MEMORY BOXES

FIGURE 14-4

the value of A on a card and gave it to the CRT, saying "Print 'The Average Is' and then this number." CRT wrote "THE AVERAGE IS 32." The last line was read and executed—the instructional counter was reset to zero, and the program ended.

Other techniques teachers have used include having students determine output from input; having them change programs by altering them or adding new BASIC statements; having them find and fix bugs (Figure 14-5 illustrates these type of problem); and, most important, having them solve problems and work on projects.

Programming and Problem Solving

These, then, are many of the fundamental statements of the BASIC computer language, along with simple programming problems. "But," you may say, "I thought using the computer was supposed to get kids to solve difficult problems and help them to think logically and learn subject matter." Let's look at an actual example of how several fifth-grade children did just that. In math class their teacher had challenged them with an exploratory problem:

"Now that you're all teamed up in pairs, here's a problem for you to solve. Each of you write the numerals from 1 to 10 on the cards I gave you. Then combine your cards and find out how many ways you can make each number from 1 to 10 by adding any pairs of numbers. Let's try to do the first few numbers together."

The class found that no combinations equaled 1; they also found that only $1 + 1 = 2$. They then decided that they would consider $1 + 2$ and $2 + 1$ to be distinct combinations. Their teacher reminded them to look for patterns, both because they are interesting and because they can help solve problems. Two boys who had been excited by the computer programming unit the class had been working on for several months asked if they could try to solve the problem on the microcomputer. Their teacher (not trying to repress her enthusiasm for the idea) agreed.

First they discussed how they would go about doing it without the computer. They decided that they would try to add up every card (number) with every other, writing only those pairs that equaled 1, then 2, then 3, and so on. Talking about it, they discovered that they never even had to try cards larger than the total they were trying to make. They first wrote a basic (no pun intended) outline in English, which helped them write the BASIC program. As you might guess, there were a few bugs in their first attempts. For example, they originally forgot to reset the variable name which represented the first card to 1. But feedback from the computer ("Hey, this doesn't have $1 + 2 = 3$! Something's wrong!") helped them debug their own thinking, and then their program.

That would have been accomplishment enough; but excited by their success, they took the problem a bit farther on their own.

"You know, I was thinking about it, and we don't need to try out

Figure 14-5

BASIC PROGRAMS: TROUBLE SHOOTING

1. Find the bug in the following programs.

```
10 REM A PROGRAM THAT SHOWS HOW TO COUNT BY TWO'S
20 LET C = 0
30 LET C = C + 2
40 GOTO 30
50 END
```

```
10 REM A PROGRAM THAT COUNTS TO 10
20 FOR N = 1 TO 10
30 PRINT N
40 END
```

```
10 PRINT "WHAT IS YOUR NAME?"
20 INPUT N
30 PRINT "HI, "N
40 END
```

```
10 REM A PROGRAM TO ADD TWO NUMBERS
20 PRINT "GIVE ME TWO NUMBERS"
30 INPUT A,B
40 PRINT "A + B = A+B"
50 END
```

2. Will the following program fulfill its purpose?

```
10 REM A PROGRAM TO COUNT FROM 1 TO 100
20 LET C = 1
30 IF C < 100 THEN END
40 LET C = C + 1
50 GOTO 30
60 PRINT C
```

3. Is the following a valid statement in BASIC?

```
10 LET N = "Cherie Meriman"
```

4. Are the outputs of the following programs accurate?

```
10 LET A = 7
20 LET B = 5
30 LET C = A - B
40 PRINT A + C - B
RUN
 4
```

```
10 LET A$ = "DOM"
20 LET B$ = "GALLO"
30 PRINT A$+" Q. "+B$
RUN
DOM Q. GALLO
```

```
10 LET A = 30
20 LET B = 10
30 GOTO 50
40 PRINT A + B
50 PRINT "FINISHED"
60 END
RUN
 40
 FINISHED
```

201

every pair. When I was checking our first program, I didn't add up 1 + 1 to see if it was 5."

"Yeah? So what?"

"Well, what I really did was to take one number at a time, starting at 1, and subtract it from the total number."

Using this line of reasoning, they wrote a program that would do just that: After learning more about BASIC, a group consisting of the same two children and some of their friends returned to the problem, spurred on by a new challenge from their teacher.

"Why don't you try to see how many ways you can add up two or three numbers from one deck of cards to make each number?"

Expanding on their subtraction strategy, the group came up with a new program (part of the printout is shown in Figure 14-6). They were excited that their program ran; and their teacher was wise enough to entice them to further discoveries.

"Look at the total number of ways you found to make each number. That's an unusual pattern: 0, 0, 2, 2, 4, 10, 12, 18, 26, 56. . . ." What do you think the "rule" is that would make that pattern?"

After a lot of experimentation and discussion, Sonya and Michelle exclaimed, "Ah, look! If you make a table showing how many ways we made each number by adding two numbers and by adding three numbers together you get a pattern." (See Figure 14-7.) "See, in the two-number column there is a pattern—the same, then two more; the same, then two more; . . . like that. The three-number column is funnier . . . it's a lot of zeros, then six more; then the same, then six more; then six *more*."

"That's quite interesting," said their teacher. "Why do you think that happens? What do you think the pattern is for numbers higher than nine?" With that, the whole group was off on another mind-stretching exploration—which, incidentally, took them far into their recess period. These children were fortunate. Without the power of the computer to stimulate their thinking (and their "thinking about their own thinking") and to perform lengthy computations quickly, *and* without the guidance of a teacher wise enough to step in, help, and challenge just enough (but not too much), they probably would never have discovered these number patterns. And they would not have felt quite so good about their thinking, mathematics, computing, and schoolwork.

More BASIC for You.

You can learn a lot about BASIC programming from one of the excellent books that are available. Find one that makes you work a little, figuring out how to solve problems for yourself. It is also beneficial to find written sources of good programs. Studying them and typing them in can teach you a lot about good programming practices. And as an additional reward, you end up with a usable program! For example, you might enter some instructional programs and games that have been pub-

```
]RUN
HOW MANY WAYS CAN A PAIR OF
CARDS FROM TWO DECKS MAKE 1?

HOW MANY WAYS CAN A PAIR OF
CARDS FROM TWO DECKS MAKE 2?
1 + 1 = 2

HOW MANY WAYS CAN A PAIR OF
CARDS FROM TWO DECKS MAKE 3?
1 + 2 = 3
2 + 1 = 3

HOW MANY WAYS CAN A PAIR OF
CARDS FROM TWO DECKS MAKE 4?
1 + 3 = 4
2 + 2 = 4
3 + 1 = 4

HOW MANY WAYS CAN A PAIR OF
CARDS FROM TWO DECKS MAKE 5?
1 + 4 = 5
2 + 3 = 5
3 + 2 = 5
4 + 1 = 5

HOW MANY WAYS CAN A PAIR OF
CARDS FROM TWO DECKS MAKE 6?
1 + 5 = 6
2 + 4 = 6
3 + 3 = 6
4 + 2 = 6
5 + 1 = 6

HOW MANY WAYS CAN A PAIR OF
CARDS FROM TWO DECKS MAKE 7?
1 + 6 = 7
2 + 5 = 7
3 + 4 = 7
4 + 3 = 7
5 + 2 = 7
6 + 1 = 7

HOW MANY WAYS CAN A PAIR OF
CARDS FROM TWO DECKS MAKE 8?
1 + 7 = 8
2 + 6 = 8
3 + 5 = 8
4 + 4 = 8
5 + 3 = 8
6 + 2 = 8
7 + 1 = 8
```

FIGURE 14-6
A partial run of two fifth-grade
children's program.

```
]
```

Sum (N)	Total Number of Combinations	Combinations with a Specific Number of Addends		
		Two	Three	Four
1	0			
2	0			
3	2	2		
4	2	2		
5	4	4		
6	10	4	6	
7	12	6	6	
8	18	6	12	
9	26	8	18	
10	56	8	24	24
11	64	10	30	24
12	100	10	42	48
13	132	12	48	72
14	192	12	60	120

FIGURE 14-7   A table of addition combinations created from the children's program.

lished that you would like to use with your students; or you might type in a grade book program like those mentioned in Chapter 7 for yourself.

More BASIC for Your Students

Children, especially those in the intermediate grades and above, also benefit from reading and typing others' programs. They can type in simulations, tutorials, educational games, and (if you're persuasive) some class management programs (for example, an attendance program) for you.

There are several books available that are written for children which teach programming in BASIC; several are cited at the end of the chapter. They range widely in quality, but generally the offerings are improving. Be sure to have enough copies so that students can refer to them even if they are not sitting in front of the computer. Don't feel you have to know everything about programming to work with your children on it. Read one of these children's books (and maybe the BASIC programming tutorial that came with the computer), run through the activities, and try them out with your pupils. It's fun and beneficial to discover some things alongside the children. They see that you too want to learn new things, and that you enjoy learning. They see a *reason* for reading (books) and for reading carefully. Their self-concept is given a boost if they can help teach you something. They benefit—on both sides—from peer teaching. (Remember, too, that sometimes, the more you protest that you don't know something at all—"Really, I *DON'T* know how to do that!"—the more they secretly think you *do* know but want them to find it out for themselves!) If you have the resources, you may be interested in one of the courseware offerings (for example, CAI) that teach children to program in BASIC.

As a teacher, you are an expert in children's learning. Many of the lessons you have learned from other areas also apply to the learning of programming. The following reminders may help you plan for positive experiences.

1. Even if you plan to learn alongside your students, avoid frustration by being familiar with operating your computer at the most basic level—turning it on, loading a disk and/or program, and so on. You might want to display these directions next to the computer for your students.

2. A growing list of BASIC statements that have been learned might also be posted. Other lists might include the computer's rules for performing each statement, such as described earlier. As another illustration, the computer's rules for GOSUB 2000 and RETURN would be:

   a. When GOSUB is encountered, remember the line number of the statement after the GOSUB statement.

   b. Go to line 2000 and do what it says there.

   c. RETURN to the line number remembered in "a."

3. You may want to place the computer so that (a) the monitor can be seen only by those using the computer, so as not to distract others; (b) it can be used all day (again, it must not distract others; this is also a scheduling problem—but why waste the computer by having it sit idle?); and (c) it is away from potentially harmful substances, such as chalkdust, water, sand, and the like.

4. As with any skill or ability, children need to *use* and practice programming to achieve competence. If possible, provide at least two or three sessions of about one hour (one half-hour minimum) every week for elementary grade students. This is best done throughout the year, but if it must be done as a unit, try to provide at least nine weeks of hands-on experience.

5. Students can be encouraged to "double up" on the computer. This extends students' time with the computer. It also encourages social interaction, as children will learn from each other and catch and correct each other's typing mistakes. Usually, the presence of more than two at a time makes sharing difficult; three at a time is about the maximum.

6. Remember, too, that some children will need additional challenge, while some will need an extra bit of empathy and encouragement—and maybe a slower pace. All students should understand that the great speed of computers does *not* mean that programming is a quick endeavor—it takes time. We certainly do not want to place pressure on students, producing a whole new phenomenon—learning-disabled programmers.

7. Don't let below-average reading ability interfere with a child's success. Sometimes the most successful programmers are children who are not particularly high-ranking in math or reading. If working with a book on programming, pair a below-average reader with a proficient reader. If given a good reason for reading, and material that is difficult but not impossible, even poor readers will extend their limits and increase their abilities.

8. Children learn best when they do things for themselves. Encourage them to write their own programs and to solve their own "problems." Encourage the use of graphics at first. Conduct art and design "shows"; invite parents.

9. Students can contribute to their class through individual projects. For instance, a group of students might construct a chart of BASIC statements and commands along with their meanings. They might want to sign the list as "experts" to whom others can come for assistance.

10. Keep a list of "qualified tutors." Students who want help sign up for a tutorial. Such lists can be very popular. They can help with organization, and everyone involved may benefit. Those who are tutored learn what they want to know from those who understand intuitively what is "bugging" them and their attempts at programming. The tutors (who may not be especially high-ranking in math or reading) gain feelings of self-confidence and competence. They also learn a lot themselves. Teachers gain time to work with other children and groups of children; they can enjoy teaching a class of children who are that much more eager to come to school; and (they will freely admit) they learn a lot about programming eavesdropping on some of the tutorials.

11. *Always* utilize active, understandable models, such as those described in this chapter. Research indicates that they are a powerful aid to learning (Mayer, 1979, 1981).

    a. Develop an understanding of the series of steps each single command involves (such as described in 2, above, or in the section on fundamental BASIC statements; that is, LET X = 25 tells the computer, "Find the mailbox with 'X' on it. If there is a number in it, throw it out. Put the number 25 in the mailbox.")

    b. Use dramatizations and discussions which translate computer programs into English language equivalents.

    c. Do not neglect the "big picture." Use "chunking" in discussing programs and sections of programs as wholes. For example, "This program will ask you a riddle, wait for your answer, check if your answer is the same as its answer, then tell you if you're right or wrong." Or "This section of the program checks to see if an *a* or *an* should go before the user's response."

    d. At a more advanced level, students can begin to understand that some combination of three basic "chunks"—actions (straight-ahead list of instructions), loops (performing the same block of instructions repeatedly), and branching (a computer decision that involves an either-or situation)—can solve *every* programming problem (see Luehrmann and Peckham, 1983, for a complete discussion).

THE ISSUE OF STRUCTURED PROGRAMMING

Cathy Farnham liked BASIC. Joe Fraser, the other ninth-grade math teacher, thought it was outdated but used it because more modern languages were not available on their school's microcomputers. Joe always grumbled that BASIC encouraged his students to be sloppy programmers. Cathy said she encouraged her students to "mess around" a bit with programming. "Try it out," she would say. "You won't know what happens if you don't." She admitted that some of the students' programs were not elegant; however, she argued first that these were just beginning students who needed some time to explore this new activity, and second that the discoveries they made while exploring were more valuable than preconceived ideas about "good programming" that she could have lectured about.

Joe had other ideas. "Sloppy programming is sloppy thinking," he told his students. "Plan first, on paper. Later, enter your well-planned program into the computer. It will work more often and more efficiently, and other people will be able to understand it and modify it if they want."

Students in the classes of both these teachers learned a considerable amount about mathematics and programming. (It is interesting to note that Joe and Cathy worked together to have their school buy the LOGO programming language. Joe is using it to help his students use the structured techniques of modern programming languages such as Pascal. Cathy is, as you might guess, allowing her students to explore their own ideas—however, due to the structure inherent in the language, they are simultaneously learning modular programming. Both are pleased.) While using BASIC may make full, structured programming more difficult, anyone, using any language, may have difficulty solving problems effectively. While it is beyond the scope of this book to fully elaborate on these ideas, the following suggestions may serve as a helpful guide to the kinds of procedures that could be developed with students. Interested readers can find many sources which will help develop their understanding of these ideas.

1. Begin with paper in front of you rather than a computer.
2. Make a clear statement of the problem. Make sure you know what it is you are trying to do.
3. Write down the objective of the program. It may help to work out a simple example yourself. Ask: Is the computer the right place for the problem to be solved or the activity conducted?
4. Decide on an approach to solving the problem. Construct a plan. This may take the form of a flow-chart, outline, or some other form of organization. For many programs, such as CAI programs, it is very helpful to create a storyboard as they do in television or movie production. This forces the designer to ask, What exactly will the user see? It is a set of five- by eight-inch cards, each of which illustrates a "frame" of the program. Each contains an illustration of the screen (most effectively written on squared paper labeled to match the grid of the particular computer screen) as it would appear to the user of the program. The cards are tacked to a bulletin board so that they can easily be moved around, altered, or replaced.
5. Using the plan, list of objectives, and storyboard, write down the program in English. Begin with the major steps. Then, through a process of "stepwise refinement," break each of these steps into their component parts (and these parts into smaller parts as necessary), until no more refinement is necessary (that is, when each part is easily translated directly into a statement in computer language). This is called top-down programming (or planning, or problem solving), and it is one of the powerful and useful ideas that have come from the fields of computer technology and artificial intelligence. First the problem is comprehended at the general level of major steps. Then these tasks are broken down into smaller parts which are more intellectually manageable ("mind-sized bites").

6. Decide on a list of variables needed. List their names, content (and type—numerical, integer, string—if necessary), and purpose.

7. "Walk" through this program following each command, just as the computer would. Return and take every branch, if possible.

8. For the first time, translate the plan into computer language. If this is overly difficult or unclear, go back and revise your plan. Construct your program in *modules* with plenty of remarks. These modules should usually include the following:

   a. Remarks that identify the name of the program, its purpose, and the programmer.

   b. A list of the variables as in 6, above (also in remark statements).

   c. The main program. This contains a stepwise refinement showing the major steps which are followed by GOSUB statements that cause the main program to branch to the module where that task will actually be performed.

   d. The modules or procedures that constitute the parts of the program that perform each of these tasks. Each should also be labeled with their name and purpose. There should be a minimum of GOTO statements. Each procedure should be self-contained and fairly short, having only one entrance (its beginning, which is called by the GOSUB statement of the main program) and one exit (the RETURN statement that sends control back to the main program).

   e. User-friendly constructions: Good instructions, prompts, clear writing on the screen, "error traps," opportunities for the user to check his or her input, and understandable structure.

9. Enter the program into the computer. With this kind of preparation, debugging should be minimal.

10. Detailed documentation (printed information) should be provided with the program.

Because factors such as computer availability, level of students' knowledge, and basic curricula vary widely, it is not possible (nor wise) to dictate a single scope and sequence by grade level for every school. However, Table 14-3 presents guidelines that two schools used, which you may adapt for your own purposes. The suggested grade levels at the left are for schools using BASIC only in the upper grades. Some schools use LOGO or PILOT in the lower grades, others do not engage children in programming activities before grade 4. This column could serve as a guideline for these schools. Schools which only have BASIC available and plan to do programming starting at grade 1 could use the suggested grade levels at the right. Looking at this column, it appears that all the primary grades use the same commands. This is true; the difference among these grades is the way in which these commands are used. Students in grade 1 may not memorize nor fully understand the commands, but they can create short (one- to three-line) programs. Students in grade 2 may create four- to six-line programs, and those in grade 3 may start experimenting with their own programming ideas. More complicated programming logic and structure are employed in the later grades.

TABLE 14-3 Scope and Sequences for Teaching BASIC

	BASIC IN Upper Grades (LOGO IN PRIMARY)	ONLY BASIC
PRINT	4–9	1–9
RUN	4–9	1–9
LET	4–9	1–9
GOTO	4–9	1–9
INPUT	4–9	2–9
Strings	4–9	4–9
IF-THEN	5–9	4–9
READ-DATA	5–9	5–9
REM	5–9	5–9
FOR-NEXT	6–9	5–9
Problem solving	6–9	5–9
GOSUB	6–9	5–9
Graphics	6–9	6–9
Sound and color	7–9	6–9
Random numbers	7–9	7–9
Arrays	7–9	7–9
Functions	7–9	7–9
Arrays (two-dimensional)	8–9	8–9
Simulation programming, matrices, files	9	9

As teachers begin to become involved with programming and start teaching it to their students, they often need ideas for problems which are appropriately solved with computers. Table 14-4 presents some programming challenges for you and your students. The educational emphasis for teaching any programming language should be on (in increasing order of importance): understanding the capabilities of the computer, developing the ability to make the computer do what you want it to do, gaining wider knowledge about subject matter, and developing problem-solving abilities.

Self-Test

1. A variable in BASIC keeps the same value for the duration of the program.
2. Say a microcomputer can execute about a thousand BASIC statements every second. If a program contains ten statements, is it possible to estimate how long it will take the program to run?
3. While dramatizing the workings of computers is motivating, it is not necessary for understanding how to program computers.

TABLE 14-4 For Teachers and Their Students: Write A Program Which . . .

will create an addition table for any number
will ask for and add any three numbers
asks for the user's name and then greets the user by name
will average any seven (or whatever you wish—computers are for *YOUR* use!) scores
provides drill and practice on some arithmetic problems
draws a picture of your choosing
draws the picture at any location, after asking the location in terms of coordinates
asks the user which of two pictures he or she would like to see; draws the corresponding picture
draws a simple moving picture (animation), such as a box, by erasing the end of it and adding a
  new section to the front.
asks for the user's name and prints it a hundred times
provides simple drill and practice on a skill you believe students need more practice with
asks for three "strings" (words, phrases, or sentences) and then prints each of them
lists all the odd numbers from one to one hundred and the number's square
calculates the sales tax for any amount input by the user
asks the user for the name of the team and the number of touchdowns, extra points, safeties, and
  field goals for each team in a football game; computes and prints the two scores and then
  prints the name of the winner
asks the user questions, giving positive feedback if the answer is correct, giving hints if the
  answer is wrong the first time, and giving the answer if the answer is wrong the second time
asks for any two (later, three or more) numbers and prints them in order
prints the greatest common factor of any two numbers
asks the user for the price of an object and the amount of money given in payment; outputs the
  change for the purchase
asks the user his or her birthday and prints out the age
asks the user's age and prints out the user's grade. Asks if that is correct. If not, prints out another
  possibility
asks the user's name and prints the user's initials
asks for three digits or letters and prints all the permutations, or combinations, or letters possible
  (e.g., for a b c prints a b c, a c b, b c a, b a c, c a b, c b a)
prints an ever-enlarged sentence, such as
  That mountain was big
  That mountain was big, big
  That mountain was big, big, big,
  That mountain was big, big, big, big,
  That mountain was big, big, big, big, big,
asks for the dimensions of a box and prints its surface area and volume
asks for a sentence and prints the number of words in it, the number of characters, and the
  average length of the words
provides practice in the user's choice of the four arithmetic operations
writes a "personalized form letter" to parents which includes their name as well as that of their
  child, and information about the child's grades or performance. Uses input statements to
  request this information
solves problems that *are really problems you would like the computer to help you with*

4. To understand the statements in a computer language, students should understand the steps a computer follows in carrying out the statements.
5. It is unwise and unfair to "team" students at the computer.
6. Poor readers can be expected to have difficulty programming.
7. To develop good programming habits, students should copy model programs rather than create their own.
8. In response to PRINT 3+5, the computer would print 8.
9. In response to PRINT "8-2", the computer would print 6.
10. Before starting a new program, a BASIC programmer should type NEW.
11. The BASIC command LIST provides a list of all the variables in the program and their values.
12. Students cannot learn good programming practices with BASIC.
13. Lines of a BASIC program must be typed in correct numerical order.
14. BASIC language may be different on different makes of computers.
15. The INPUT statement allows BASIC programs to be interactive.
16. To use good programming techniques, children should be encouraged to use many GOSUB but few GOTO statements.
17. Numbers can be manipulated in BASIC, but letters and words cannot.
18. In BASIC programming, IF-THEN is the main decision-making process.
19. It is best to have two children program at a computer at one time. One child too often makes typing errors or gets stuck (and social interaction is not encouraged), whereas three or more tend to argue about who is to type.
20. Most microcomputers presently have the BASIC language built in.
21. Computers with built in BASIC cannot be programmed in any other language.
22. Children can profitably teach each other about programming.
23. Structured programming involves more work on paper than on a computer keyboard.
24. The process of structured programming is very similar to the process of good instructional design.
25. Well-written BASIC computer programs should contain a minimum of REM statements, as they tend to clutter any listing of the program.
26. The BASIC statement FOR is always followed by the statement NEXT.
27. Variables in BASIC programs must be given values by the programmer.
28. BASIC is an ideal language for structured programming.
29. The name BASIC rightly implies that this language is the foundation for all other computer languages.

Think About

1. Would your approach to programming align more closely with that of Cathy's or of Joe's, as presented in this chapter?
2. What would you say to a teacher from a senior high school who says, "What are we supposed to teach them if you teach computer programming?"
3. What experiences do you already provide for your students that could be used (or modified to be used) to develop the kind of thinking that is necessary for programming a computer? What others can you think of?

4.   Attack or defend:

Computer programming should be taught to every student as a necessary skill for living in a technological society.

If computer programming is forced upon all children, we will soon start seeing a new phenomenon: children with a learning disability in programming.

Since most programming languages are evolving quickly, it makes little sense to teach a programming language to elementary and middle school students—especially BASIC.

Good programming is good problem solving.

Learning BASIC now, and Pascal or FORTRAN later, will confuse children.

Children should learn to program to meet the needs of the "second literacy" required in a modern society.

Pre-algebra students cannot understand the concept of "variables"; therefore, this should be omitted from their training in BASIC or other languages.

Even teachers with little knowledge of computer science and programming can teach children important concepts and abilities in programming.

Allowing students to use preprogrammed materials, especially games, discourages them from learning how to program.

When you program a computer, you rarely get it right the first time. In recognizing this, and in debugging programs, children become less easily discouraged and more insightful into their own problem-solving processes.

Why make everything a "requirement"? Computer programming should be a free-choice activity for students, so that it is enjoyable to them. Those who do not wish to learn programming should not be forced to do so.

Any problem can be solved by a computer if it is programmed correctly.

If provided with appropriate experiences and lessons in structured programming, most fifth- to ninth-grade students could learn the concepts that are presently taught in a beginning college course in computer programming.

Programs in BASIC require such a painfully complicated structure that only bright students, or those who are highly motivated, can learn to program to solve real problems.

Suggested References

Aiken, Robert, and Moshell, Michael. Computer power. *The Computing Teacher,* April 1982, pp. 12–14.

If you are a middle school teacher (especially in mathematics, science, and/or computer science) you might be interested in this introductory curriculum in which children learn to program in a graphical, interactive dialect of Pascal (a modern, "structured" computer language). It is described in a series of articles beginning with this reading and is for sale from Gregg/McGraw-Hill. Whether you would want to use it or not, most teachers will find its approach to programming—emphasizing student experimentation, design, and discovery ("the Suzuki Method of Computer Programming") — interesting.

Bork, A. Computers and learning: Don't teach BASIC. *Educational Technology,* 1982, 22(4), 33–34.

Luehrmann, Arthur. Don't feel bad about teaching BASIC. *Electronic Learning,* 1982, 2(1), 23–24.
Whose arguments do you find more persuasive, Bork's or Luehrmann's? Why? Is there some truth in each position? What? What would (do) you plan to do?

Boss, Jacqueline. Teaching computer literacy through low resolution graphics. *The Computing Teacher,* March 1982, pp. 41–44.
After reading this article, construct an outline of how you might introduce computer programming in BASIC to a class of fourth graders.

Brown, Jerald. *Instand BASIC.* Beaverton, Oreg.: Dilithium Press, 1982.

Clark, James, and Drum, William. *Structured BASIC.* Cincinnati: South Western Pub. Co., 1983.

Dwyer, Thomas, and Critchfield, Margot. *BASIC and the personal computer.* Reading, Mass.: Addison-Wesley, 1978.

Faulk, Ed. *How to write a computer program.* Chatsworth, Calif.: Datamost, Inc., 1982.

Friedman, Paul. *Computer programs in BASIC.* Englewood Cliffs, N.J.: Prentice-Hall, 1981.

Jones, Aubrey, Jr. *I speak BASIC to my . . . [versions for many models of microcomputers].* Hasbrouck Heights, N.J.: Heyden, 1982.

McDermott, Vern, and Fisher, Diana. *Learning BASIC step by step.* Rockville, Md.: Computer Science Press, 1982.

Monro, Don. *Start with BASIC on the Commodore VIC 20.* Reston, Va.: Reston Pub. Co., 1982.

Moursund, David. *BASIC programming for computer literacy.* New York: McGraw-Hill, 1978.
These readings provide other sources of programs, ideas for teaching programming, and programming hints. Also check a local computer store, magazines, and so on for new releases. Which do you think are most applicable to education?

Feeney, John E. A microcomputer minicurriculum. *Arithmetic Teacher,* 1982, 29(5), 39–42.
This reading presents ten activity cards introducing BASIC programming while reinforcing mathematical concepts. Work through them, asking yourself: Would these benefit my students? How could each activity be extended to provide a real problem-solving situation?

McCunn, Donald H. *Computer programming for the complete idiot.* San Francisco: Design Enterprises of San Francisco, 1979.
This book provides an explanation of several BASIC statements and commands and lists useful (often business) programs. Read the section describing guidelines as to when it is wise to create original programs. What problems or jobs do you have that fit these guidelines?

Pattis, Richard E. *Karel the robot: A gentle introduction to the art of programming.* New York: John Wiley and Sons, 1981.
A prelude to learning the popular structured computer language Pascal, this work encourages sophisticated, modern programming techniques while moving Karel through the streets of a city (all simulated on a CRT screen, of course). Its approach is intuitive and easy to understand.

The following are programming books, filmstrips, and so on written for children. Review a few.

Books:

Van Horn, Royal. *Computer programming for kids and other beginners.* Austin, Texas: Sterling Swift, 1982.

Richman, Ellen. *Spotlight on computer literacy.* New York: Random House, 1982.

Larsen, Sally. *Computers for kids.* Morristown, N.J.: Creative Computing Press, 1984.

Richardson, Kay. *Everybody's BASIC.* Indianapolis, Ind.: Meka Pub. Co., 1982.

Richardson, Kay. *1 Computer. 30 Kids.* Indianapolis, Ind.: Meka Pub. Co., 1980.

Luehrmann, Arthur, and Peckham, Herbert. *Computer literacy: A hands-on approach.* New York: McGraw-Hill, 1983.

Carlson Edward H. *Kids and the Apple.* Reston, Va.: Reston Publishing Company, 1982.

Filmstrips:

"Computer Programming—BASIC for Elementary grades (3–7)." By K–12 Micro Media, P.O. Box 17, Valley Cottage, New York 10989, 1982. Five color filmstrips with cassettes and a teacher's handbook.

"BASIC" for Microcomputers: Step by Step Instruction." By Educational Activities, Inc., P.O. Box 392, Freeport, New York 11520.

Which do you think is the best for your children? Order it for your classroom.

Bibliography

Aiken, Robert, and Moshell, Michael. Computer power. *The Computing Teacher,* April 1982, pp. 12–14.

Bork, A. Computers and learning: Don't teach BASIC. *Educational Technology,* 1982, 22(4), 33–34.

Boss, Jacqueline. Teaching computer literacy through low resolution graphics. *The Computing Teacher,* March 1982, pp. 41–44.

Dwyer, Thomas, and Critchfield, Margot. *BASIC and the personal computer.* Reading, Mass.: Addison-Wesley, 1978.

Friedman, Paul. *Computer programs in BASIC.* Englwood Cliffs, N.J.: Prentice-Hall, 1981.

Luehrmann, Arthur. Don't feel bad about teaching BASIC. *Electronic Learning,* 1982, 2(1), 23–24.

Luehrmann, Arthur, and Peckham, Herbert. *Computer literacy: A hands-on approach.* New York: McGraw-Hill, 1983.

McCunn, Donald H. *Computer programming for the complete idiot.* San Francisco: Design Enterprises of San Francisco, 1979.

Mayer, Richard E. A psychology of learning BASIC computer programming: Transactions, prestatements, and chunks. Series in Learning and Cognition, Technical Report No. 79–2. Santa Barbara, CA: Department of Psychology, University of California, 1979.

Mayer, Richard E. The pschology of how novices learn computer programming. *Computing Surveys,* 1981, 13(1), 121–141.

Moursund, David. *BASIC programming for computer literacy.* New York: McGraw-Hill, 1978.

Pattis, Richard E. *Karel the robot: A gentle introduction to the art of programming.* New York: John Wiley, 1981.

15

Programming in LOGO

Scott sat down in front of the computer and typed READ "SCOTT'S STUFF." The programs he had invented up to that day were read into the computer. After a few seconds, he typed FLOWER. A small triangle on the screen began drawing lines, producing the picture seen in Figure 15-1.

Scott has planned what he wanted to do. He typed TO BOUQUET. The screen cleared, and the computer got ready to "learn" how to make a bouquet by clearing the screen and printing TO BOUQUET. Scott typed in:

FIGURE 15-1

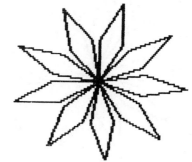

```
TO BOUQUET
  REPEAT 4 [PENUP  LEFT 90  FORWARD 90  PENDOWN  FLOWER]
END
```

Scott typed "CTRL-C" to tell the computer he had Completed his idea. He then typed BOUQUET, and the small triangle created Figure 15-2.

Scott was pleased . . . almost. "A real flower would have a circle in the middle, with the pistil in it," he muttered. He typed EDIT FLOWER and saw:

```
TO FLOWER
  REPEAT 9 [PETAL  RIGHT 40]
END
```

Using a few simple keystrokes, he changed this to read:

```
TO FLOWER
  CIRCLE
  REPEAT 9 [PETAL  RIGHT 40]
END
```

Still conversing quietly with himself, he said, "Now I gotta tell it how to do a circle . . . a little circle." He typed:

```
TO CIRCLE
  REPEAT 36 [FORWARD 2  RIGHT 10]
END
```

FIGURE 15-2

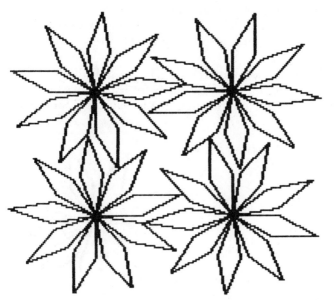

Scott excitedly typed BOUQUET, and the screen showed the picture in Figure 15-3.

Scott laughed as he stopped the triangle from drawing any more. "Oh yeah, I gotta change the place the petals start so they go around the circle now." He never noticed his classmates as they came in from recess, yelling, "Come on, Scott, my turn!"

WHAT IS LOGO?

Scott has been working with the computer language LOGO. LOGO has been called "a language for learning." Other languages, such as BASIC, were written for computers of the 1960s, which had small memories. Therefore, variable names were kept short, data structures had to be "declared," and primitives—the basic words the computer understood— were kept to a minimum. Some considered it advantageous to have a small number of basic words. It was argued that this made the language easier to learn. But consider: Could you express yourself more easily with a language limited to a hundred-word vocabulary?

Not accepting these limitations, Seymour Papert and several of his colleagues developed a language that is simple and powerful, that can be used by preschoolers and college graduates, and that allows a person to create interesting programs the first time he or she sits down. Let's ex-

FIGURE 15-3

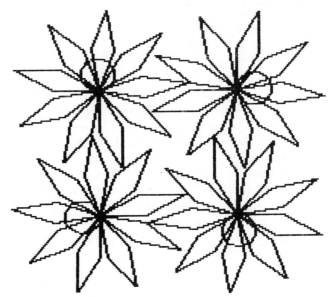

plore that part of LOGO which often serves as an introduction to the language, "turtle graphics." The triangular pointer in the middle of Scott's screen is called the turtle. This is because the first turtle was an actual computer-controlled robot—called a tortoise or turtle by its inventor—that scurried around on large sheets of paper, drawing shapes and the like.

The turtle responds to a few simple commands. If you type FORWARD 50, the turtle moves forward (in whatever direction it is pointing) 50 turtle steps (about one-quarter of the height of the screen). RIGHT or LEFT rotates the turtle a given number of degrees; RIGHT 90 commands the turtle to turn at a right angle. PENUP and PENDOWN tell the turtle to stop and start leaving a trace of its path on the screen. Interesting drawings can be created just using these commands. But the truly beneficial explorations come from teaching the computer new words. For instance, one second grader taught the computer how to make a square:

```
TO SQUARE
  REPEAT 4 [FORWARD 40 RIGHT 90]
END
```

SQUARE is now a new LOGO *procedure*. The first line specifies the name (which didn't have to be SQUARE—it could just as well have been called BOX or HI). The rest tells the computer how to carry out the procedure. It is a list of instructions. SQUARE tells the turtle to go forward 50 steps, turn right 90 degrees, go forward 50 more steps, make another right turn, and so on, until it has done that four times. Procedures can also have inputs. For example, SQUARE might be written this way:

```
TO SQUARE :SIDE
  REPEAT 4 [FORWARD :SIDE  RIGHT 90]
END
```

Now the person (or another procedure) that types in, or "calls" SQUARE can specify a certain length for the side. The variable :SIDE— the colon (:) means "the thing or number associated with the name SIDE"—is called a *local variable*. It is "known" only to the procedure SQUARE. Other procedures could have their own number associated with :SIDE. In the analogy used in the previous chapter, each procedure has its own set of mailboxes. SQUARE has a mailbox named SIDE, and the person can place any number into it. SQUARE will draw a square, and the length of each side will be that number (see Figure 15-4).

WHY LOGO?

. . . the first computer language you learn has a lifelong effect on how you think, computerwise. Thus, the computer language we choose for use in the

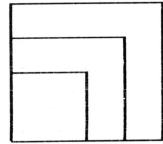

FIGURE 15-4

schools becomes vital. . . . Logo is a much better language to use for introducing children to computers than, say, BASIC.
(Chris Morgan, 1982)

Why are people like Chris Morgan (editor of Byte magazine), elementary teachers, college math professors, teachers of exceptional children, parents, and children (of all ages) so enthusiastic about LOGO? It was a bit hard for the authors to understand when they were first learning about computers and computer languages. They weren't very impressed with the claims that it was procedural, interactive, nontyped, structured, recursive, and a list-processing language. Just like their students, they didn't really know what those things meant—even if someone explained them—until they used the language and had some hands-on experience with these characteristics. Now they're on the other side of the computer. They want to tell you about the possibilities of LOGO and the wonderful characteristics it has. Because you are reading, they'll have to ask you to (a) make a real effort to get some actual hands-on experience with LOGO—through a store, a workshop, a friend, or whatever, and try out some of the ideas in this chapter; or at least (b) follow through the programs, trying to map out what is happening; and (c) resist feeling that you don't understand either the language or its "specialness" until you've given it a chance.

Characteristics of LOGO

Let's look briefly at some of the characteristics of LOGO, then study a few more examples.

Like other modern languages, LOGO is *procedural*. Instead of the long lists of commands you see in the BASIC language, LOGO programs consist of small, understandable procedures, each of which has a specific job to do. In Scott's program FLOWER drew a flower.

One procedure can call another. In Scott's program FLOWER called PETAL eight times.

```
TO FLOWER
REPEAT 8 [PETAL   RIGHT 40]
END

TO PETAL
FORWARD 30
RIGHT 30
FORWARD 30
RIGHT 150
FORWARD 30
RIGHT 30
FORWARD 30
RIGHT 150
END
```

Try to walk yourself through the steps to understand how they work. Remember, the BOUQUET procedure called the FLOWER procedure, and so on. (Go back and look at those procedures and walk through them, too.)

Let's look at another example. A learning-disabled sixth grader wanted to draw a clown's face. She had been expertly guided by her teacher to do careful planning. She started by writing:

```
TO CLOWN
HEAD
HAT
EYES
NOSE
MOUTH
END
```

Now she saw that she had to tell the computer how to draw each part. For instance:

```
TO HEAD
REPEAT 4 [FORWARD 70 RIGHT 90]
END

TO HAT
RIGHT 30
FORWARD 70
REPEAT 3 [FORWARD 70 RIGHT 120]
END
```

She then defined eyes, nose, and mouth, finally producing the drawing in Figure 15-5.

It can be seen that this process allows children to look at the "big picture" first, planning what they want to do and then breaking down this large plan into "mind-sized bits." LOGO is a structured language.

This is one of the most important characteristics of LOGO. Problems can be divided into small pieces, and a separate procedure can be written for each piece. In this way, children can "divide and conquer" problems as they being to see, in a concrete fashion, how tasks can be broken down into procedures, how procedures can be combined to form superprocedures, and how procedures interact.

FIGURE 15-5

This also illustrates that LOGO is *extensible*—children "teach" the computer new words. As another simple example, a popular early project of children is to draw a house. Children first "teach" the computer to draw a square, possibly naming the procedure SQUARE (they could just as well name it BOX or any other word). They then construct another set of commands to draw a triangle. Finally, they assemble these procedures in a superprocedure they might name HOUSE, which uses the SQUARE procedure to draw a square, moves into position, and then uses the TRI-ANGLE procedure to draw a triangular roof. As an extension, one child might write another superprocedure that uses the new word HOUSE as a procedure to draw a house, then moves to the side, draws another house, moves again, and so on; this new superprocedure was entitled CITY by one child (see Figure 15-6).

LOGO is also *interactive*. Unlike Pascal—another modern, procedural language—the LOGO programmer can type in a command or program and see it executed immediately.

Further, LOGO is *recursive*. A procedure can "call itself" or make a "copy" of itself. Look at the procedure DESIGN, which Scott wrote:

```
TO DESIGN
PETAL
RIGHT 30
DESIGN
END
```

FIGURE 15-6

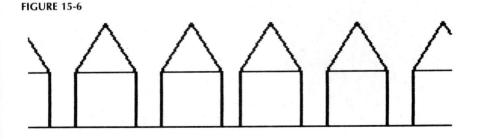

It's a bit tricky at first, but walk it through. DESIGN begins by drawing a PETAL. Then it instructs the turtle to turn right 30, and then . . . it calls itself. This means that it instructs the turtle to do a DESIGN again. This produces the design in Figure 15-7.

LOGO is a language for learning. It has been specially designed, with features such as turtle graphics, to encourage learning and problem solving by children. It is user friendly. Instead of getting a message such as SYNTAX ERROR, a person might be told, THERE IS NO PROCEDURE NAMED FOWARD 10" (because you forgot the "R"); or if your program said PRINT 13 + TWO, LOGO might tell you, + DOESN'T LIKE TWO AS INPUT (you tried to add a word to a number).

We'll look at these and other characteristics in more depth as we go on. For now, notice that because children can "play" with the turtle, they can solve more abstract problems by using their intuitive knowledge. For instance, they can ask, "If I were the turtle, what would I do next?" Working with turtle geometry, they can develop this intuitive sense even further, laying a foundation for later studies in geometry, trigonometry, calculus, and even physics.

SETTING UP FOR LOGO EXPLORATIONS

LOGO is not just a computer language. It is a philosophy of education. Whatever our own individual philosophies and methods, it is often beneficial for us to add exploratory, problem-solving activities. This is the heart of LOGO programming and LOGO learning. The following paragraphs briefly describe the philosophy of LOGO and some classroom activities based on this philosophy.

Seymour Papert, one of the creators of LOGO, based his ideas on the theories of Piaget, with whom he studied. Papert (1980) has argued that the most beneficial learning is what he calls "Piagetian learning," or "learning without being taught." He has proposed that computer programming can allow children to learn ideas previously believed to be too abstract for their level of cognitive development. Computers can make the

FIGURE 15-7

abstract concrete and personal as they help children learn by helping them think about their own thinking. By programming the computer to do what they want it to do, children must think about how one might do the task oneself—and therefore, about how they themselves think (Papert, 1980). In this way, LOGO programming holds the promise of being an effective device for teaching how, rather than what, to think.

Of course, these ideas must be examined cautiously. For example, some of Piaget's ideas would actually seem contradictory to this optimistic view. For example, Piaget writes that you cannot teach young children to deal with abstract concepts before they reach the period of formal operations. He also maintains that biologically determined development, not learning, must come first. Piaget did believe that people develop cognitively from interactions with their environment, however, and the interactions children have with LOGO can be exciting.

Classroom turtle walks are an effective way to introduce LOGO programming. Have one child be the turtle while one or more others give directions. Make sure the steps are very small "turtle steps." You might have LEFT and RIGHT represent 90-degree turns at first, or have 90 "tiny turtle turns" be right angles. Children who need more experience with circles and degrees may benefit from playing "turtle turns" in a large circle laid out on the floor and marked in degrees (possibly in twelve sections, similar to a clock). The child-turtle at HOME is facing 0 degrees (that is, twelve o'clock). Turns of different degrees can be commanded by others. This can later serve as the basis for more complicated designs, such as the FLOWER procedure.

After a couple of gamelike practice sessions, have the computer available. While one child acts out the commands, have the LOGO computer do likewise on the screen. Let the activity itself emphasize that the turtle does exactly what the programmer(s) tell it to do. Use the children's own movement to show them that direction is relative to position. Have them imagine that they are the turtle. This will take advantage of their own knowledge of their bodies in space and encourage them to continue using this knowledge in their explorations of geometric ideas.

Programming in LOGO can now begin. At first, the teacher will demonstrate simple processes fairly often. Children then take turns trying out their own ideas. Teachers may wish to use support programs which help children build procedures (see Clements, 1983b). The next step is planning specific movements, or procedures. Have the children tell the child-turtle and the LOGO-turtle (simultaneously) how to walk a square or other simple shape. Write down the program at the same time. Debug the procedures as necessary. It is through this debugging, rethinking process that people become reflective, precise thinkers. Children can then experiment with building more complex programs based on these procedures. This kind of planning and whole-class work encourages not only social interaction but also planning ahead. This advance planning helps students become better problem solvers, *and* it allows more students to get more programming experience with limited computer resources. Many children can be acting out the turtle, making small paper cut-out turtles act out their programs, drawing their designs with pencils as they study the movements they make, writing their procedures, discussing solutions to problems, and so on, while one or two are actually typing in and executing their programs.

Now that your students and the turtle are "rolling" (that would be an interesting project—how does a computer turtle roll?), you might supply disks (on which students can store their programs), rulers and graph paper, and printouts (or handwritten records) of projects, challenges, and children's procedures and designs in the LOGO learning lab. The day could be divided into fifteen- to twenty-minute periods, and children might sign up for LOGO time on the computer (each is responsible for leaving on time and quietly informing the next person that it is his or her turn). Each student should receive three or four turns per week if possible.

When he is free, the teacher can say: "What are you working on? What does this procedure do? Tell me exactly what you want the turtle to do. You need to. . . . How do you think you could do that? Do you have an idea about why that didn't work? What did you try already? How could you test your idea? You could ask Sandy; she had a similar problem." Students often ask others without their teacher's suggestion. Some teachers have certain students (interestingly, not always those with the highest grades) serve as weekly "LOGO Experts," resource people for other students needing assistance.

At specified times the class gathers together around the computer and discusses students' programs, problems, and solutions. Interaction is guided by the teacher. "Can you figure out what made Chuckie's program work?" "Bob, would that help you with your program? How?" "Could Chuckie make his program different? How?" "Chuckie, are you going to build more onto your work? What?" "Class, how might he do that?" "That's a tough one. No one seems to have an answer. Let's put tape on the floor to draw the design. You tell Terry how to walk the pattern while I write what you say on the board." "How is this similar to other programs we have made? How is it different?"

This is an excellent time for the teacher to note strengths, areas of need, directions for future work, interests, and the like. He notices that Chuckie is growing in self-confidence and initiative, that Bob might profit from working a bit with Chuckie or with him to get "over the hump," and that several students might be ready for an introduction to random selection. He makes a note to speak briefly with these students tomorrow. Maybe he can suggest a project that will require this; with the right hints, they might just discover the need for it themselves. He observes that several students are still enjoying just "fooling around" with variations of their procedures, whereas some are planning elaborate projects, and two seem hesitant to experiment. Maybe showing them pictures and descriptions of programming projects will help.

MORE EXPLORATIONS FOR YOU
AND YOUR STUDENTS

Figure 15-8 presents some procedures and results that show the power of explorations in LOGO. Note that many, like POLYGON, contain inputs. Walk through several of the POLYGON drawings. With a computer (or at least with paper and pencil), try out some other inputs. What figures can you create? A single procedure and the almost endless explorations that it can generate is the LOGO concept of the microworld. The microworld is a small, controllable "problem space" similar to an almost infinitely explorable learning center. It allows the great freedom to experiment within the structure of simplicity. In other words, the model or activity is kept as simple or as easy to understand as possible (while retaining its essential characteristics), yet it allows almost endless creativity and flexibility within its boundaries. POLYGON and INSPIRAL are two examples (the turtle itself, with its limited rules, is, of course, one slightly larger example). Others suitable for young children will be discussed later in the chapter.

FIGURE 15-8

```
TO POLY :SIDE :ANGLE
  FORWARD :SIDE
  RIGHT :ANGLE
  POLY :SIDE :ANGLE
END
```

POLY 40 90

POLY 40 140

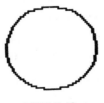

POLY 5 10

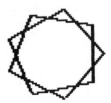

POLY 40 280

JUST TURTLE GEOMETRY?

"As fascinating as this is, I can't see that doing turtle geometry alone is enough. I thought you said LOGO was a great language for everything. Can LOGO work with words and numbers like BASIC? What is 'list processing' "? We shall explore these questions below.

LOGO is an interesting and useful language for explorations of graphics and geometry, but its power does not stop there. Instead of handling data as numbers or strings of characters like BASIC does, LOGO uses lists composed of words. In LOGO a *word* is a string of characters. A *list* is a sequence of words or of other lists. How is this different from a character string as in BASIC? In the latter the string must be manipulated on a character-by-character basis. In LOGO lists can be manipulated as wholes or on a word-by-word basis. Let's look at some simple LOGO programs which use lists (lists must always be in square brackets). Notice that LOGO has many more commands than BASIC, and recall that you can define and add your own original commands.

```
TO FADEOUT :LIST
  IF :LIST = [ ] THEN STOP
  PRINT :LIST
  FADEOUT BUTLAST :LIST
END
```

A sample run—the person types the first line, giving a "list" to the procedure FADEOUT, and thus asking FADEOUT to do its job using that list.

```
FADEOUT [I AM GOING FAST!]

I AM GOING FAST
I AM GOING
I AM
I
```

This defines a procedure which takes a list as input (:list means "the thing that is called list"). If the list is empty, it stops. Otherwise, it prints the list. Then it does something very powerful. *The procedure calls itself* (recursion). But when it does, it uses a list which is the list it started with minus (BUTLAST) the last word. That list is printed, and the procedure calls itself again, with a list again shortened by one word. When the list is empty, the procedure stops. Now let's combine some procedures:

```
TO DISAPPEAR
  FADEOUT [I AM THE DISAPPEARING PERSON!]
  PRINT [ ]
  PRINT [XXXXX  POOOOOOOF!!!  XXXXX]
END
```

Now all you have to type is:

```
DISAPPEAR
I AM THE DISAPPEARING PERSON
I AM THE DISAPPEARING
I AM THE
I AM
I

XXXXX  POOOOOOOF!!!  XXXXX
```

With LOGO, children can easily design simple drill-and-practice programs for each other (see Clements, 1983a). When they do this, they and their friends get practice in using the program; but more important, they learn about the thinking that goes into designing such a program, they learn programming, and they learn about some very sophisticated mathematical notions.

Another powerful application of words and lists involves programming projects in which the goal is to produce random sentences. To tell the computer how to write syntactically correct, but endlessly random sentences, the child has a deeper, more demanding purpose for understanding and using the notions of parts of speech. A sample run of one such program, written by an intermediate-grade child, follows.

```
TALK

BLUE ELEPHANTS WALK
SORRY GIRLS RUN
LARGE BUILDINGS WIGGLE
MANY ELEPHANTS PLAY
SORRY BUILDINGS CRY
```

There were some procedures she needed for this project that were probably too advanced for her. This presented no problem, as her teacher merely supplied them. She experienced a mixture of thinking, programming, academic content, and fun.

Properly planned, LOGO projects can also have a beneficial effect on children's learning of conventional academic content. For instance, in a major project students may design an "intelligent" program that categorizes types of life on our planet, an essential concept in science. To do this, they must use LOGO's capability to manipulate lists in a hierarchical structure. Thus, to construct and use the program, students must learn (in a painless, purposeful, intrinsically motivated way) about the hierarchical categorizational system of biology, about hierarchical categorization itself, about grammar, and about logic, modules, data management, and programming. This program is "intelligent" not only for the information it has but for its ability to put *a* or *an* before words appropriately, and so on. Most important, the program can learn. Figure 15-9 illustrates a sample run of one version of such a program.

Thus, LOGO is not merely a good way to teach programming and other aspects of computer literacy. It provides opportunities to present the core subjects—reading, language arts, math, science, social studies,

```
YOU THINK OF SOMETHING LIVING.

I WILL TRY TO GUESS WHAT KIND IT IS BY
ASKING YOU QUESTIONS.

CAN IT MOVE ON ITS OWN?
YES
IS IT A WARMBLOODED ANIMAL WHICH NURSES ITS YOUNG?
NO
OK, IS IT A MOLLUSK?
NO
THAT'S NOT IT. WHAT IS IT?

SNAKE
PLEASE TYPE IN A QUESTION WHOSE ANSWER
IS "YES" FOR A SNAKE AND
"NO" FOR A MOLLUSK
DOES IT HAVE A BACKBONE?
O.K. WE'LL TRY AGAIN
YOU THINK OF SOMETHING LIVING.

I WILL TRY TO GUESS WHAT KIND IT IS BY
ASKING YOU QUESTIONS.

CAN IT MOVE ON ITS OWN?
YES
IS IT A WARMBLOODED ANIMAL WHICH NURSES ITS YOUNG?
NO
DOES IT HAVE A BACKBONE?
YES
OK, IS IT A SNAKE?
YES
I GOT IT!
O.K. WE'LL TRY AGAIN
YOU THINK OF SOMETHING LIVING.

I WILL TRY TO GUESS WHAT KIND IT IS BY
ASKING YOU QUESTIONS.

CAN IT MOVE ON ITS OWN?
```

FIGURE 15-9

music, and art—in new and exciting ways. Instead of asking, "Where will I fit LOGO programming in my crowded day?" you might more profitably ask, "How can I improve the learning/teaching in my classroom so as to take advantage of the new approaches to subject matter content, skills, and problem-solving abilities offered by LOGO?"

WORKING WITH DIFFERENT AGE GROUPS

Working with Very Young Children

If you teach very young children, you might have been thinking, "But preschool and kindergarten children may not even be able to type 'forward' accurately," or some similar objection. There are two responses to this. First, children do not have to read. There are several options. Some people have invented modified keyboards with pictures instead of letters. This works well with tots. However, it necessitates additional hardware. You can also type in a few programs which will make the turtle advance, turn, draw, and even save and repeat programs, with just a single keystroke. (These are available within the suggested references.) By merely typing F, the children will be able to make the turtle draw a line forward a set amount (you can set the distance); typing R tells the turtle to turn right a certain amount (usually 30 degrees is a useful start). You might put stickers over the keys for even easier use. When a child has created a program he or she likes, pushing one key will save it; pushing another will run the entire graphic program (see Clements, 1983b).

A second response to the objection about requiring reading is: How long does it take your children to learn to do something when they are just "burning" to do it? If a small thing like reading a few words is all that is between a child and making a computer do what she wants, watch the child tackle those words. This is a meaningful reading experience, too: The child gets immediate feedback; it is interactive; it is purposeful; and it puts the child in a position of power. Take advantage of peer teaching here. The amount of knowledge, techniques, words, and skills that children pass around when they are intensely involved is amazing. So don't dismiss the programming that involves several words; it might just serve as a teacher's aide for reading/reading readiness instruction. In a similar vein, kindergarten children have been observed within another modified learning environment. Here the computer was programmed to display an entire word (and the space after it) at the touch of one key. Keys were covered by stickers bearing the name of the corresponding word. Other keys were programmed to erase whole words and save finished sentences for instant replay. Another key printed the child's sentences. Children repeat words often, but in the context of meaningful communication. The basal's repetitive practice was combined with the motivation and purpose of real communication.

Obviously, this was just a start, but a good start. Soon the children wanted to type the whole words in themselves, and with the help of an easy-to-use word processing program, they were on their way to creative writing and reading, in a modified, electronic language-experience approach.

What other activities can the young child program the computer to do? The concept of microworlds is important here. Many implementations of LOGO employ sprites, "invisible beings" that "carry" shapes in varying directions and at varying speeds across the screen. With very little effort, the LOGO-controlled computer can be programmed to display a screen, say a city street, and the child can create a world. By typing in

SUN and UP, the child makes a yellow circular region rise to the sky. Typing STOP freezes it, or SLOW might make it travel leisurely across the clouds. Cars, trucks, people, and so on are all moved in the same way—and they keep moving while the child creates more of her micro-world. The possibilities are almost endless; and the effects on reading, thinking, and self-concept are potentially quite powerful.

As a teacher, you know the truth in the old saying that to truly understand something, you must teach it. In teaching LOGO new proce-dures (new words, shapes, tasks, ways of doing things, and so on), chil-dren also build stronger understandings. They develop clear ideas about the descriptions of tasks. Working with LOGO combines teaching, learn-ing, and programming into an integrated, personal experience.

What About Advanced Children?

Of course, many advanced children will virtually challenge them-selves with programming projects that are extensions of those listed above. Music explorations are also fruitful (see Bamberger, 1982). LOGO can be used to implement a programming language that is a generative grammar—a set of rules that can be used to describe, manipulate, and explore languages, drawing, chemistry, music, and so on (see Rowe, 1978). There is no limit to the learning that LOGO can generate. College students have even used it to investigate Einstein's theory of relativity (see Abelson and diSessa, 1981, for a description of these—and other more accessible—ideas for exploring mathematics). References listed at the end of this chapter will provide you with a wealth of explanations, descriptions of activities, and examples.

A SCOPE AND SEQUENCE?

There are several reasons why the presentation of a scope and sequence model for learning LOGO would not be appropriate.

1. LOGO programmers create their own words for their own purposes. There-fore, there is no set sequence that each should follow.
2. Many third graders have been observed programming at higher levels of sophistication than some ninth graders or even adults. No predetermined grade-level placement would be universally appropriate.
3. The LOGO educational philosophy is not based on a strict sequence of skill acquisition. To capture the power of the LOGO guided-discovery approach, most teachers do not prescribe instruction.

Those teachers needing guidance are advised to use one or more of the books or other sets of materials which are listed at the end of the chapter and in the appendix. In helping you and your students learn LOGO, these references provide some step-by-step instructions.

PROGRAMMING CHALLENGES FOR YOU
AND YOUR STUDENTS

Try some of the following projects out yourself and with your students. (Examples of how the programs would actually look are provided for some.) Can you write a program which . . .

draws a house? (Try combining a triangle and a square.)
draws a spiral?
draws a stairway of any size?
re-creates a picture you drew yourself?
doubles any list given to it? For example,

```
DOUBLE.SENTENCE [BANG]
BANG BANG

DOUBLE.SENTENCE DOUBLE.SENTENCE [BANG]
BANG BANG BANG BANG
```

reverses any list given to it?

```
REVERSE.SENTENCE [I AM GOING OUT]
OUT GOING AM I
```

checks if a word or number is a palindrome (reads the same way backwards and forwards)?

```
PALINDROME.CHECK? "MADAM

YES IT IS A PALINDROME.
PALINDROME.CHECK? "ADAM
NO, THAT'S NOT A PALINDROME.
```

makes a palindrome out of any (can it be done with any?) number?

```
MAKE.A.PALINDROME 59
```

properly prints "a" or "an" before words?
asks for a person's name and his or her friends' names, then prints out sentences that state that every person named likes every other person (permutations)?

```
WHAT IS YOUR NAME?
MARYJANE
TELL ME THE NAME OF ONE OF YOUR FRIENDS.
BOBBY
HOW ABOUT ANOTHER FRIEND?
DONNA
THANK YOU.
MARYJANE LIKES BOBBY
MARYJANE LIKES DONNA
BOBBY LIKES MARYJANE
DONNA LIKES MARYJANE
BOBBY LIKES DONNA
DONNA LIKES BOBBY
A LOT OF FRIENDSHIPS!
```

asks for the user's name and outputs a "secret number code" equivalent to the letters of that name?

averages any given number of grades?

permits children to type in their names, then maintains and prints out an attendance list?

draws houses of random size and shape?

adds to the above a random number of windows?

provides the English names of any number given it up to a million?

Self-Test

1. LOGO is an easy language for children to learn, although to solve difficult problems, they would have to learn a more "adult" language, such as BASIC or Pascal.

2. The advantage of LOGO is that it is based on modules, or procedures.

3. LOGO is fine for drawing pictures, but it has limited power for developing sophisticated mathematical understandings.

4. The "list" in LOGO is the precise equivalent of the "string" of characters in BASIC.

5. Not only can children invent and define new words (procedures) in LOGO, but teachers can easily provide (especially younger) students with difficult procedures to allow them to work on a project.

6. Although young children can use LOGO, one must, of course, wait until they can read and spell.

7. Although we call working with LOGO "programming," it should be recognized that the activity is more playing than actual computer programming.

8. Perhaps the best use of LOGO involves children solving problems—from their work in school subjects or from their personal lives.

9. LOGO is designed to solve only easy problems. This makes it ideal for young children.

10. Probably the best use of LOGO is in the teaching of geometric ideas.

Think About

1. Do you believe children who program computers in LOGO are using *more* or *less* concrete models to think about thinking?

2. The use of learning environments that languages such as LOGO make possible will allow teachers to design curricula in which students solve "real life" problems and participate in more adultlike activities. Is this true? Is it desirable?

3. Will the required debugging of computer programs lead children to be less critical of their own mistakes, to be higher in self-esteem, and to be more willing to experiment and learn? Or will it lead to sloppiness in thinking and planning?

4. Most students do not really discover much about the process of problem solving until late in their lives, if ever. Can computer programming change this? What effect will this have on students?

5. Papert studied with Piaget before participating in the development of the

LOGO language. But according to Piaget, formal thinking does not occur until about age twelve years. This means something as abstract as computer programming is not appropriate for younger children. Papert did not consider this aspect of the theory in his plans for elementary students. What do you think?

6. Should computers and LOGO programming be used primarily to stimulate planning and problem solving, or to teach subject matter? Why do you think so?

7. Do you believe computers will change the way people think and solve problems? Is this merely another "bandwagon" optimists jump on? Defend your answer.

8. Will (should) the availability of languages like LOGO mean that the dream of the progressive movement and open classrooms—children learning without a prescribed curriculum, each designing his or her own—can finally be realized?

Suggested References

Abelson, H., and diSessa, A. *Turtle geometry: The computer as a medium for exploring mathematics.* Cambridge, Mass.: MIT Press, 1981.

Howe, J. A. M., and O'Shea, T. Learning mathematics through Logo. *ACM SIGCUE Bulletin, 1978, 12(1).*
The authors provide ideas on using turtle geometry as a medium for exploring mathematics.

Bamberger, Jeanne. Logo music. *Byte,* August 1982, pp. 325; 328.
The author provides insight into how Logo might be used in music education.

Bitter, Gary, and Watson, Nancy. Apple Logo Primer. (Also CyberLogo Primer.) Reston, Va.: Reston Pub. Co., 1983.
Bitter and Watson provide a readable introduction to Apple Logo and also provide brief but useful descriptions of how Logo is used in schools.

BYTE, August, 1982.

D'Angelo, John, and Overall, Theresa. Learning with LLLogo. In C. Hernandex-Logan and M. Lewis (eds.), *Computer support for education.* Palo Alto, Calif.: R and E Research Associates, 1982.
Of the applications in the schools described by Daniel Watt ("Logo in the Schools") and R. W. Lawler ("Designing Computer-Based Microworlds") in this issue of *BYTE,* which do you think would fit your situation the best? See also D'Angelo and Overall.

Classroom Computer News, April 1983.

The Computing Teacher, November 1982.
These issues were dedicated to Logo in the classroom and could serve as an introduction. Particularly noteworthy is the listing of different Logo programs that are available and "Logo Library," a listing of resources and references.

Lewis, Coleta. Talking turtle: A game for Logo learners. *Electronic Learning,* March/April 1982, pp. 48; 50.
This provides other ideas on introducing Logo to children.

Papert, S. Mindstorms: Children, computers, and powerful ideas. New York: Basic Books, 1980.

Rousseau, J., and Smith, S. Whither goes the turtle? *Microcomputing,* September 1981, pp. 52–53; 55.

Watt, Daniel. Should children be computer programmers? *Popular Computing,* September 1982, p. 130.
What programming projects do you think would add to your curriculum? Do you think Papert is correct in assuming that proper programming experiences can change the way children think? Is he too optimistic? Does he forget Piaget's warning that learning cannot precede development, or can powerful experiences change the "natural" course of development? Will children still need drill and practice in the "basics," or will they learn these effortlessly as they pursue more meaningful projects?

Papert, Seymour, and Solomon, C. NIM: A game-playing program. Memo 254, MIT Artificial Intelligence Laboratory, 1970.
This fascinating paper illustrates how middle school children can become involved in planning and writing a program which can play a game (one-pile NIM, or 21) at increasingly intelligent levels. How do you think students could benefit from this type of exercise? In programming? In thinking strategies? In self-concept? What simple game do you and your children know that you could work on in a similar manner?

Riordon, Tim. Creating a Logo Environment. *The Computing Teacher,* November 1982, pp. 46–50.
Riorden provides helpful suggestions for creating a Logo environment as well as a brief scope and sequence.

Rowe, Neil. Grammar as a programming language. *Creative Computing,* January/February 1978, pp. 80–86.
Many "languages" use grammars besides those that are strictly linguistic (human speech). Rowe provides a framework of generative grammar, implemented with Logo, which can be used by teachers and children to explore writing, modifying, and using grammars (systems of rules) in English, drawing, music, and so on. Experiment with these programs. How would you use these ideas with children so that the children would learn about programming, grammars, and subject matter?

Solomon, Cynthia. Introducing Logo to children. *Byte,* August 1982, pp. 196; 198; 200; 202; 204; 206; 208.

Watt, Daniel. A comparison of the problem-solving styles of two students learning Logo: A computer language for children. *Creative Computing,* December 1979, pp. 86–88; 90.
Do you think any of your students would "fit" the categories of different styles of learning Logo as described in these readings? How would you go about teaching them?

Thornburg, David. *First book of robots and computers.* Greensboro, N.C.: Compute! Books, 1982.
Thornburg presents ideas for beginning programming of turtles and Big Trak.

Watt, Daniel. *Learning with Logo.* New York: McGraw-Hill, 1983.
This book provides teachers with a tutorial on Logo, and provides suggestions for helping children learn the language and the "powerful ideas" it contains.

Bibliography

ABELSON, H., AND DISESSA, A. *Turtle geometry: The computer as a medium for exploring mathematics.* Cambridge, Mass.: MIT Press, 1981.

BAMBERGER, JEANNE. Logo music. *BYTE,* August 1982, pp. 325; 328.

CLEMENTS, DOUGLAS H. Programming, problem solving, and practice. *Arithmetic Teacher,* 1983, 31(4), 32–35. (a)

CLEMENTS, DOUGLAS H. Supporting young children's Logo programming. *The Computing Teacher,* 1983, 11(5), 24–30. (b)

D'ANGELO, JOHN, AND OVERALL, THERESA. Learning with LLLogo. In C. Hernandex-Logan and M. Lewis (eds.), *Computer support for education.* Palo Alto, Calif.: R and E Research Associates, 1982.

HOWE, J. A. M., AND O'SHEA, T. Learning mathematics through Logo. ACM SIGCUE Bulletin, 1978, 12(1).

LEWIS, COLETA. Talking turtle: A game for Logo learners. *Electronic Learning,* March/April 1982, pp. 48; 50.

MORGAN, CHRIS. Editorial. *BYTE,* August 1982, pp. 6; 8; 10; 16.

PAPERT, SEYMOUR. *Mindstorms: Children, computers, and powerful ideas.* New York: Basic Books, 1980.

PAPERT, SEYMOUR, AND SOLOMON, C. NIM: A game-playing program. Memo 254, MIT Artificial Intelligence Laboratory, 1970.

PAPERT, S., DISESSA, A., WATT, D., AND WEIR, S. Final report of the Brookline Logo Project: Project summary and data analysis. Logo Memo 53, MIT Logo Group, 1979.

ROUSSEAU, J., AND SMITH, S. Whither goes the turtle? *Microcomputing,* September 1981, pp. 52–53; 55.

ROWE, NEIL. Grammar as a programming language. *Creative Computing,* January/February 1978, pp. 80–86.

WATT, DANIEL. A comparison of the problem solving styles of two students learning Logo: A computer language for children. *Creative Computing,* December 1979, pp. 86–88; 90.

WATT, DANIEL. Should children be computer programmers? *Popular Computing,* September 1982, 130.

Constructing CAI Programs: Authoring Systems and Languages

Sandy Marong was not satisfied. She had searched through several books and magazines which catalog and review software for microcomputers and had requested and received literature from several companies. But the specific program she wanted was not to be found. She wanted to provide her first-grade students with additional lessons on classification. She also wanted them to have to figure out some categorizations for themselves. As far as she could tell, no such program was available. Feeling a bit exasperated, she talked to Mrs. Brooks, who was the school's own "expert and enthusiast" in the realm of microcomputers.

"I'm sorry, I couldn't come up with anything that fit your exact needs either," Mrs. Brooks apologized. "Why don't you write your own?"

"Oh come on now! You're the programming specialist. I'm not going to try to write a lesson that includes text, shapes of different colors and sizes, and branching. I just started learning BASIC."

"Actually, Sandy, I was thinking about having you program it in an entirely new computer language, one . . ."

"Forget it! I'm barely managing to find the time to learn the first one."

"Wait!" laughed Mrs. Brooks. "You didn't let me finish. This is a language that's easy to learn and helps you write CAI programs. It's called an authoring language."

"Easy? What you call easy may be a bit different from what I call easy. You'll have to convince me first. What exactly is an authoring language?"

"It's a special computer language that attempts to help a person who is not familiar with the intricacies of programming write courseware for use in the classroom. Using statements of only one or two letters, you can present information, ask questions, accept and store responses, and branch to different parts of the lessons, depending on those responses. A particularly useful feature of many authoring languages is their ability to provide special methods of drawing graphics, special characters, and music, as well as to integrate these into the lesson."

"OK, you've got me interested. But be honest with me—*how* easy is it to learn to use?"

"Well, I learned to use one authoring language moderately well in five or six sessions of an hour or two each, with a bit of reading on the side. It depends on the particular language, of course. Some are more complex than others. You might also want to look at some authoring systems that ask you what you want to do and then write the CAI lesson themselves."

"What can the different systems and languages do? I'd better think first about what I want to do and what they can do."

"You're wise. But as an introduction, let me describe each of them. An authoring language is a computer programming language with simple commands which are designed specifically to help teachers construct lessons. An authoring system provides more of a structure. It asks you a series of questions about what information you want to present, what questions you want to ask, what the correct answers are, what feedback to give, and so on. The system then creates the lesson for you. Here's a list of the capabilities of several systems and languages."

These are a few of the descriptions Mrs. Brooks showed Ms. Marong:

1. This package allows teachers to develop lessons immediately upon sitting down at the microcomputer. The program asks the teacher for the information it needs to create and present the material. The teacher types in the information to be presented to the student, questions to be asked, hints to be given, correct and incorrect answers and responses to these, and so on. Each exercise is made up of units that begin with a text page. Questions are then posed. When students type in their responses, they are provided with feedback directly related to these responses. After a certain number of incorrect responses, the student receives hints. The units can go on as long as the teacher desires (Courseware Development System, from Bell and Howell; with a package called GENIS, this system can be used with an authoring language, providing the advantages of each).

2. In this system the teacher constructs lessons from modules consisting of text pages, graphs, and graphics. Hints can be offered. Revision questions, presented if the student responds incorrectly on the main question, can be

inserted. Student records can be maintained (Zenith Educational System, from Avant-Garde Creations).

3. Students working with this system have some control over the form of presentation that they receive. Pushing special keys, the learner will be presented with advice, a rule, an example, help, practice, and the like.

4. This system is comprised of a series of "shells" in which teachers can create their own quizzes. Three forms are available: multiple choice, matching, and true/false. With no programming knowledge, teachers can substitute their own quiz material into any of these formats (The Shell Games, from Apple).

5. This system has a tutorial format with drill-and-practice quizzes, fill-in-the-blanks, matching, multiple choice, or true/false, to test the material taught. Teachers can preset lesson branching patterns for students based on their performance on the quizzes, or they can assign specific sequences of lessons for students. Management (CMI) is also available (AIDS, by Instructional Development Systems).

6. This authoring language allows a teacher to type in short commands and write interactive CAI lessons. (This is the route Ms. Marong decided to take.) This authoring language, PILOT, is available from several companies for most major makes of microcomputers. Newer versions, such as Super-PILOT, have even more advanced editing features, plus the capability to control video tapes and disks, allowing a remarkable range of lessons to be presented.

USING AN AUTHORING LANGUAGE

After reading and practicing a bit with the language called PILOT (Programmed Inquiry, Learning, Or Teaching), Ms. Marong was ready to create her lesson. Wisely resisting the temptation to begin programming the lesson immediately, she took the time to plan the lesson carefully. Her first outline looked something like this:

Shape Sorting

1. Randomly select sorting by shape, color, or size.
2. Shape
   A. Draw a group of geometric shapes in no particular order at the bottom of the screen. Type: "Watch. Some shapes will be sorted."
   B. Draw shapes at the top of the screen, at each side or in the middle, categorizing according to shape.
   C. Draw a shape just below the center of the screen.
   D. Type: "Does this shape go . . ."
   E. Erase shape in middle. Draw identical shape near one of the sorted groupings. Type: ". . . here?"
   F. Accept response. If *not* yes, or no, then type: "Please type in yes or no" and go to beginning of F.
   G. If shape was in correct category
      (1) and response was yes, type: "Right! Let's try another one." Go to the beginning (1).
      (2) and response was no, type: "Yes, it does. Try again." Go to I.

H. If shape was placed incorrectly
   (1) and response was no, type: "That's right. Let's try another place."
       Go to E.
   (2) and response was yes, type: "No, it doesn't. Try again." Go to I.
I. If child responded incorrectly, the first time type: "Look at the sorted
    shapes. Try to figure out how they are alike." The second time, type:
    "Do you think the shapes are sorted by color, size, or shape?" The third
    time, type: "They are sorted by shape." Return to E.
J. Start over (go to 2).
3. Size (similar to shape)
4. Color (similar to shape)

If you trace Ms. Marong's program through step by step, you might
find—as she did, checking it over herself—that there are some errors in
the logic of the program. After a bit more planning and debugging,
however, she was ready to start programming. She first translated the
program into PILOT on paper. Let's look at just a few of the statements
she used (taken from the middle of the program).

`*NEWTRY`	(This is a label for this section of the program)
`U: PLACE`	(*U*ses another section called *PLACE which places the shape near one of the sorted groups and then returns here)
`T: ...here?`	(T: means "*T*ype this")
`A:`	(*A*ccepts student's response)
`M: YES!Y!YEA!NO!N`	(*M*atch—checks if the student typed any of these. The exclamation point is just a separator.)
`JN: YESORNO`	(*J*ump if No, i.e., if there was no match, to the label *YESORNO, which will request a yes or no answer and then return here.)

The program continued. A similar Match command checked to see
if the answer was correct. If not, the student was given a prompt. This
section, labeled I in Ms. Marong's outline, looked like this in PILOT

`T1: Look at the sorted shapes.`	(**T1** means type this for first wrong answer)
`Try to figure out how they are alike.`	
`T2: Do you think the shapes are sorted by color, shape, or size?`	(Type this for the second wrong answer
`T3: They are sorted by shape.`	(Jump back to NEWTRY)
`J: NEWTRY`	

Of course, these are only a few of the statements. To draw the shapes, Ms. Marong used several G: (Graphics) commands. There are many other commands for sound, computations, storing records on disks, linking one program to another, waiting, and so on. One of the powerful features of a good authoring language like PILOT is its editors. These are special programs which allow you to draw shapes, pictures, and characters, or create sound and music for your lesson, using simple commands. When the graphics were ready and the program was first used by a child, it looked like this:

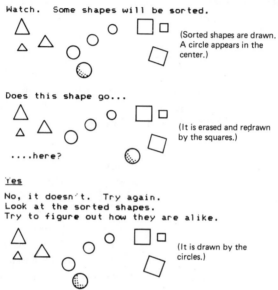

```
Watch.  Some shapes will be sorted.
```

(Sorted shapes are drawn.
A circle appears in the
center.)

```
Does this shape go...
```

(It is erased and redrawn
by the squares.)

```
....here?
```

```
Yes
```

```
No, it doesn't.  Try again.
Look at the sorted shapes.
Try to figure out how they are alike.
```

(It is drawn by the
circles.)

Ms. Marong was still interested in working on the program. She didn't think the children interacted with it enough. A later version responded like this:

```
No, it doesn't.  Try again.

Do you think the shapes are sorted

by color, shape, or size?

color

Are all the yellow shapes together?

no

What IS the same about the groups?

All the squares are together

Yes, the squares are all in one place.

They are ALL sorted by...

shape

Shape!  That's right!...
```

USING AN AUTHORING SYSTEM

An authoring *system* takes advantage of the fact that many lessons follow the same format: Information is presented, questions are asked, and feedback is given based on the student's responses. Authoring systems ask the teacher questions based on this format; that is, the teacher is asked what information is to be presented, what questions are to be asked, and so on. Then the system is able to create a lesson automatically. Systems vary in format. Some use multiple-choice questions, others use blocks of text followed by questions, and some have specific game formats, such as a matching game or a TV show game. Some allow branching or hints to be offered if a student gives an incorrect response. Some permit several correct answers: for example, they allow for an incorrect spelling or will accept either *true* or *t.*

For example, The Shell Games (from Apple) are written in BASIC and require that the teacher replace specific lines of the program (data statements) with new material. For one of the games, the match machine, the teacher types in pairs of items that could be matched into specific lines of the BASIC program. The machine sets up the matching activity, mixing up the options, presenting them in two columns, asking the student for a match, and providing praise or correction.

The Game Show (from Computer Advanced Ideas) is a take-off on the TV show *Password.* Given a set of clues, each player attempts to guess a word or phrase. A number of possible subjects to choose from is already provided; however, teachers and students can insert their own subject area, words, and clues. The program asks you for the name of the subject, the "target" word or correct answer, and a set of clues. You type these in, and a new game is ready to be played. Many more authoring systems are listed at the end of this chapter.

CRITICISMS OF AUTHORING SYSTEMS
AND LANGUAGES

While the idea of writing instructional programs using a language designed specifically for this purpose is appealing, criticisms can be made. Most languages such as BASIC or Pascal have very similar commands. While they usually consist of more than one letter, they may not be that much more difficult to learn to use, if the programmer wants to become proficient in a language. Additionally, learning such a high-level language might be more useful to the teacher in a variety of settings and applications than learning an authoring language, with its more limited application.

Basically, an authoring language is easier to use because it has fewer commands than a computer language. But while this makes the program easier to use, it also restricts the range of possibilities. Some commands, such as PILOT'S M, or MATCH, command, are very helpful and not immediately available in other languages. However, commands for other functions may not be available.

In an authoring language, commands are included that are designed specifically for instructional applications. While this can be helpful, it can also encourage users to adopt and utilize only one instructional strategy—presenting content, questioning, checking answers, giving feedback, going to the next section, and so on. If programs end up as technological page turners, or as endless sequences of the same pedagogical approach—even good Socratic questioning can be tedious if there is no other approach—they will not lead to increased student achievement or improved attitude. Variety is possible, but the nature of the language and commands tends to encourage repetition.

In authoring systems the user fills in material to be presented, as well as questions, examples, answers, hints, and so on, in response to computer prompts. Therefore, the order and method of presentation is preset, or programmed, into the computer. While this gives the user more help, it should be noted that it also reduces the possible teaching strategies he or she can use.

MAXIMIZING THE ADVANTAGES AND MINIMIZING THE DISADVANTAGES

Questions to Ask

A potential user of an authoring system or language might want to ask the following questions:

1. Would I benefit from learning a more powerful computer language with a wider range of applications? Do I have the time to do that?
2. Are the commands available in the system I am considering adequate for the type of courseware I want to write?
3. What are the teaching strategies that are "built into" or encouraged by the program? Are these too limiting? Do they match what teaching strategies I would want to employ?

Avoiding the Pitfalls

When writing computer programs with an authoring language, the following suggestions may help you avoid the pitfalls:

1. Start by considering what you want to teach and how you intend to teach it. Before beginning programming, a well-developed model should exist which includes content and teaching strategies. Where appropriate, have the learner attempt to figure something out for him- or herself. This planning, or design, stage is actually quite extensive. Specifically, it should involve:
   a. Analyzing the instructional needs of your students
   b. Stating the instructional goal
   c. Outlining the instructional program

d. Designing a detailed plan for the program. Depending on the program, you may wish to (1) perform a task analysis, (2) specify objectives and entry behaviors, and (3) develop testing strategies. You will want to plan and sequence specific learning activities and plan how the instruction will be conducted; that is, what teaching methods and strategies will be used. Remember the public speaker's advice: Tell 'em what you're going to tell 'em, tell 'em, then tell 'em what you told 'em.

2. Use "structured programming techniques." Using the model as a guide, break down the project into "mind-sized bites." First, develop structured outlines or flow charts detailing the sequence of activities. Second, lay out the screen presentations or "frame storyboards." Review and revise as necessary. Plan each of the sections in detail as well as the order and branching sequences of the various sections.

3. Document this first draft of the program adequately.

4. Develop each section on the computer as a first draft. Try to

   a. Use simple menu selection when presenting options.

   b. Let the student determine the pace of the program; for example, by pressing RETURN to advance.

   c. Use a variety of types of presentation.

   d. Avoid overusing sound or graphics.

   e. Avoid too much print on the screen at any one time. Double space.

   f. Design the activity so as to involve the learner as often as appropriate. Make requests for learner input clear.

   g. Avoid correction for incorrect answers that is "fun."

   h. Highlight main concepts and ideas.

   i. Debug each section before going on.

   j. Ensure that the learner cannot cause the system to "crash" by typing in an unexpected or unusual response. Check what happens if the learner presses RETURN when entering any information.

   k. Ensure that the sequence you plan—branching and looping back for slow learners, branching ahead for fast learners and those who already know the material—determines to a large extent the effectiveness and efficiency of the lesson. About 80 to 90 percent of the students should correctly answer the mainline questions on the first try.

   l. Plan how performance will be monitored, if that is desired. You may want to plan an assisted quiz with lots of feedback, followed by a lesson summary and a final quiz.

5. Ask colleagues to try out the program and offer suggestions for improvement. Note that if possible, it would probably be beneficial to use a team approach to the development of the lesson. Flaws tend to be caught sooner; and the various suggestions given usually enrich the material. Ideally, one member of the team may be a subject matter expert, another a programming expert, and the last an authority on instructional design.

6. Formatively evaluate first-draft materials. Revise as needed.

7. Field test your program by (a) sitting down one-on-one with one or two students while they use the program, (b) using with small groups, and (c) letting others use it with their classes.

8. Produce final product.

9. Write helpful documentation.

Most of all, be realistic. It would be far easier for most of us to write an entire student textbook for a particular subject for our grade level than to write an extensive, high-quality CAI program. However, programming in authoring languages can still be valuable for several reasons. First, it allows us to experience directly, and thus to really learn about, the thinking that should go into CAI materials. This makes us better critics—we can choose the best from among the wide variety of offerings. Second, we can write programs that we cannot find commercially. Ms. Marong's case provides one example. However, new courseware is being produced daily, and programs that meet her—and your—needs might now be available. It is not as likely, though, that tests that are tailored to your diagnostic needs will be as readily available. It is quite easy to write a PILOT program which will administer tests to children individually, ensure that they are responding logically according to the format (for instance, in a multiple choice, typing in one of the numbers that constitute the optional choices rather than a word, and so on) skip portions they do not seem to need, and record their performance for you to examine at your convenience.

Let's look at brief sections of one such test. Mrs. Ferris wanted a diagnostic instrument for reading that would tell her how her students could perform on the reading materials she was using and that would involve a specific group of skills and abilities with which she was concerned.

A student taking this test was presented with multiple-choice questions. Some were independent, "stand alone" questions; many followed the presentation of a passage taken directly from one of the levels of materials Mrs. Ferris planned on using that year. Students began the test at a level which would be relatively easy for them. Often they read a selected passage, then answered comprehension questions based on it.

If the student typed in anything but a number corresponding to one of the choices, the program would prompt him or her accordingly and ask the question again.

```
WHICH ANSWER IS THE BEST?   (PLEASE TYPE IN A NUMBER.)

HE FELT SAD

I'M SORRY.   I ONLY UNDERSTAND THE NUMBER IN

FRONT OF THE ANSWERS.   PLEASE TYPE IN 1, 2, OR 3.

2

CORRECT.   HE MUST HAVE FELT SAD.
```

If the student ever answered less than 50 percent of the comprehension questions correctly, the test was terminated in a friendly manner. Otherwise, the next higher level was begun.

In the second section of the test, students were asked questions requiring them to use specific reading skills. Only five items dealt with any one skill. If the student did not answer at least four (80 percent) of the items dealing with that skill correctly, he or she was immediately branched to another section of the program which presented a more extensive and diagnostic selection of items. Then Mrs. Ferris would know exactly what the student did and did not know. With this information she could plan special-needs groups and assignments meaningfully and efficiently. If the student answered four or five of the questions correctly, he or she would pass immediately to the items assessing skill in another area.

Mrs. Ferris admitted that developing this test was not easy; however, she has said that she is proud of it and pleased with its benefits, which include the following:

1. She gets a measure of each child's reading level *in relation to the materials he or she will be using.*
2. She gets an extensive picture of each child's strengths and weaknesses.
3. This information is automatically recorded.
4. The program is permanently stored and can be used immediately with children who were absent or who join the class at any point during the year.
5. The program can be added to, or otherwise modified, at any time. With or without these changes, it is "ready to go" the next year.
6. Children enjoy taking the computerized test much more than a paper-and-pencil version—at least in part because of the fun inherent in the medium. Several of the students remarked that they liked when the presentation was personalized with their name and "dressed up" with graphics and sound. Also, and more important in Mrs. Ferris's eyes, the students have not been given items that are too easy, unnecessarily repetitive, or too difficult. This maximizes student time for learning and minimizes boredom and frustration.

Mrs. Ferris is now modifying the program so that it will provide the students with a series of assignments tied to individual performance. These will be used in setting up instructional "contracts" between the students and herself.

Mrs. Ferris used an authoring language. To save time, you might want to use an authoring *system* instead. With a loss of flexibility, this would achieve about the same results with considerably less effort. You need only look for one which closely matches your needs; many are listed at the end of this chapter.

If you have given thought to questions such as those posed above and have decided that an authoring language or system—properly used— would help you in the classroom, you will also undoubtedly find yourself challenged to create more and more useful applications.

Self-Test

1. All authoring languages ask the users what they want to say and write a program for them.
2. Authoring systems, as their name implies, are used for printing out text.

3. Some authoring systems have more structure than others.
4. There is little real difference between an authoring language and high-level languages like BASIC.
5. When the authoring system gives more help, the user's choices are usually decreased.
6. Although PILOT is easier to learn, it has as many commands as other computer languages.

Think About

1. Would you choose to learn an authoring language or a high-level computer language like BASIC or Pascal?
2. Defend or attack:

   Using an authoring language forces a teacher to adopt a certain (narrow?) approach to teaching with microcomputers. Why or why not?

   Children would appreciate CAI material more if their teacher made it.
3. Which of the guidelines for creating software do you think is most important? Irrelevant?
4. What specific applications or needs do you have presently that seem to indicate that you might wish to author CAI programs?
5. Would you use a microcomputer for administering a test you made? Why or why not?

Suggested References

Atherton, Roy. Software standards in BASIC and COMAL. In I. C. H. Smith (ed.), *Microcomputers in education.* New York: Halsted Press, 1982.

Camuse, Ruth. An Apple PILOT primer. *Educational Computer Magazine,* September/October 1982, pp. 20–23.

Christensen, Borge. COMAL—An educational alternative. In I. C. H. Smith (ed.), *Microcomputers in education.* New York: Halsted Press, 1982.

Doyle, Danny. PETCAI: A system for development and delivery of computer-assisted instruction. In I. C. H. Smith (ed.), *Microcomputers in education.* New York: Halsted Press, 1982.

Jelden, D. L. A CAI "coursewriter" system for the microcomputer. *AEDS Journal,* 1981, 14, 159–168.

Smith, Mike. PILOT for the Apple. *Creative Computing,* July 1982, pp. 62; 64; 67–68.

Further descriptions of PILOT can be found in Camuse and Smith. Other authoring languages can be found in Atherton, Cristensen, Doyle, and Jelden.

Bockman, F. Creating your own software with mini-authoring systems. *Electronic Learning,* March 1983, pp. 72–75.

Lubar, David. Authoring systems for the Apple. *Creative Computing,* November 1981, pp. 34; 36; 38.

These readings describe other authoring packages you might be interested in.

Hartman, Ken. **Authoring considerations in writing instructional computer programs.** *The Computing Teacher,* September 1982, pp. 27–29.

Hirschbuhl, John J. **The design of computer programs for use in elementary and secondary schools.** *Journal of Educational Technology Systems,* 1980/1981, 9(3), 193–206.

Isaacson, Daniel. **How to design microcomputer educational programs.** In N. Watson (ed.), *Microcomputers in education: Getting started* (Publication No. 2). Proceedings of the Ninth Annual Math/Science Conference, Arizona State University, January 16–17, 1981.

Magel, Kenneth. **Software engineering principles for courseware development.** *AEDS Journal,* 1980, 13, 144–155.

Roblyer, M. D. **Instruction design versus authoring of courseware: Some crucial differences.** *AEDS Journal,* 1981, 14(4), 173–181.

Schoen, H. L. **CAI development and good educational practice.** *Educational Technology,* 1979, 14(4), 54–56.

Spitler, C. D., and Corgan, V. E. **Rules for authoring computer-assessed instruction programs.** *Educational Technology,* 1979, 19(11), 13–20.

All these readings set up guidelines for construction quality CAI materials.

Representative Authoring Systems

Adaptable Skeleton, from Micro Power & Light Company

Blocks Author Language System and Graphics Library, from San Mateo County Office of Education

CAI-Manager, from Mathware/Math City

CAIWARE, from MicroGnome

Create (series), from Hartley

Educators' Lesson Master, from Aquarius Pub.

Eureka Learning System, from Eiconics

GENIS, from Bell & Howell

Jabbertalky, from Automated Simulations

Magic Spells, from the Learning Company

Micro Test Administration System, from SRA

Microteach, from Compumax

Professor, from Monument Computer Service

Quick Quiz: A Mini-Authoring System, from Radio Shack Outlets

Square Pairs, from Scholastic

Super-CAI Authoring System, from Fireside Computing, Inc.

Teacher Authoring System, from Kyd Tyme Project

Teacher Utilities, from MECC

T.E.S.T and Individual Study Center, from TYC Software

TRS-80 Author I, from Radio Shack Outlets

Authoring Language

COMAL (COMmon Algorithmic Language)

PETCAI (i.e., CAI authoring for the PET microcomputer)

PILOT (many versions for most microcomputers)

SuperPILOT

17

Utility Programs

For many children and their teachers, using the computer as a tool will involve using "canned" programs. Many of these programs are now available, and many more are being created every week. The wide variety of available programs will help you file recipes, phone numbers, and other materials; keep records of your diet and exercise programs; balance your checkbook or generally manage all your home finances; analyze the stock market; write music or create pictures; and so on. Several of the programs we will discuss in this chapter are widely used in homes and businesses. They are called general-purpose, or utility programs, in that they turn the computer into a tool that can be used to solve many problems of a similar type. They can help teachers and students do a variety of tasks while simultaneously familiarizing them with computer applications from the real world.

ELECTRONIC SPREADSHEETS

After word processing and data base management, or filing systems, possibly the most useful "canned" program for professionals would be the electronic spreadsheet. These programs, often termed Calc programs, have for a long time been the most popular microcomputer software packages.

They handle jobs that involve a table of rows and columns filled mostly with numbers that need to undergo numerous repetitive computations.

For example, Mrs. Schifano, an eighth-grade mathematics teacher, decided that rather than purchasing one of the grade book programs (see Chapter 7, Computer-Managed Instruction), she would buy an electronic spreadsheet program. It might take her a bit more time to learn to use, she realized, but then she would be able to use the same tool to do her inventory valuation, home budgeting, and the like. Further, she would illustrate to her principal how it would save hours on budget preparation and requisitions, inventory, enrollment projections, and so on, and to her husband how it could help him with all his income tax calculations. It wouldn't hurt, after all, to have more computers and computer enthusiasts at home and at school. Most important, she was already thinking of some very worthwhile projects her students could do using the program, such as setting up spreadsheet models to solve various problems.

To give us a better picture of how one program could help in so many areas, let's examine how an electronic spreadsheet works. After practicing for a couple of hours with the manual, Mrs. Schifano entered her students' names in the first two columns, followed by the name of assignments and tests. In the appropriate places she entered each student's grade. She was impressed by the ease with which she could move the "window"—the screen can be thought of as a movable window which views one section of a much larger electronic worksheet—and the cursor—which indicated where the next entry would be—to any location she desired, just by touching the arrow keys. She was a bit dismayed when she noticed that she left a student's name off inadvertently; but she then remembered that a whole new row could be inserted, in proper order, by pushing only three keys.

Mrs. Schifano then decided she would like to know what the highest mark, lowest mark, and average was for each assignment or test. She entered these rows. Some of the real power of the program became evident when she decided to compute quarterly grades. She had only to enter a formula for a new column, weighing each assignment and test in any way she chose. For instance, she wanted to weigh the unit test twice as heavily as the other grades. She entered this formula into column G for row 3 (Keith's row): (C3 + D3 + E3 + (2 * F3))/5. This meant, "In this location add up the first three grades plus two times the unit test ("*" is the computer's sign for multiplication) and divide it ("/" is the sign for division) by five." Then, instead of having to write this formula in for every student (row), she merely pressed the keys for the replicate command, which extended the formula to every row she wanted.

Stopping for a minute to think, she printed out a hard copy of her spreadsheet. Sections of this are illustrated in Figure 17-1. Note that she now has a properly weighted average for each student and a minimum, maximum, and average for each test *and* for the student's averages.

G3

$(C3+D3+E3+2*F3))/5$

	A	B	C	D	E	F	G
1	NAME		PAPER 1	PAPER 2	PROJECT	TEST #1	QUAR GR
2							
3	ANDER	KEITH	82	83	77	76	79
4	ANDREWS	CATHY	65		70	51	44
5	BELL	SHARON	95	96	88	83	88
6	BISSEL	DARLENE	85	86	84	82	83
7	CONDOR	CHUCK	94	96	96	91	93
8	CAFFE	BETH	80	93	92	88	87
9	CRANE	DEBBY	80	83	84	83	82
10	DUNES	ALICE	88	89	88	81	84
11	EGLER	GORDON	72	90	94	76	78
12	FRANK	BRIAN	77	82	78	73	76
13							
14	NUMBER		10	9	10	10	10
15							
16	MINIMUM		65	0	70	51	44
17	MAXIMUM		95	96	96	91	93
18							
19	AVERAGE		82	89	85	78	79
20							

FIGURE 17-1   Using the electronic spreadsheet to calculate grades.

For her own information she then proceeded to see what the averages would have been using a different marking plan. She added a column that omitted assignment one and did not give more weight to the unit test. (She could just as easily have changed column G—and, since she saved her work on a disk, she could still reload the old worksheet.) For this she could simply use the AVERAGE function for columns D to F. In this way, she could quickly and effortlessly see "What if . . . ," allowing her to study the effect of different grading plans. At the same time, she was becoming excited about the possibilities for her students to play numerous "What if" exploratory games with projects.

Other changes were just as easy. Several students took a second version of a mastery test, which altered their grade for test number 1. Mrs. Schifano changed these marks and the computer—automatically and almost instantly—recalculated all the statistics, including the maximum, minimum, and average for test 1, each of the student's averages, and so on. When any number is changed, all the other related numbers on the worksheet are changed automatically.

The computer has been beneficial to Mrs. ,Schifano beyond her original expectations. First, everyone—students, parents, teacher, principal—can see students' standing and progress clearly. Just as clearly, the students see how real problems are solved with the help of the computer. They have begun to understand the computer's capabilities and have started working with it on their own projects. This interest has taken many forms. One student impressed his mother by quickly calculating her budget and balancing her checkbook for her home-based retail business.

Others have used the programs just to "play" with data—exploring the effects of different ways of manipulating numbers, formulas, and formats. Still others, to their teacher's delight, have volunteered to help put her inventory of supplies on the computer. Others in the school are beginning to use it for mapping time on tasks, for enrollment projections, and for budget development and maintenance. A junior high school teacher is having his students use it just as an executive would, as a direct simulation of business applications.

There are many arithmetical explorations electronic spreadsheets make possible. One idea is the Multiple-Multiplication Table. (The computer file and full explanation is available in Volume 1, Number 2 of *Window*.) This table shows how an entire table of numbers can be generated from a single number and a set of relationships. In the electronic spreadsheet the first numbers in each row—that is, the top row—and column—the left-hand column—are merely defined as one more than the previous one. Each intersection of these numbers is their product (see Figure 17-2). By changing any of the first numbers, the entire multiplication table is recomputed (see Figure 17-3). The tables that can be generated can help students learn facts and explore relationships—the number patterns that emerge can be fascinating. What patterns can you find?

Older children might use the spreadsheet to investigate conversions, for instance, placing selected numbers representing a certain temperature in Fahrenheit in one column, then defining the next column as Celsius (5/9 of the difference between the first column and 32). Wishing to have his students understand the way changes in the dimensions of two- and three-dimensional shapes affect areas, perimeters, and volumes, one teacher had his students explore this topic with the spreadsheet. For example, one group chose a cube. In the first column (column A) they entered the length of the sides of different cubes. The other columns were defined as the perimeter (12 times A), the area (A times A times 6),

FIGURE 17-2 Using an electronic spreadsheet to explore mathematical relationships: "Multiple-Multiplication Table" (Courtesy, WINDOW, INC.).

MULTIPLE		–	MULTIPLICATION			TABLE						
	1	2	3	4	5	6	7	8	9	10	11	12	13
1	1	2	3	4	5	6	7	8	9	10	11	12	13
2	2	4	6	8	10	12	14	16	18	20	22	24	26
3	3	6	9	12	15	18	21	24	27	30	33	36	39
4	4	8	12	16	20	24	28	32	36	40	44	48	52
5	5	10	15	20	25	30	35	40	45	50	55	60	65
6	6	12	18	24	30	36	42	48	54	60	66	72	78
7	7	14	21	28	35	42	49	56	63	70	77	84	91
8	8	16	24	32	40	48	56	64	72	80	88	96	104
9	9	18	27	36	45	54	63	72	81	90	99	108	117
10	10	20	30	40	50	60	70	80	90	100	110	120	130
11	11	22	33	44	55	66	77	88	99	110	121	132	143
12	12	24	36	48	60	72	84	96	108	120	132	144	156
13	13	26	39	52	65	78	91	104	117	130	143	156	169

```
MULTIPLE  -  MULTIPLICATION    TABLE
      -5   -4   -3   -2   -1    0    1    2    3    4    5
  ----------------------------------------------------------
-5  !   25   20   15   10    5    0   -5  -10  -15  -20  -25
-4  !   20   16   12    8    4    0   -4   -8  -12  -16  -20
-3  !   15   12    9    6    3    0   -3   -6   -9  -12  -15
-2  !   10    8    6    4    2    0   -2   -4   -6   -8  -10
-1  !    5    4    3    2    1    0   -1   -2   -3   -4   -5
 0  !    0    0    0    0    0    0    0    0    0    0    0
 1  !   -5   -4   -3   -2   -1    0    1    2    3    4    5
 2  !  -10   -8   -6   -4   -2    0    2    4    6    8   10
 3  !  -15  -12   -9   -6   -3    0    3    6    9   12   15
 4  !  -20  -16  -12   -8   -4    0    4    8   12   16   20
 5  !  -25  -20  -15  -10   -5    0    5   10   15   20   25
```

FIGURE 17-3   The same table with the first two numbers changed to −5.

and the volume (A times A times A). Entering different lengths for different sides in column A, they were able to explore the effects of changing that length on the other measures (for example, for a side of 1, the columns were 12, 6, and 1; for 2, they were 24, 24, and 8; for 4, they were 48, 96, and 64; for 8 they were 96, 384, and 512). They compared their observations to those of students investigating similar effects on other shapes. Many formulas can be studied in the same way; for example, students learning about interest might vary the rate or time while keeping the principal constant to observe how this affects the interest ($I = P \times R \times T$).

Information from the electronic spreadsheet program also can be transferred to and from a data base management, or filing, system. Now Mrs. Schifano is maintaining all her student information on the computer. She can transfer grades to the electronic spreadsheet program and compute weighted averages and the like. These can then be transferred back into the "files" on the data base management system. This one teacher's success and enthusiasm are spreading. Already the school nurse is keeping immunization records with a similar system; the secretary has used it for enrollment projection; the basketball coach is maintaining and organizing performance statistics and eligibility information; the secretary is planning to store demographic data on students; and the counselor is interested in keeping transcript, interest, and aptitude information on each student. These uses combine two tools, the electronic spreadsheet and a computer-based information system.

FANCY FILING: COMPUTER-BASED INFORMATION SYSTEMS

Recall the students working with the filing system in the chapter on social studies. This section will explain in more detail what an information system is and how a computer-based information system can be utilized in the schools.

Educators everywhere have to be able to store and have access to large amounts of information about students—their names, addresses, dates of birth, parents' names and place(s) of work, medical history, subjects studied, test scores, and so on. All this information is usually kept on cards in filing drawers or in folders in a filing cabinet. Periodically it has to be brought up-to-date. It also has to be referred to for writing reports on a student, charting progress of a group of students, assigning students to classes, determining how many students—and also which students— have scored above or below a certain level, locating all the students who live in a specific area, and so on. The storage of this information, along with the method of organizing and using it in these ways, is an example of an information system.

It can easily be seen that virtually every person and every business uses an information system of some type. Chapter 4 described several uses of such systems. The information itself is coded in some way—usually through words, letters, numbers, and other symbols. These codes represent the information and are called *data*. Updating or otherwise changing this data, sorting or ordering it, and getting hold of some part of it are the kinds of activities which are known as data processing.

To be useful, data must be structured in some way. Consider a list (file) of all the names, addresses, and telephone numbers (records) of all the children in your school system. If they were listed in the order in which they were typed, they would be near useless. You would have to look through thousands to find the one you wanted. If they were in alphabetical order, you would not need to look at more than, say, five or ten. This is a data structure. Most schools would not use just this simple sequential ordering; rather, they would use a hierarchical structure in which the records were first separated by school, then by grade, then by teacher. A computer might use a similar data structure. To find the records of Jonathan Herbeck in Mrs. Demar's sixth-grade class, it would first look at the list of grades, then find Mrs. Demar's class, and finally examine her class list to find Jonathan's records. And it would do this with incredible speed and accuracy. This is still a simple structure. But no matter how complex, it makes it easier to store, retrieve, and process data. A computerized data base system consists of a base of information and computer programs that make it easy to make needed changes in this information or to answer certain questions about the information.

Mrs. Schifano, then, created a file for her student records. Each student had a *record,* or one unit of a *file.* She developed *fields* (the structural parts of the file) for the students' names; for each test, paper, and assignment she gave them; and for their reading level, their interests, and other information—for example, results from a sociogram. (The records and fields that make up a file are often called a data base—hence the term *data base management system* or DBMS.) Part of some students' records, when printed out, looked like Figure 17-4.

```
                    CLASS FILES
                    M. SCHIFANO

DATA FILE: SCHIFANO
DATE OF PRINTOUT: JANUARY 19, 1984
-----------------------------------------

NAME          DARNELL WHITE
READ LVL      9.0
TEST #1       96
PAPER #1      A
ASSIGN #1     99
QUAR 1 GR     95
COMP WEAK     STYLE
INTERESTS     ELECTRONICS VIDEO COMPUTERS
OTHER         BUILDS OWN ROBOTS

NAME          DON ROBERTS
READ LVL      7.5
TEST #1       89
PAPER #1      A
ASSIGN #1     87
QUAR 1 GR     88
COMP WEAK     SPEL SENT PARA
INTERESTS     VIDEO FOOTBALL PUNK MUSIC
OTHER         ALLERGIES

NAME          FRANCIS WILLIAMS
READ LVL      6.6
TEST #1       87
PAPER #1      A
ASSIGN #1     95
QUAR 1 GR     87
COMP WEAK     PRON-AN SUBJ-VE ORGAN
INTERESTS     DANCING   BABY SITTING
OTHER         PARENTS DIVORCED

NAME          JANELL SMITH
READ LVL      8.0
TEST #1       85
PAPER #1      A
ASSIGN #1     95
QUAR 1 GR     91
COMP WEAK     ORGAN PUNC PRON-AN
INTERESTS     BABY SITTING VIDEO   PUNK
OTHER         PARENT DECEASED, WITH MOM

NAME          JAY MEYERS
READ LVL      5.0
TEST #1       82
PAPER #1      B
ASSIGN #1     90
QUAR 1 GR     84
COMP WEAK     SENT PARA SPEL PRON-AN
INTERESTS     HOCKEY TV
OTHER         SEVERAL INTERMUR TEAMS
```

FIGURE 17-4 Using a data base for students' records.

FIGURE 17-4 *(cont.)*

```
NAME        JOE STUDENT
READ LVL    7.5
TEST #1     92
PAPER #1    A
ASSIGN #1   87
QUAR 1 GR   93
COMP WEAK   PUNC SENT
INTERESTS   STAR WARS VIDEO ADVEN BOOKS
OTHER       WRITES ON OWN

NAME        LISA EVANS
READ LVL    5.5
TEST #1     80
PAPER #1    B
ASSIGN #1   78
QUAR 1 GR   77
COMP WEAK   PUNC SPEL PRON-AN
INTERESTS   GYMNASTICS
OTHER       OLYMPIC CONTENDER

NAME        RENE JOHNSON
READ LVL    3.0
TEST #1     78
PAPER #1    B
ASSIGN #1   75
QUAR 1 GR   74
COMP WEAK   PUNC SPEL SENT PARA SUBJ-VE
INTERESTS   ROLLER SKATING PUNK
OTHER       LD NEEDS HELP ON ALL BASICS

NAME        TONY SHARTRO
READ LVL    5.0
TEST #1     80
PAPER #1    B
ASSIGN #1   83
QUAR 1 GR   82
COMP WEAK   ORGAN PARA
INTERESTS   VIDEO MOTORCYCLES MUSIC
OTHER       PLAYS GUITAR IN BAND
```

Using this system was a good way for Mrs. Schifano to store, organize, and retrieve all this information faster and more accurately than she could without the computer—but that's only the beginning. With simple commands she could "call up," or display, any record. She could search the whole file by any field; for instance, she could instruct the computer to find and display the records of all the students who had not completed an assignment, who had averages in math under 75 percent, or who had completed level 18 in reading.

Notice that one field covers weakness in writing. In that field Mrs. Schifano wrote such characteristics as subject-verb agreement, pronoun-antecedent agreement, punctuation, spelling, sentence structure, paragraphing, and so on. When she was ready to teach a lesson on one of these areas, she simply had the computer print a list of all the students who needed this work. This also allowed her to choose specific composition assignments for students which would evoke practice in certain skill areas. She could group children for independent study by sorting them in terms of their interests, or possibly by interest *and* reading level. In the unstructured, or unnamed, category, she would put important, but miscellaneous, information such as home-school correspondence, critical personal information—for example, the recent death of the student's father—and the like.

She could also generate and print out reports. Figure 17-5 illustrates a report of all the students who had completed a science test, ordered by their mark on that test. She could sort her file according to several criteria. For example, she could easily instruct the computer to print out a list of all the students that scored over or under a certain percentage on their final grade, *and* she could have that information sorted in alphabetical order by last name. Or the computer could be told to provide a list of all the students who had completed their special projects in science and social studies *and* were "walkers." She was planning on working after school with whichever students were interested, teaching them to put their project resources on the computer's filing system.

Using such packages with students has many advantages. First, learning to find information is one of the most important goals of education, especially with the present-day information explosion. Students learn to use dictionaries, encyclopedias, and numerous library sources. Increasingly, computers will be used to store and retrieve information. Therefore, teaching children to use computerized sources of information teaches them an important real-world application of the computer. It helps them to better understand the subject matter they are working with. Most important, the data will have to be structured in a certain way,

CLASS FILES
M. SCHIFANO

FIGURE 17-5 A report generation by the data base.

DATA FILE: SCHIFANO
DATE OF PRINTOUT: JANUARY 30, 1984

NAME	TE
RENE JOHNSON	78
LISA EVANS	80
TONY SHARTRO	80
JAY MEYERS	82
JANELL SMITH	85
FRANCIS WILLIAMS	87
DON ROBERTS	89
JOE STUDENT	92
DARNELL WHITE	96

according to set rules. In understanding this structure and applying it, students learn much about informational systems, classification, problem solving, and so on. Since these students will grow up in a world of huge data bases, it is essential that they understand that the knowledge that can be gained from these bases depends on the ways in which the information is structured, stored, and retrieved, as well as the user's comprehension of this structure.

First activities might involve discussions of data and data bases similar to those in the preceding paragraphs. Then talk with students about how a dictionary or phone book is organized. How does one look up a phone number? An address? What do you do if two people have the same first and last names? Suppose you are a detective who has discovered a phone number but does not know who the number belongs to. Would the phone book help you? Why or why not? Would a computerized phone book help more? How?

One teacher had half his social studies class use a DBMS to enter events that occurred in nineteenth-century Europe; the other half entered the major events that occurred in the nineteenth-century United States. The class then instructed the computer to print out all the events for five-year periods. This allowed them to study the relationships between events on two continents. They then analyzed this information to discover facts, and relationships between the facts. Based on these new discoveries, they returned to the data base and asked it for other information, such as a summarization of the war activity and economic state of both continents for specific decades. This tool allowed the students to honestly discover historical ideas for the first time.

An excellent way to use a DBMS is to have students cooperatively enter data for a major unit of study. The entire class first decides what the records and files are to be. For a unit on mammals, the records would be different mammals and the fields would be various characteristics of the mammals. Individuals or small groups of students would then be responsible for entering the information for specific mammals. After the data base has been created, children then use it as a resource for papers or presentations. For example, one student may wish to study only those mammals living in Africa. He could use the SEARCH function of the DBMS to quickly locate and print out reports on every animal that was entered which comes from Africa. Of course, this information—the place of origin—would have had to have been one of the fields the class decided on. Another student might want to investigate the running speeds of the various mammals. She would instruct the system to print out a report in which all the animals were listed, ordered by running speed. Later she might decide to instruct the system to print out a report including only mammals living in the United States, ordered by speed.

The data base of mammals could be used to answer a variety of questions: What is the tallest mammal? Which mammals live in caves?

Which suckle their young (quite a long list!), and so on. What mammals weigh more than 100 kilograms? What about the speed of various animals? Is it true that the more the animal weighs, the faster it can run? (The system could print out a report listing each mammal in order of weight, including only the following information: the animal's name, weight, and running speed. Because the animals would be ordered by weight, it would be easy for the students to ascertain the relationship between weight and speed.) Other similar questions might include: What is the relationship between gestation period and average life span? size? intelligence? Are any characteristics related to the number of young?

Similar data bases and activities could be organized alongside virtually any curriculum area, especially in science and social studies—for example, dinosaurs, plants, or other life forms; planets, geographic regions; or a more focused topic, such as famous mountains; cultures or countries; cities or states; historical figures; and so on.

One DBMS is exceptional for several reasons. First, it was written specifically for children's use. Second, it is quite inexpensive. Third, it is accompanied by an adventure game in which you must learn to use the system to solve a mystery, and it includes several example files and suggestions for school use. The name of the program is Notebook (from *Window*, a learning magazine on a computer disk). The following are just a few of the ways one class used it.

The students kept track of books they had read in a file called Bookfile. Each file represents a report on one book. Students used it to find out what others were reading, to locate books on favorite topics, and to select their next book based on the evaluations of others. Spelling Demons was a simple file that allowed students to enter the spelling words with which they were having trouble. Math Plans allowed the teacher to keep track of where different math groups were in their individualized math plans. The Interest File was used constantly. Almost daily, students retrieved, changed, added, deleted, and sorted information. They used a numerical sort to find out who had the highest Pac-man score. They used the alphabetical sort to learn the range of interests in the class. A few examples of these files can be found in Figure 17-6.

Soon students will be communicating with data bases in schools using computers equipped with a modem, a device that allows communication between computers over phone lines. These data bases will be the encyclopedias, card catalogs, and libraries of the technological society. Again, the ability to understand the use and structure of these data bases will be crucial life and study skills. Furthermore, the challenge of using the computer to find the information they need, and the motivating and positive feeling of quickly and easily satisfying their curiosity, may help students become "hooked" on learning.

```
                    NOTEBOOK BY BILL CROUCH
                    A PRODUCT OF WINDOW, INC.
           469 PLEASANT ST, WATERTOWN MA 02172
           DATA FILE: SPELLING DEMONS
           DATE OF PRINTOUT: AUGUST 9, 1983
           ------------------------------------------------

                    NAME        JANE BREWSTER
                    WORD1       SUCCESS
                    WORD2       SINCERELY
                    WORD3       ABCESS
                    WORD4       CORSAGE
                    WORD5       RECEIVED
                    WORD6       EMBARRASS
                    WORD7       APOLOGIZE
                    WORD8       BARREL
                    WORD9       FINALLY
                    WORD10      HEIGHT
                    UPDATED     9/28/82

                    NAME        SANDRA WHITE
                    WORD1       SPEECH
                    WORD2       BENEATH
                    WORD3       LENGTH
                    WORD4       INVITATION
                    WORD5       GYMNASTICS
                    WORD6       FUNERAL
                    WORD7       THEIR
                    WORD8       DISEASE
                    WORD9       NIECE
                    WORD10      NICKEL
                    UPDATED     9/29/82

                    NAME        KEN APPLETON
                    WORD1       ARRANGE
                    WORD2       RECEIVED
                    WORD3       DISEASE
                    WORD4       FAVORITE
                    WORD5       FOREIGN
                    WORD6       NEITHER
                    WORD7       JOURNEY
                    WORD8       ADVANCE
                    WORD9       THEIR
                    WORD10      BARREL
                    UPDATED     9/29/82

                    NAME        TOM SINCLAIR
                    WORD1       EMBARRASS
                    WORD2       GYMNASTICS
                    WORD3       FOREIGN
                    WORD4       BICYCLE
                    WORD5       INVITATION
                    WORD6       SYSTEM
                    WORD7       RADIATION
                    WORD8       DESSERT
                    WORD9       IDLE
                    WORD10      AISLE
                    UPDATED     9/29/82
```

FIGURE 17-6 Several ways one teacher used *Notebook* (Courtesy, WINDOW, INC.).

A PRODUCT OF WINDOW, INC.
469 PLEASANT ST, WATERTOWN MA 02172
DATA FILE: MATH PLANS
DATE OF PRINTOUT: AUGUST 9, 1983

```
NAME          BARRY FRANK
PLAN          FRACTIONS +/-
WK BEGUN      10/4
WK FINISH     10/25
TEST GR       100
COMMENT       EXCELLENT GRASP OF CONCEPTS

PLAN          PROB/SOLVING
WK BEGUN      11/1
WK FINISH     11/15
TEST GR.      N/A
COMMENT       USED COMPUTER TO DO PS BKLT

PLAN          FRACTIONS X & /
WK BEGUN      12/4
WK FINISH     12/20
TEST GR.      92
COMMENT       RETAINS CONCEPTS

NAME          SANDRA JONES
PLAN          DIVISION 2
WK BEGUN      9/15
WK FINISH     10/8
TEST GR       70
COMMENT       PROBLEMS WITH ESTIMATING

PLAN          ADDITIONAL DIV.
WK BEGUN      DAILYGRP
WK FINISH     DAILYGRP
TEST GR.      88
COMMENT       GRP WITH STUDENT TCHR

PLAN          INTRO. FRACTION
WK BEGUN      10/22
WK FINISH     11/1
TEST GR.      100
COMMENT       UNDERSTANDS EQUIVALENCY

NAME          PAUL O'CONNOR
PLAN          DECIMALS X & /
WK BEGUN      11/6
WK FINISH     12/20
TEST GR       92
COMMENT       EXCELLENT UNDERSTANDING

PLAN          PERCENT
WK BEGUN      1/4
WK FINISH     1/29
TEST GR.      100
COMMENT       GRASP OF %, DECIMAL & FRAC
```

FIGURE 17-6 *(cont.)*

```
                    PLAN          PROBLEM-SOLVING
                    WK BEGUN      2/5
                    WK FINISH     2/25
                    TEST GR.      N/A
                    COMMENT       DESIGNED PS BKLT FOR CLASS


                    NAME          LAUREL HANFORD
                    PLAN          MULTIPLICATION
                    WK BEGUN      9/15
                    WK FINISH     10/10
                    TEST GR       80
                    COMMENT       NEEDS DRILL ON 9&12 TABLES


                    PLAN          INTRO DIVISION
                    WK BEGUN      10/15
                    WK FINISH     10/30
                    TEST GR.      95
                    COMMENT       CAN DO SHORT DIVISION WELL


                    PLAN          2# DIVISION
                    WK BEGUN      11/4
                    WK FINISH     11/30
                    TEST GR.      75
                    COMMENT       KNOWS CONCEPT CARELESS


                    NAME          KAREN GREMLEN
                    PLAN          GRP WK #THEORY
                    WK BEGUN      10/4
                    WK FINISH     10/19
                    TEST GR       95
                    COMMENT       KNOWS PRIMES & COMPOSITES


                    PLAN          GRP WK FRACTION
                    WK BEGUN      10/22
                    WK FINISH     11/2
                    TEST GR.      62
                    COMMENT       PROBLEMS WITH EQUIV.CONCEPT


                    PLAN          GRP WK FRACTION
                    WK BEGUN      11/4
                    WK FINISH     11/18
                    TEST GR.      85
                    COMMENT       UNDERSTANDS EQUIVALENCY


                    NAME          ELIZABETH ORBUN
                    PLAN          DECIMALS +/-
                    WK BEGUN      11/4
                    WK FINISH     11/18
                    TEST GR       100
                    COMMENT       RETAINS CONCEPTS WELL


                    PLAN          DECIMALS X
                    WK BEGUN      11/20
                    WK FINISH     11/27
                    TEST GR.      95
                    COMMENT       UNDERSTANDS CONCEPTS


                    PLAN          DECIMALS /
                    WK BEGUN      12/1
                    WK FINISH     12/14
                    TEST GR.      100
                    COMMENT       EXCELLENT COMPREHENSION
```

```
        NOTEBOOK BY BILL CROUCH              FIGURE 17-6 (cont.)
        A PRODUCT OF WINDOW, INC.
   469 PLEASANT ST, WATERTOWN MA 02172
   DATA FILE: INTEREST FILE
   DATE OF PRINTOUT: AUGUST 9, 1983
   ------------------------------------------

   NAME        MARILYN SMART
   GRADE       6
   FAV.SPORT   BASKETBALL
   VIDEO GME   PAC-MAN
   TOP SCORE   45,569
   DATE T.S.   10/3/82
   FAV.ACTVY   SWIMMING
   FAV.GROUP   LED ZEPLIN
   BEST REC.   I LIKE ROCK & ROLL
   COMMENT     I TAKE MODERN JAZZ. I LIKE
               TO READ BOOKS ABOUT ANIMALS
```

STATISTICS AND GRAPHING PROGRAMS

One other "canned" program which turned out to be useful to all the members of the school—from students, to teachers, to administration—was a plotting and statistics package. It also can send information between the electronic spreadsheet and the data base management system, or it can be used on its own. For instance, by the next quarter Mrs. Schifano was doing much more with her electronic spreadsheet program. She had mastered transferring the information from it to a program which analyzed the data with preset, sophisticated functions, and presented the information in graphic displays such as pie charts, bar graphs, and line graphs. She is now analyzing her test scores more completely, getting standard deviations and correlations with ease. As a result, she is able to show the class and individuals how they are doing in an easily understood, pictorial form. Figure 17-7 shows a printout of one student's progress throughout the first half of the year.

Some of Mrs. Schifano's students have used the electronic spreadsheet and the statistics/plotting program to analyze information they have collected. One group of students conducted a survey of the height of their peers in the school and graphed the results. The definite suggestion of the familiar bell-shaped curve, *and* the deviations from it, provoked quite a bit of thought and discussion. Students used the graphs to help them find and better visualize the mode and median.

The combination of the spreadsheet and the plotting program can lead to many interesting investigations. For example, one class used the spreadsheet to create several series. Starting with the counting numbers in the first column, they defined each succeeding column based on a different transformation of the first column. The second column was twice the first column; the third was the first multiplied by itself, and so on. These series were then plotted, providing a visual representation of the concept of a function, and allowing the comparison of linear to nonlinear functions.

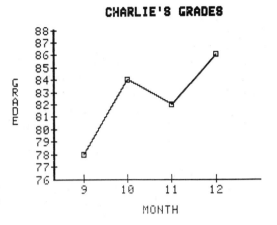

CHARLIE'S GRADES

FIGURE 17-7 Using a graphic program to represent a child's grades.

After three students in Mr. Richman's science class collected data for their pendulum experiment, they entered it into the plotting program, creating a scatter graph. They then decided to change it to a line graph with grid lines. They also changed the scale along the vertical axis. They did this in a matter of two minutes. For other projects they drew graphs with two or three lines, pie charts, bar graphs with one or two bars, and so on. This particular program also calculated statistics for the data, such as the average, the maximum and minimum, correlations, and so on.

As with other utility programs, one of the main advantages of the plotting program lies in the freedom and interest it generates for productive playing or experimenting with the data students have collected. Simultaneously, students are learning a "real world" application, and they are getting a feel for fairly complex mathematical ideas—similar to the feel a young child gets for the idea of the relationship between the heights and widths of containers by pouring water or sand from one to the other. For Mr. Richman's students, the computer conducts the complex calculations, while the students immediately see the results of the graphs or calculations they requested. At a later time they will understand more fully the mathematical basis for the calculations—but now they are building an intuition about them that they could *not* have developed without the support of the computer and the program.

Teachers of mathematics in the middle school know that children often have difficulty understanding how one extreme number can affect the mean, or average, of a group of numbers. One teacher had her students use the statistics program to compute their average and range, mode, median, standard deviation, and so on—which are automatically supplied by the program—add a very low or high number, and compute the average and other statistics again. This allowed them to concentrate on the effects of different quantities on a distribution. Then students entered figures representing people's wages, heights of girls and boys, prices of houses in a neighborhood, and so on. Again they investigated the effects of an extreme value. Furthermore, they discussed which measure of central tendency— the mean, median, or the mode—was the most appropriate for a given situation. For example, for the prices of real estate in a neighborhood with many middle-range houses and two $250,000 houses, the median or mode would be more appropriate. Students could easily see this by examining the figures from the statistics program.

The program can, of course, be used in many ways. Students might graph their progress in spelling. Others might use it to display the results of their school poll (Figure 17-8). An illustration of how the meaning of graphs themselves depends on how they are structured or formatted can be dramatically shown on the microcomputer. With Charlie's permission, Mrs. Schifano showed the graph of his grades to the class (Figure 17-7) and asked them about the impressions they got from it. With a few keystrokes she changed the range of the vertical axis, and within seconds the students were looking at the same information on the same type of graph, with only one alteration (Figure 17-9). But it was clear from the ensuing conversation that they received a very different impression of Charlie's progress—and gained a deeper understanding of data representation.

The students are not alone in their delight with this program. Teachers are using it to develop visuals for their classes; and the principal and superintendent can show board members and parents, pictorially, where money is spent.

UTILITY PROGRAMS: SOME GUIDELINES

The following are suggested guidelines for using any utility program.

1. Regardless of the subject area you are teaching—reading, language arts, mathematics, science, or social studies—consider how utility programs such as those described in this chapter might be used.

FIGURE 17-8   Student-generated graph: The result of a poll.

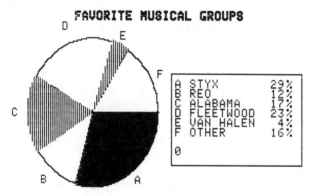

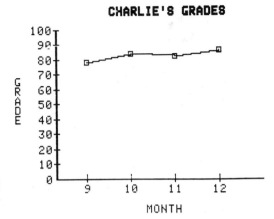

CHARLIE'S GRADES

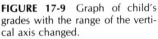

FIGURE 17-9 Graph of child's grades with the range of the vertical axis changed.

2. Emphasize use of the programs by students. When they actually have to decide on how to use the program, they gain deeper knowledge of the program as well as of computers, computer applications in the world, *and* of the subject matter. This kind of active, guided-discovery learning should be a high priority.

3. As applications arise in particular subject matter areas, ask first, "What is the important structure of this information?"

   In electronic spreadsheets the structure to be thought out involves (a) the content of the rows and columns and their relationships and (b) the mathematical formulas to be employed.

   In information systems the structure includes the content and relationships of the file, the records, and the fields, as described above.

   In statistical/graphing programs, the relationships between the data sets, and between the data sets and the format of the graph(s), needs to be considered.

4. Maintain a balance between teacher-controlled projects (useful especially when introducing a new tool or extending children's knowledge of the tool or of a specific facet of subject matter knowledge) and student-initiated projects.

Self-Test

1. An electronic spreadsheet program is useful, but only to administrators.
2. Numbers and formulas for each cell of an electronic spreadsheet program have to be carefully entered one at a time.
3. All information systems structure their data (information).
4. One of the big advantages of using an electronic spreadsheet is the ability to experiment; to ask "What if."
5. Using utility or "tool" programs helps students connect schoolwork with the real world.
6. Filing programs would be useful to school staff, although children could not have much use for, nor interest in, these programs.

7. Most teachers have never used *any* type of information system.
8. An electronic spreadsheet works primarily with numbers.
9. An information system works primarily with numbers.
10. Children should be taught about data processing and its use in larger businesses, but it is not an appropriate activity for the elementary and middle schools.
11. Data base management systems and filing systems are two completely different things which should not be considered as similar.
12. Symbols that represent information are called data.

Think About

1. How would you construct a social studies project for students which would encourage them to use a data base? What prerequisite abilities would your students have to have? How about you?
2. What lessons or units do you teach presently which would be enhanced by the use of an electronic spreadsheet, a filing system, or a plotting program? What place could the "computer as tool" play in these lessons?
3. List three uses you would have at school or home for tool programs such as those discussed in this chapter.
4. If you had to choose one tool program to use with your class, what would it be? Why?
5. Learn about a filing or data base management system by using one. Possibilities include Notebook (especially written for children from *Window*); VisiFile (from Personal Software); PFS (from Software Publishing Company); and many others.
6. Attack or Defend:

    There is too much subject matter to be covered in most content areas to spend time working with computers.

    "Real" books and libraries will never be replaced by electronic means.

    If children do not learn how to use real encyclopedias, card catalogs, and dictionaries first (before using a computer to look up information), their study skills will never have a firm foundation.

    More "tool" programs requiring little or no knowledge about computers will be available in the future. Therefore, use of these tools should be taught rather than programming itself. Most children will not be computer programmers.

    Since the tool programs will become increasingly user friendly and therefore easier to use, it is unwise to teach children to use the relatively "primitive" ones of today.

    Having children draw a graph with a computer is (a) a waste of valuable computer time and (b) poor educational practice—children would learn more by drawing the graph themselves.

    The use of tool programs such as the electronic spreadsheet should be taught in business courses, not in elementary and middle schools.
7. *Window* contains a series of electronic spreadsheet applications you might wish to investigate.

18

Are There Dangers
in the Computer World?

Besides providing the opportunity for better living, each of the new developments of the twentieth century has also caused difficulty. For example, while the automobile has increased our standard of living and provides a great deal of pleasure, it also causes death, crippling injury, pollution, and depletes our natural resources. Television was hailed as a major breakthrough in communications. There was the suggestion that with television there would be a giant leap in the educational level of the general population. Television still has a great deal of potential to educate. At the present time the average person in the United States spends more hours in front of the television than at work or at any other activity (about forty-eight hours a week). However, the top-rated programs are adult soap operas, sports programs, and situation comedies.

Educators are faced with a similar problem when considering the computer. Several of the questions to be considered by the thoughtful teacher are listed below. In the remainder of the chapter, we discuss each question more fully.

1. Is the computer always right? What are the problems of blindly accepting computer information?
2. How do we decide when we should and when we shouldn't use the computer?

3. How much time should we spend with computers? In instruction? For our work? For our leisure?
4. How much can we use the computer in decision making?
5. How are video games to be used? Are they harmful? Are they helpful?
6. What are the ethics of reproduction of computer disks?
7. What effect will automation have on our lives? What can be done?
8. Can the computer be held responsible? How?
9. What is "computer crime"?

IS THE COMPUTER ALWAYS RIGHT?
WHAT ARE THE PROBLEMS OF BLINDLY ACCEPTING
COMPUTER INFORMATION?

Computer excuses have come to replace the "lost in the mail" and "my secretary must have forgotten" explanations for not following through on a task.

For example, several months ago a student came to one of the authors and said, "I tried to register for your class and couldn't. It was filled, so I came tonight to see what I could do."

There were twenty-five people in the class, and the author felt that he could take up to thirty, so he called registration and asked for help.

The person reached said, "The room you're assigned to is listed as holding twenty-five. The computer is programmed to allow no more than twenty-five to register. You'll have to change the room you are in to get the student registered."

This wasn't a major problem, and the author was able to use an alternate procedure to register the student; but this is representative of the many times a computer is incorrectly programmed and the information is considered as unalterable. Also, there is somewhat of a mystique concerning the computer. Many people think it can do almost magical things. They don't associate the things a computer does with the programmer who developed the procedures for its use.

The problem of reliance on nonhuman information has been with us for quite a while. Students in many classes argue with their instructor concerning a point by suggesting that their point *has* to be right because it is in the book written by the instructor with whom they are arguing. Information can be wrong in books and certainly can be wrong in computer programs. Also, errors in computer results can occur due to weather conditions, power surges, dust, or a variety of other factors.

Joseph Weizenbaum of MIT is one of the pioneers in the so-called artificial intelligence languages. He relates a situation which caused him to completely rethink his position on computers. He developed an interactive language called Eliza (for Eliza Doolittle, of "My Fair Lady" fame). Weizenbaum used the language to develop a program that followed closely the type of counseling session Carl Rogers, the psychologist, would have conducted (Weizenbaum, 1976).

The following dialogue might occur:

Program: How are you feeling?
Patient: Not too well.
Program: Oh, you're not feeling too well? What do you think is wrong?
Patient: I'm upset about my daughter.
Program: What did your daughter do to upset you?
Patient: She is moving to an apartment.
Program: Do you feel your daughter shouldn't move to an apartment?

The program continues on in a similar manner, making use of the comments made by the individual at the terminal.

Weizenbaum demonstrated his program at a meeting of psychiatrists as an example of artificial intelligence. Several of the physicians came up to him after the presentation and asked about the availability of the program and indicating that they would like to use it with their patients. Weizenbaum was upset; he did not believe that the program was at all ethical for use with patients. Incidents such as this caused Weizenbaum to take a year off for study and consider the role of computer and humans.

Here are several suggestions for getting children to consider the relationship between the computer and the human programmer.

1. Have the students keep track of computer errors mentioned in newspapers, on television, and by persons around them. Have them consider the question: What caused the error? A programmer? Computer malfunction? Error unknown? To motivate the children, give a prize or a title to the one who finds the most cases.
2. Discuss the role of the people who work on programs. For example, the Scott, Foresman CAI programs are developed by from ten to twenty persons. If a program has an individual author, emphasize the author's name. Get some of the students who like the program to write to the author.
3. If you're playing a game on the computer, suggest that they are playing the programmer rather than the computer. For example, when playing chess on the computer, find out who your opponent is; that is, who developed the chess program.

HOW DO WE DECIDE WHEN WE SHOULD
AND WHEN WE SHOULDN'T USE THE COMPUTER?

This question is closely tied to the previous question. The comments of Weizenbaum are as appropriate for this question as for the last. Let's look at a teaching situation which got to the heart of the issue.

Janet's fifth-grade class was studying Michigan as part of the social studies program. One of the children asked (in a question-raising session),

"I read that many auto workers are being replaced by computer robots. Should this be done?" Her question caused a good deal of discussion, from which a series of questions concerning computer use came forth. They included the following:

1. Should computers replace human beings in work settings? If so, when and when not?
2. Should computers be used to store information on people—even if they don't want it stored?
3. How can we prevent our personal life from being invaded by computers?
4. How much "thinking" should we let computers do?
   Sub Questions:
   a. Can computers think?
   b. What do we mean by "think"?
   c. How are computers different from people?

These questions were of so much interest that it was decided to spend a week at the end of the Michigan unit trying to find answers to the questions. In the mean time, the children were challenged to try to find information that would help them arrive at some answers to the questions.

As can be noted, the majority of questions involve opinion as well as facts. The children first gathered facts concerning the amount of jobs that were being lost to computers, what authorities believe "thinking" to be, and the difference between relative statements and absolute statements.

Janet had done some work with "philosophy for children," developed at Montclair State in New Jersey, and she made use of a few of the exercises from that program to help the children in their thinking. The exercise on fairness, below, is one example.

Fair or Right?

A. In the space provided, fill in either "fair," "unfair," "right," or "wrong."

1. Every citizen should have an equal vote.
2. Every man is entitled to have his wife prepare a home-cooked meal for him every day.
3. All prisoners must be flogged twenty times each evening at 4 P.M.
4. All firstborn males shall be put to death.
5. The defendant was tried by a jury of his peers.
6. The teacher allowed James to take the exam before it was given to the rest of the class. (Lipman, 1983)

(Note: The original exercise contained twelve questions.)

After a great deal of study, discussion, and several planned debates, the children arrived at the following generalizations:

1. We face a very real problem as concerns computers replacing people. It is not new—the problem first occurred with machines driven by animals, then with steam and gas machines, and now with computers.
2. Each new replacement of people adds to the growing total.
3. It would be good if there were some criteria developed for ethical limits of machine use.
4. Machines do store too much private information. We should limit these big data machines. It would be preferable to have "private" computers.
5. If we don't want computers to invade our lives, we need to do less things that computers have control over—credit cards and the like.
6. Can computers think? It depends upon what you consider thinking to be. Some computer authorities say yes; some say no.

HOW MUCH TIME SHOULD WE SPEND WITH COMPUTERS? IN INSTRUCTION? FOR OUR WORK? FOR OUR LEISURE?

There are a variety of opinions as to how much time children should spend in computer-assisted instruction. However, the issue is still academic, since there aren't enough computers at the elementary/middle school level to go around. But in the future we will need to answer this question. The question is closely related to an older question concerning individualized instruction. There were those who felt that it was sound to have children work on their own for the entire day.

Nevertheless, research revealed that the large majority of plans for individualized instruction produced poorer achievement. There have been several reasons suggested for this phenomenon. For example, it has been proposed that children learn better in a social, interactive setting than they do by themselves. This would appear to be true. Several years ago I toured a computer-assisted-instruction facility with about twenty terminals and a group of twenty students. It was late in the school year. The children had been working on drill-and-practice material in mathematics for about seven months. I found that many of the children sitting in the same area were on the same computational example. They were not copying each other's work but were staying at about the same place so they had someone to work with and with whom they could talk about their work.

Another reason for the failure of completely individualized programs is the lack of teacher involvement. A leading developer of individualized materials who decided that the approach didn't work concluded that the children worked harder and learned more when the teacher was actively involved, leading discussions, testing, and so on. He felt that the children considered the instruction important because the teacher took the time to be involved. They felt the individualized time was considered less important because the teacher was not actively involved.

What about CAI? There is no doubt that a good CAI program can make the student feel involved in dialogue. Thus, some of the problems of pencil-and-paper individualization are removed. However, the writers believe that individual CAI involvement should not exceed an hour a day—perhaps longer, if two or three children work together.

Too much time viewing a computer video monitor may cause eyestrain. This would suggest that only a portion of the day should be spent in this way. Also, if any great length of time is to be spent on word processing or on CAI, it is important to use a monitor rather than a converted TV set. The monitor gives higher resolution, which makes letters and numerals much easier to read.

If children are involved with computers in school for CAI and for programming, it is probably wise to suggest a very moderate amount of involvement outside the classroom. If a child has ready access to a computer at home, it may be well to have the child take part of the CAI or programming work home and work in a more social setting at school.

HOW MUCH CAN WE USE THE COMPUTER IN DECISION MAKING?

A fine set of materials for introducing children and adults to BASIC is produced by the Center for the Humanities. One of the slide tape presentations has a BASIC program that computes the batting average of a baseball player and then prints out GO or STAY—if they are to be sent down to the minor leagues based on their average. Almost everyone using the material recognizes that no one would make such a decision based on one piece of information. However, that material would be a good place to start a discussion concerning computers and decision making (Communications Park Group, 1981).

One teacher used the baseball program and then asked, "Would you send whole groups of persons down to the minor leagues if their batting averages dropped below a specific score?" The students interested in baseball indicated that they would want much more information. They would want to know the fielding of the player. Another mentioned that it would be impossible to decide without watching the player in action for a long period of time. For example, a player could have a good fielding average but not be good enough to attempt very hard plays which would result in errors.

Next the teacher asked, "Are there decisions that we could make by putting the information in our computer and then asking for a decision based on that information?" One of the children suggested that the teacher might use it for making out grades. She suggested that each of the grades could be recorded, and a program could be developed by which the teacher could give added weight to certain projects or tests and could put in a grade for class participation. The teacher indicated that there were programs of this sort developed for the majority of microcomputers. The next day the teacher brought in three such record-keeping programs and demonstrated them to the class. She asked, "Do you think I could grade you fairly using one of these programs?"

The class discussed the merits of each of the programs and indicated a difference of opinion as to whether or not it would be a good idea to use the program. They developed a brief set of criteria for deciding whether or not a computer program could be used as a major means of decision making. Their list included the following:

1. Write down the information you use in making decisions.
2. Decide if the information could be indicated by numbers. Could a grade be given in numbers—could the various traits of a football player be put into numbers?
3. How much does your overall experience go toward deciding something? Can this be put into numbers?
4. Is it fair or "right" to make a decision based on a computer composite?

As they continued their discussion, one of the class members interested in football said he thought the coaching staff of his favorite professional team used a computer to help in deciding about the draft choices they were going to make. He believed that they fed the information into the computer with numbers given to the specific traits, and then the staff sat down and decided if they agreed with the rating.

This particular class agreed that they would use the computer to help them decide—but they would then review the information given by computer analysis.

HOW ARE VIDEO GAMES TO BE USED?
ARE THEY HARMFUL? ARE THEY HELPFUL?

If you are beginning a discussion of the helpful and harmful effects of the computer on everyday life, it is probably well not to begin with the subject of computer games (video games). By and large, children are quite positive about video games, and a large portion of the adult population has very mixed feeling about these games.

One teacher used video games as a topic in a social studies unit at the sixth-grade level concerned with "controversial issues." One committee decided to explore the issue and present the information in a round-table discussion. As part of the exploration, each committee member was to treat the issue using the following approach:

All agreed that they needed to listen and to have respect for other opinions. They needed to think about such matters as

1. What is my position on the issue?
2. What do I believe to be true without thinking about the issue?
3. Are there other beliefs that have as much validity as mine?

4. How else might I look at the issue?
5. How much does my past experience affect how I think about the issue?
6. How do others I like think about the issue?
7. What evidence (other than opinion) do I have about the issue?
8. Can I find "real" evidence to back up my point of view?
9. How can I decide if evidence is true?
10. I must avoid fallacies such as
    a. attacking the person who makes an argument rather than the argument itself. For example, "I don't believe him. His dad is out of work."
    b. appealing to an authority who is not an authority on the particular topic. For example, "One of the NFL coaches thinks that video games improve kids' timing" (but hasn't any information other than his opinion).
    c. jumping to a conclusion about cause and effect. For example, "There have been drugs found at video game rooms. Therefore, I better not let anyone play video games in my home, for they will want to use drugs."

The children gathered information from magazine articles and books. They asked the librarian for help in exploring all sources of information. One group phoned a professor who was making a study on the question, Are video games helpful or harmful?

One of the major points that came out of their work was the need for individuals to make good decisions about the use of their time. As an outgrowth of the committee work, a one-week study called "How I spend my time," was conducted by the class. Class members were amazed at the amount of time spent watching television. The students then made priorities for using their time and compared their use of time with their priorities. Many found that they spent much of their time on low-priority items, while they had little time for high-priority items.

A Note: I believe that we teachers have a responsibility to help children look at the way they spend their time. Whether or not a family spends three to four hours each evening playing video games, reading, working on crafts, or in community service is a decision that each family or person must make. However, we can help children decide whether or not they wish to engage in a variety of activities. At present, I find that most children spent either very little or very much time on video games.

WHAT ARE THE EFFECTS OF THE COMPUTER ON THE HOME?

A group of eighth graders were looking at the merits of a variety of microcomputers for home and school use. The teacher asked, "What is the effect on a family of having a microcomputer at home?" After a discussion the class developed a questionnaire to be administered to a sample of families that had home computers. In order not to invade the privacy of the families, each questionnaire was placed in unmarked envelope.

The class asked questions such as:

About how much time per week do you use your computer for

Games
Word processing
Financial work
Other business activities
Home filing

Who uses the computer—hours per week?

Father
Mother
Son
Daughter

Add other sons and daughters—mark out the names if they do not apply to your family. For example, if the family is a mother and two daughters, put a line through father and through son and add another daughter.

Are you glad you have a computer?

(The directions indicated that each family member, whether or not they used the computer, was to assign a number from 1 to 10 to their feelings about the computer. One (1) indicated that they wished they didn't have the computer, and 10 indicated that they enjoyed the computer.)

WHAT ARE THE ETHICS OF REPRODUCTION OF COMPUTER DISKS?

This is one of the major problems facing the developers of instructional materials. While the majority of commercial computer disks are "protected" from being copied, thousands of microcomputer users have found ways of copying the programs. In many ways it is a bigger problem than the unauthorized xeroxing of written materials and the reproduction of audio tapes. If a book is 200 pages long and costs $15, the cost per page is under 8 cents. Xeroxing in great quantities is not very economical. On the other hand, a particular computer disk may cost from $10 to $400, depending on the developmental costs and the sales potential. For example, the majority of word processing programs for the popular microcomputers range in price from $85 to $350, with a median of about $150. It has been estimated that there are two unauthorized copies of each program for every one that has been sold. This is probably a conservative estimate. These disks aren't like xeroxed copies of books. For if they have been copied correctly, they are exact copies of the original and are every bit as good.

Teachers need to explore the questions that follow for themselves and help children to understand the problem.

1. Why do some programs cost so much, when they are so easy to reproduce? Is it due to developmental costs, limited audience, greed, distribution costs, some other factors?
2. What is the law concerning reproduction of copyrighted disks? (Note: if the distributor indicates that the disks are not to be reproduced, the purchaser usually has the right to reproduce one disk for a back-up.)
3. What is the role of the teacher in dealing with this problem?
4. What are both sides of the disk reproduction controversy? (Several references are given at the end of the chapter).

WHAT EFFECT WILL AUTOMATION HAVE ON OUR LIVES?

One middle school teacher had a class that was studying the Industrial Revolution as part of seventh-grade social studies. The teacher led the class to consider the effect of the current computer revolution. Among the areas that were explored were (a) current robots in the auto industry, (b) computers in the telephone service, and (c) future questions such as

> Can computer-assisted instruction be developed to the point where we won't have school in the traditional sense? Will most children study at home on a computer? What might happen to teachers? Will they do anything other than develop computer programs?
>
> Will secretaries be replaced by computers that can directly type out dictation? (We now have attachments to computers such as the Apple II that can recognize up to a hundred words and act upon them—and these attachments are not prohibitively expensive.)
>
> Will computers do all the cleaning in large buildings?
>
> How many people will work at home on computer terminals?
>
> Will computers replace books?

While many of these questions seem a little far out, they really are not—if things change as rapidly in the next twenty years as they did in the past twenty years. Some sociologists indicate that changes in society occur as rapidly in ten-year periods today as they did in hundred-year periods up until the 1900s. Consider the changes between 1940 and today: atomic energy, television, radar, jet planes, rocket ships, computers, changes in family lifestyle, changes in morals, changes in the economy, and on and on.

To be responsible members of society in this changing world, the elementary/middle school student of today must learn a host of thinking, deciding, and valuing skills that were not as crucial in the past. Is the school the proper place to develop these skills?

WHAT IS "COMPUTER CRIME"? HOW DOES IT AFFECT THE COUNTRY?

There are numerous forms of computer crime, but the one most often discussed involves having one computer change the response of another computer. Crimes have included both drawing money from banks and putting nonexistent money in banks. Too often the computer criminal has been considered a clever "Robin Hood." This notion needs to be faced head on in the classroom. A discussion of the effects of such crime upon others needs to be carefully explored. Teachers cannot wink at computer crime any more than they would condone the same crime committed with a gun.

Self-Test

There is no self-test on this chapter because of the subjective nature of the material. The Think About section should provide any needed "self-test."

Think About

1. The chapter has dealt with a number of sensitive issues. Does the school have the right or the responsibilty to deal with each of these issues? If not, which issues should be considered?
2. How would you handle this comment, "My dad duplicates game disks for all the families in our area. One family buys one and dad makes twenty copies. Should he do this?"
3. How do you feel about video games? Why? What evidence do you have? What is your responsibility to get more information?
4. Should there be a standard sequence of topics concerned with ethics and computers developed for each school system?
5. If you answered yes to question four, how would you go about developing them?
6. How would you develop a laboratory that would help children decide when and when not to use a computer?
7. What do you think the role of computers should be in teaching?
8. Should we ever limit computer use when the computer can do a job better than a person can?
9. Some computer-oriented persons believe that given the choice between saving a computer that has helped them and saving others or a person of little achievement, the computer should be saved. What are the ramifications of such thinking?
10. Do computers take something away from the dignity of humans?

Suggested References:

Conniff, Richard. Computer war. *Science Digest,* January 1982, pp. 14–94.
Conniff comments on computers and war. How do you react to his notion of using the computer to "foul up" an opponent's economy?

Grout, Bill. Piracy—A serious threat or unfounded fear? *Microcomputing,* July 1982, pp. 76–82.
Study Grout's suggestions concerning software piracy.

Howe, Charles L. Coping with computer criminals. *Datamation,* January 1982, pp. 119–128.
Howe makes suggestions for reducing computer crime. How can his suggestions be used by teachers in the classroom?

Peterson, Ivars. Computer crime: Insecurity in numbers. *Science News,* July 1982, pp. 12–14.
Peterson suggests that computer crime may cost $5 billion a year to American citzens. Study his data. What implications does this have for teaching computer ethics?

Robinson, Sharon P. Questions for teachers. *Today's Education,* April/May 1982, pp. 27–28.
Robinson raises some issues concerning teachers and computers. What are the ethics of teacher replacement by computers?

Westin, Alan F. Information abuse and the personal computer. *Popular Computing,* August 1982, pp. 112–116.
Westin gives an overview of invasion of privacy by computer data banks. Study his material carefully.

Bibliography

BASIC: An introduction to computer programming. Mount Kisco, N.Y.: Communications Park Publishing Group, 1981.

LIPMAN, MATTHEW, SHARP, ANN MARGRET, AND OSCANYAN, FREDERICK S. *Instruction manual to accompany LISA.* Upper Montclair, N.J.: Institute for the Advancement of Philosophy for Children, 1983.

WEIZENBAUM, JOSEPH. *Computer power and human reason.* San Francisco: W. H. Freeman and Co., 1976.

Keeping Up-to-Date

In studying an issue such as the use of computers in elementary/middle school education, there is always the problem of staying current, or keeping up-to-date. While there is no easy way to solve this problem, if you heed the suggestions that follow, you should be able to effectively function in this ever-developing field.

1. Read, read, read. In the appendix there is a rather long list of published materials available in this area. Probably the most important source of material is the journals; while books are crucial for obtaining the general principles and basic ideas and for studying in depth, in a rapidly developing field they are not as current as are journals.

The journals are constantly changing. For example, the authors began with a subscription to one computer journal in their math center four years ago and have had three different journals from this order. A journal may be taken over by another journal, it may go out of business, or it may change its name.

It is not possible to subscribe to all the journals, so try to select one or two that you feel are most helpful to you. Try to have your building subscribe to others. If this is not possible, visit libraries, local colleges and universities, and magazine stands. Once or twice a year buy a copies of a journal that gives a different focus than those to which you subscribe. For example, *Byte* magazine deals with hardware in a rather technical fashion but has many good articles on software. It also has many, many advertisements for the current new hardware and software. Once a year there is an issue which emphasizes education. We purchase the education issue and usually one other issue.

On the other hand, *Classroom Computer News, The Computing Teacher, Electronic Education,* and *Electronic Learning* all have articles in each issue that are helpful in keeping up-to-date on computers in education. Try to find three or four interested teachers and each subscribe to one of the computer education journals—then exchange the journals on a monthly basis.

Develop the skill of skimming articles. Often there are a number of articles which basically cover the same topic. Each month we find several articles dealing with teaching the LOGO language. While some contain new ideas, many repeat information we already know. We quickly skim the article (taking about two minutes) looking for ideas we haven't seen before. If we begin to see a new approach, we start over and read the article thoroughly.

2. Keep a notebook. Use whatever type you find to be handy. We often find that a steno pad is useful. When you skim an article in a journal that you don't own, make a brief annotation of the sources and a sentence on the unique content. Then several days later, when you decide you want to see the article or suggest it to someone else, you will be able to check in your pad for information. Once you become proficient with the microcomputer, you can make use of one of the many filing systems (often called data base management systems) to keep your notes. In fact, if you have a machine like the TRS 80 100 or the NEC lap computer, you can take your electronic notebook along with you. (By the way, these two very small computers are effective for word processing and programming as well as for note keeping.) Here's a format we've found useful. First we'll provide the complete format and then our shorthand summary.

Long Form:

Lias, Edward J. Which micro? It's academic. *Electronic Learning,* January 1983, pp. 20–22.

Lias, a manager of education marketing at Sperry Univac, argues that the computer you buy today is not crucial, but what you want to do with it is. He suggests evaluation on (1) word processing, (2) problem solving with BASIC, (3) data bases, (4) network data banks, (5) electronic spreadsheets, and (6) statistical calculation systems (also perhaps LOGO and CAI below grade four).

Reaction: For elementary school I believe LOGO, CAI, and word processing are top priority, with data file next. HARDWARE.

Short Form:

Lias, E. J. (at Sperry Univac). Which mic.? It's academic. *El Lear* 1–83 p. 20 (6 criterion select:WP;BASIC;data B;network;visc.;stat.(LOGO and CAI)secondary.HARDWARE.

Take your notebook along and jot down comments from others you are talking with. Take notes on new products as you read magazines or get information from a computer store.

If you have a computer available, you may want to keep your notes on a data file system. Then you can quickly get your information together by asking for a key word such as *hardware*. There are a number of file programs available for the current crop of microcomputers. They vary in their complexity; some can alphabetize as well as search. As mentioned previously, they are also useful for a number of teaching and pupil activities.

3. Attend conferences. Pick these with care. It is very important that there be others you can talk with and share information with, that there be good displays of hardware and software, and that there be good speakers. You will find that the more you learn and the more you keep up-to-date, both the conversations you have with others of like interest and the displays are of greater use than many of the presentations. Remember to keep your notebook handy.

4. Develop ways of remembering information. Many of the companies and products have very similar names. Recently a coworker couldn't find out about an order because he received taped messages each time he called the company from which he had bought a computer. When the company called back a day later, he found that it was not the company with which he was doing business. His company was Computer Systems Center, Inc., and he had called Computer System Center. Many word processing programs have similar names, for example: Word Wizard and Text Wizard; Magic Screen and Magic Wand; Word Juggler and Word Handler.

5. Attend credit courses and workshops. If you attend credit courses, be sure to work out (with your instructor) ways in which your papers and projects will have relevance to your interests, your work, and the equipment you have available. Be creative in getting the most out of courses and workshops.

6. Try out new ideas in your classroom. Make use of children as resources: As children of the computer age, they can often be of real help in getting started on projects.

7. Work closely with administrators; let them know your interests and needs. If you are able to get equipment from a principal or curriculum director, be sure to invite these individuals to your room for a demonstration.

8. Keep close contact with parent groups and interested parents. They can often be of help in obtaining materials and in helping you "keep up."

9. Make use of intermediate district resource centers. They often have materials that can be checked out for trial use. Also, they may give workshops.

10. Make use of salespeople for various software companies. Get on

their "new product" mailing list. Get trial disks from them. Many will loan out a disk for up to a month. Be sure to handle the disks with care, and do not attempt to duplicate them (unless given permission by the salesperson).

11. Join local and national organizations concerned with computers in the elementary/middle school. Take an active part. You will find many people with whom you can discuss issues and share information.

Self-Test

1. Keeping up-to-date on the topic of computers in the elementary/middle school requires more effort than keeping up-to-date on a typical subject matter area.
2. You can be reasonably certain that all the information of interest will appear in two, or at most three journals.
3. It is suggested that you subscribe to at least four computer-oriented journals.
4. Sharing information is an important means of keeping up-to-date.
5. The computer itself can help you keep up-to-date.
6. Be certain to spend all your time at conferences attending the scheduled sessions.
7. Read each article in depth.
8. Skimming is a key skill to develop.
9. Magazines are quickly dated.

Think About

1. What type of record-keeping system do you think would be best for you? One that you would actually use for reference?
2. How could you use the children to help you keep up-to-date?
3. If you could attend any conference next year, which would you attend? Why?
4. If you could only read one computer-oriented magazine each month, which one would you read?
5. Who do you know that really is "up-to-date"? Ask this person how he or she is able to accomplish this feat.
6. Look at three current educational computing journals. Rate the articles in each.
7. What is your major interest as regards computer use in the elementary/middle school? (Computer-assisted instruction? LOGO? BASIC? Computer literacy? Problem solving with computers?) What are the special concepts you must know and keep learning?
8. Prepare a note to parents entitled, "Computers in the Elementary/Middle School in 19XX."

Suggested References

Almost all the references contained in the appendix are helpful in keeping up-to-date. Therefore, the entire appendix is the suggested reference. However, look at the professional organizations and consider joining one.

What's in the Future?

How long do you think it will be before an intelligent computer tutor is available? Such a program would guide students' discovery. It might, for example, serve as a tutor or coach for students playing an educational math game. It would keep students from forming incorrect ideas of the rules, purposes, and concepts of the game. It would help students see the limitations of their game-playing strategies, and it would suggest more effective strategies. It would be perceptive enough to make relevant comments—but not so often or intrusively that it would spoil the fun of the game.

To accomplish these ends, the program would need to be able to (a) infer students' shortcomings from whatever they do in the context of playing the game; (b) compare the students' moves to those of an expert, in order to figure out what it is the student does not know; and (c) "understand" enough about teaching and learning to figure out when and how it should coach the students. Try to place a date on the emergence of this program.

The actual date: 1975 (Burton and Brown, 1979). While the above paragraphs may have presented an overly optimistic picture of the program's abilities, they do represent a description of an actual computer system designed to coach people playing a mathematics game, How the

West Was Won. While there are complex problems in creating computer tutors (and some that defy solution), progress is definitely being made. What might we expect in the future?

VISIONS

One Vision

In *Education and Ecstasy* George Leonard (1968) describes a utopia in which lifelong learning and lifelong creative change exist as the main purposes of life. Computers play an essential role. In one section of the futuristic school, the BASICS Dome, children sit at individual learning consoles that form a ring within the dome. The children face outward toward a laser-produced three-dimensional learning display.

When a child first sits down, the computer taps in to her learning history. The child puts on combination earphones and brain wave sensors. The latter analyze the wave patterns of the learner and immediately influence the ongoing dialogue between the student and the computer. If she is responding neurologically, the dialogue moves on. Pace is adjusted. Learning is efficient and steady. General states of emotion, consciousness, and short-term memory are taken into consideration.

After reading these patterns, the computer quickly reviews the child's last session. If she wants to continue, she pushes the "yes" key on the modified typewriter keyboard. If she presses "no," the computer searches rapidly for other material appropriate to her level of learning, flashing alternatives in front of the child until she presses "yes."

Taking into consideration a full bank of basic cultural knowledge (which most children learn from ages three to six), other interesting material which allows for individual discovery, the child's brain wave pattern, the child's typed or spoken responses, and even the material from the displays of the child's friends sitting around her, the computer constantly creates and re-creates an appropriate dialogue. A four-year-old girl is "conversing" about primitive cultures. A six-year-old boy is deep into a simple calculus session. A three-year-old girl is learning standard spelling and trying out alternative forms (this experimentation gradually leads most children into a key project—inventing their own language). For instance, the computer asks for a spelling of *cat* in response to the girls's recognition of a displayed cat and her verbalization of the word *cat*. After she provides the standard spelling, she is asked for a few alternative spellings (for example, "Kat" or "Katte"). The following dialogue ensues:

Computer: A cat is a Kat is a Katte.
Girl (typing): A Katte is a Kat is a cat.
Computer: Copy cat.
Girl: Koppy Kat.

At that time the girl notices the display from the child in the next console. This is taken into account by the computer. For a few moments the microworlds of several children interact and influence each other. The jungle from the "primitve cultures" dialogue of the other girl spills over into the three-year-old's display. She types, "A cat hiss a Kat hiss a Katte." The computer says, "Wild!!!" Reacting to a leopard in the scene, she types "A tiger is a tigger./A gunne has a trigger." The leopard becomes a tiger before her eyes. The two girls exchange delighted glances.

> Computer: Why not "leopard"?
> Girl: "Leopard" doesn't rhyme with "trigger."
> Computer: Okay, How about some alternative spellings for "leopard"?
> Girl: That's easy. Leppurd.

The computer compliments her but reminds her that she doesn't have to stay with sound correspondence. She tries, "Leap-heart."

Leonard postulates that human potential is great, learning is sheer delight, learning is life's ultimate purpose, and that educators can use computer technology to actualize that potential and that ecstasy. It is critical to note that Leonard's vision includes many other learning and growing situations besides the BASICS Dome. Just as essential is purely human contact. He gives an example of a group of children and adults dramatizing a historical episode, discussing it (and crying from empathy) afterward.

A Second Vision

Christopher Evans (1979) paints a picture of futuristic education that is as convincing as it is dramatic. His teaching computers will be genuinely "smart," in that they will adjust their responses in a variety of ways, giving the impression that they are interested in teaching and that they understand the subject matter and the student's grasp of it. "Lessons" will be true dialogues. Teaching devices must, according to Evans, be made available to all children; otherwise, the bright, advantaged children will benefit from the mind-stretching and information-giving potentials of the machines, while the less fortunate will be left, again, far behind. These teaching computers must be carefully prepared to motivate every child. Information is now locked in books, available only to those with the keys to their use. In Evans's future, "books will come down from their shelves, unlock and release their contents, and cajole, even beseech, their owners to make use of them" (p. 129). When they reach the stage of Ultra Intelligent Machines (more intelligent than people), their role as teacher will be unequaled. "It will be like having, as private tutors, the wisest, most knowledgeable and most patient humans on earth: an Albert Einstein to teach physics, a Bertrand Russell to teach philosophy, a Sigmund Freud to discuss the principles of psychoanalysis, and all available where and when they are wanted" (p. 229).

Can It Happen?

Is this realistic? A series of articles in *Educational Technology* (Atkinson et al., 1978) addressed this question. Atkinson postulates that by 1990 equipment and location will not be barriers to access and use of CAI programs. Computer-based intelligent video-disk systems will provide interactive programs which will automatically control for reading level and student's performances. Book-sized personal computers, as common and convenient as today's hand-held calculators, will be used for everything from art, to music, to solving complex mathematical problems. While somewhat limited in memory and capabilities, such book-sized computers are available today. Soon these machines will be more intelligent and will be able to "understand" what a student does and does not understand, assisting the student as appropriate.

With some warnings as to the complexity of the problem of wide-scale implementation of computer-based learning, most of the authors in the series agree that every student will own his or her own computer; that single chips and other memory devices will provide increasing computing power and vast amounts of information, and will be available as "plug-in" additions to any system; and that CAI will be utilized extensively. Most thoughtful authors also agree that we need more quality research on how people learn and how this can be facilitated. Only in this way can education—including computer-aided education—advance substantially.

SCENARIOS . . . AND THEIR AUTHORS

Even if much of this is realizable, is it all desirable? These issues must also be thoroughly examined. There are, of course, many scenarios we can dimly perceive as we try to look through the veil of the future. The following are just a few. Which actually materialize depends on many forces—one of which is the impact of teachers like you.

Scenario 1.   Computers made a big impact—about five to ten years ago. Now they're sitting in storerooms, decaying beside the other unused teaching machines. They made no more lasting impact on school than did movies and television. One or two teachers in a building use them for remedial help in reading and mathematics, although the programs haven't been updated in quite a while.

Scenario 2.   Schools have benefited from the application of computer technology, although the inertia of society has tended to channel their application into teaching the traditional curriculum more efficiently. Some educators are insisting that computers, used innovatively, can make a major change in the thinking and learning of children. The few implementations of their ideas seem interesting, but they have not made a large impact on most schools.

Scenario 3. Schools are controlled mainly by curriculum writers, educational psychologists, programmers, and administrators, in that order. Advances in cognitive psychology and computer science have allowed the construction of "intelligent systems" which can test, prescribe, teach, and retest students, keeping track of all their studies with impressive efficiency. Designers of the educational programs are working vigorously to create better systems, so that each student will be tutored by a computerized Shakespeare in writing and so on. Because the cost of developing ultracomplex curricula is tremendous, there is a tendency for decisions as to the nature and content of the programs to be made at the national level, as the curriculum becomes more standardized and education more centralized. Students learn as much (or more) at home as they do at school, except that the school provides certain important social and physical activities. The influence of teachers has lessened considerably, largely due to the way educational computing has grown. The school adapted too slowly—students learned about computers, and from them, at stores, at clubs, and at home. Institutions and forces outside of schools stepped in and met the growing demand.

Scenario 4. Students learn almost everything at home. With cables connecting every home to every other home and institution, schools have become unnecessary, dinosaurs in a technological age. Due to the availability of huge communication networks and the dwindling supply of energy, people live, work, and learn at home. Contacts with other children and with teachers still exist via telecommunications. Social and physical needs are met through play with other neighborhood children. As more and more curricula from commercial organizations are approved by the state, more and more children are being taught exclusively via computer or in a few non-public schools using computerized teaching.

Scenario 5. Schools have become centers for learning and communicating for entire neighborhoods. Computer-enhanced facilities are used by children and adults throughout the day. Classes are held, but their organization has been substantially changed, and attendance is usually not mandatory. Children explore and learn about their world through a variety of formats and experiences, some of which are highly technological, some of which are not complex at all. Computers are used to drill, instruct, solve problems, simulate, and stimulate. Each student has a work station where he or she can put in and receive information, solve problems, and "play." In a middle school several students play a video game that leads to an intuitive understanding of the laws of physics in space. First graders develop their own cartoon shows with computer graphics and a child-oriented computer language. Others do more advanced art, music, and writing. Virtually no children "fail," as all can find, with help, those activities in which they excel; and they have the encouragement and supportive environment to pursue those activities.

Teachers in these schools are thankful that their predecessors worked hard to become computer literate—some at the beginning, some in the middle of their careers—taking the responsibility upon themselves to give students the education they needed within the schools. They were also responsible for encouraging the development of learning style compatibility research and practice, which led to the development of computer systems which adapted to the aptitudes, interests, and personalities of learners. Similarly, they were strong proponents of monitoring carefully the self-absorption that could be generated through continuous, intense control of a powerful machine. They advocated a balance of individual and social experiences. They avoided the "panacea" machine, looking carefully at every new application of technology.

Many scenarios are possible. Every concerned educator should be knowledgeable about, concerned with, and involved in, the applications of technology to education. It is they, along with some writers and poets, who know what education and school mean to the child. By becoming authors of the future scenario, they can ensure that the future will not resemble that foretold by Isaac Asimov (1976), who describes an eleven-year-old girl who hates her expert learning machine. Finding a book ("What a waste," says her friend, for it must be discarded—unlike his television screen), she reads about the schools of the past. Although her mother explains that learning must be adjusted to fit the mind of each boy and girl, she is entranced by the schools of the past. When her mechanical teacher flashes a problem on the screen, she thinks about children of the past and *The Fun They Had.*

CONTROLLING COMPUTERS IN THE FUTURE

What about programming? Which language will be used? Will everyone program computers? While answers to these questions must remain speculative, it would seem that, just as today, people will program at varying levels. Some will, of course, still design and program computers at a technical, "machine language" level. At the other extreme, some may employ only user-friendly programs which ask them what they want done. However, even for those somewhere in between, the task may be very different from today. They may be able to talk to the computer and design programs in natural languages. However, as we have seen, our conversations can often hide ambiguity. How will this be handled? First of all, since people of the future will have worked with computers almost since birth, planning and problem solving will be more natural and more organized for them. Second, where their intentions or ideas are a bit "fuzzy," the computer they are conversing with will ask them what they mean, carrying on a dialogue which will force them to carefully think through their problem, their goals, and their methods of solution. Thus, computer programmers may write initial systems which, once written, can grow and adapt with the user. Combining work from the fields of cognitive psychology, artificial intelligence, computer science, education, and others, professionals of the not-too-distant future will create computer systems capable of interacting in conversational English. These machines will help people create programs, answer questions, discover new information, and so on.

Some of the pioneers in the construction and use of the LOGO language are already making steps toward a new, even more user-friendly language, which also overcomes some of the disadvantages of LOGO (for example, limited data storage capabilities and inability to integrate many users and/or many types of systems). Called Boxer, it is visually oriented so that "what you see is what you have." The spatial relationships among words and phrases enclosed in boxes on the screen directly represent meaningful relationships within the language. What is seen, then, is a close representation of the computational system itself. Also, the various uses of a computer, such as text processing, programming, and file management, are built into the system simultaneously.

As an example, a teacher might type the names of his students into the computer. He could then enter one of the student's data boxes by moving the cursor into it and hitting a key, "entering" that box (that is, that box would expand to fill the screen). There he could enter another data box, say "Math." Here he might enter new information directly, such as a new unit, or he might enter yet another box to add or change an existing grade or other piece of information. Notice that the spatial arrangement directly mirrors the hierarchical arrangement of information. Also note that the editing system is always present (information can be added or changed at any time). Helpful menus are no longer special, auxiliary features but rather are built into the program. They can be used, constructed, or edited by the user. Data can also be shared among different modules, and one module can "ask" another to do something for it. Statements can be typed in and executed one at a time and later built up into a program of the user's choice. While Boxer demands higher capabilities than most microcomputers possess at the present time, they should be available soon.

New ideas are coming. Watch for them.

Think About

1. Does there *have* to be some difference between the intelligent human and the ultraintelligent machine? What?
2. Read one of the futuristic works mentioned in this chapter. How comfortable will *you* be if the world described actually materialized? How could you

open yourself, and extend your own abilities and knowledge, to welcome such a world? Can you plan for this and take just the first step?

3. As programming languages become increasingly user friendly, will we lose in our ability to learn from the demanding, but fascinating, occupation of programming?

4. As machines become more and more "intelligent," will people become less so?

5. Can teachers ever be replaced? Why or why not? If we examine both what it is about our teaching that is unique and what machines are capable of, we will be able to answer this question (to ourselves and others). We will also be more aware of our own teaching—what it involves, what in it is truly important, why we should value it.

6. What if complex CAI sytems are shown in research studies to yield achievement equivalent to that of traditional schooling? What forces might attempt to replace the schools? What would you say and do?

7. Write a description of what an ideal computer teacher of the future would do. Write a description of what an ideal human teacher of the future would do.

8. Will increased use of computers in the home and school become one more way we "hurry" our children?

9. Reread scenario 2. Would centralization be an improvement or a disaster for education? Would the fears of Orwell's *1984* be more realizable under this system? If such a trend emerges, what safeguards should be constructed?

10. If huge CAI programs are constructed, should they be used to aid those who at present are not profiting from traditional instruction? If they are used in this way, do you think these children (often lower-class) could be trained into docility, obeying and believing the "master computer," while more fortunate children learn to control technology for their own ends? (If this seems contrived, note that some poorer urban school systems are presently using microcomputers to provide basic skills instruction to low-achieving students, while more affluent districts ascribe to the goal of computer literacy.)

11. How do you feel about the futuristic visions described in this chapter? Will you welcome change? Resist it? Fear it? How would this attitude affect the way you teach? If you have negative feelings, what could you do to make them more positive?

Suggested References

Asimov, Isaac. **The fun they had.** In *The best of Isaac Asimov.* Greenwich, Conn.: Fawcett, 1976.
   Asimov's story is interesting reading for adults and children alike. Discuss with your students the differences between learning in schools and learning from the computer. Ask if this type of futuristic scene is possible. How would *you* feel if you were that girl? How close is modern technology to Asimov's vision? What are the advantages and disadvantages about each type of learning?

Deken, Joseph. *The electronic cottage.* New York: William Morrow and Co., 1982. This book contains interesting insights into the computer revolution of the near future (as well as readable explanations about how computers work).

The information about programmable devices that we will all be using will be of interest to you personally and professionally, as you plan to stimulate discussion with your students. These include computer-controlled clocks that control almost all the electrical devices of the home; heat tracking devices which keep infrared lamps pointed at all the people in a room so that central heating need only be high enough to keep water pipes from freezing; computer alarms which detect burglars, fire, and so on, call neighbors, and take protective action; windows, doors, and walls that appear only when needed; refrigerators mounted out of the way (underground), which will remove and replace items through an airlock/dumbwaiter, tell you what its contents are, and even inform you what you would need to cook turkey divan (or, better yet, what you could cook without going to the store); and so on.

Evans, Christoper. *The micro millenium.* New York: Pocket Books, 1979.
Evans believes that the future will be dramatically influenced by the creation of UIM—Ultra Intelligent Machines. Computers designed by computers, these machines will far outstrip our intellectual abilities. Read these chapters. Is it possible? If so, will it lead to disaster or utopia for the human race? Will our belief in ourselves be destroyed, or can we find a new basis (not merely "we are the most intelligent beings") for valuing ourselves and our universe?

Leonard, George. *Education and ecstasy.* New York: Delacorte Press, 1968.
Read Leonard's book. Do you believe this perfect balance between technology and humanism is possible? Can education be an ecstatic experience? All the time? Do you sometimes feel better about an accomplishment that you have "sweated" over?

Levine, Carl. Electronic information: An introduction to what lies ahead. *Electronic Learning,* September 1982, pp. 66–68; 103.

Nelson, Ted. Mail chauvinism: The magicians, the snark, and the camel. *Creative Computing,* November 1981, pp. 128; 130; 134–135; 138; 140; 142; 144; 150; 156.
Nelson and Levine describe recent projects (and efforts to stop them) on improving communication between people.

Pritchard, William H., Jr. Instructional computing in 2001: A scenario. *Phi Delta Kappan,* 1982, 63, 322–325.
Another possible scenario. What do you think?

Toffler, A. *The third wave.* New York: William Morrow and Co., 1980.
Toffler is famous for helping us think about the future and our place in it. What insights into your own and your students' futures do you gain from reading this book?

Bibliography

Asimov, Isaac. The fun they had. In *The best of Isaac Asimov,* Greenwich, Conn.: Fawcett, 1976.

Atkinson, Richard C., Bitzer, Donald L., Bunderson, C. Victor, Charp, Sylvia, and Hirschbuhl, John J. Futures: Where will computer-assisted instruction (CAI) be in 1990? *Education Technology,* 1978, 18(4), 60–63.

Burton, Richard R., and Brown, John S. An investigation of computer coaching for informal learning activities. *International Journal of Man-Machine Studies,* 1979, 11, 5–24.

Evans, Christopher. *The micro millenium.* New York: Pocket Books, 1979.

Leonard, George. *Education and ecstasy.* New York: Delacorte Press, 1968.

Appendix

COMPUTER JOURNALS FOR EDUCATORS

The journals below devote the majority of their space to computers in education. Each has its own particular approach. Get a copy of each journal and see what type of material it contains. Which are most helpful to you? After careful study we suggest that you subscribe to one and find ways to review the others each month.

AEDS Monitor: 1201 16th Street N.W., Washington, D.C. 20036.

Classroom Computer News: Intentional Educations, Inc., 341 Mt. Auburn St., Watertown, Mass. 02171.

The Computing Teacher: Department of Computer and Information Science, University of Oregon, Eugene, Oreg. 97403.

Educational Computer Magazine: Educational Computer, P.O. Box 535, Cupertino, Calif. 95015.

Educational Technology: 140 Sylvan Avenue, Englewood Cliffs, N.J. 07632.

Electronic Education: Suite 220, 1311 Executive Center Drive, Tallahassee, Fla. 32301.

Electronic Learning: Scholastic Inc., 902 Sylvan Avenue, Englewood Cliffs, N.J. 07632.

School Courseware Journal: 1341 Bulldog Lane, Suite C. Fresno, Calif. 93710.

T.H.E. Journal: P.O. Box 992, Acton, Mass. 01720.

GENERAL COMPUTER JOURNALS

Study a copy of each of these computer magazines. *Creative Computing* often has articles on computers and the classroom. *Byte* has one education issue a year. The magazines vary in the number of programs they contain. Which do you think is most helpful? Which would you use to keep up to date on computer hardware?

Note that there are many month-to-month changes in the number of computer journals and in the format. This listing should be considered as representative not exhaustive.

Byte: 70 Main Street, Peterborough, N.H. 03458
Compute: 515 Abbott, Broomall, Pa. 19008
Creative Computing: P.O. Box 789-M, Morristown, N.J. 07960
Infoworld (Newsweekly): 375 Cochituate Road, Box 880, Framingham, Mass. 01701
Personal Computing: P.O. Box 1408, Riverton, N.J. 08077
Popular Computing: 70 Main Street, Peterborough, N.H. 03458

SOFTWARE DIRECTORIES

The Software Directories contain brief descriptions of software available for use with particular computers.

The Apple Software Directory (Vol. 3 Education). WDL Video, 5245 W. Diversey Avenue, Chicago, Ill. 60639.

The Blue Book for the Apple Computer. Visual Materials, Inc., 4170 Grove Avenue, Gurnee, Ill. 60031.

The Book of Apple Software. The Book Company, 11223 S. Hindryb Avenue, Los Angeles, Calif. 90045.

The Commodore Software Encyclopedia. Commodore Corporate Offices, Education Dept., 487 Devon Park Drive, Wayne, Pa. 19087.

Educator's Handbook and Software Directory. Vital Information Inc., 350 Union Station, Kansas City, Mo. 64108.

Index to Computer Based Learning. Educational Communications Department, University of Wisconsin, P.O. Box 413, Milwaukee, Wis. 53201.

International Microcomputer Software Directory. Imprint Software, 420 S. Howes Street, Ft. Collins, Colo. 80521.

Reference Manual for Instructional Use of Microcomputers. JEM Research, Discovery Park, University of Victoria, P.O. Box 1700, Victoria BC V8W 2Y2, Canada.

School Microware Directory. Dresden Associates, P.O. Box 246, Dresden, Me. 04342.

The Software Directory. 11990 Dorsett Road, St. Louis, Mo. 63043.

Swift's Directory of Educational Software, Apple II Edition. Sterling Swift Publishing Co., 1600 Fortview Road, Austin, Tex. 78804.

The TRS-80 Sourcebook and Software Directory (available at local Radio Shack stores).

Vanloves Apple Software Directory. Vital Information, Inc., 350 Union Station, Kansas City, Mo. 64108.

SOFTWARE CLEARING HOUSES

Public Domain Software (software that can be legally used and copied without fee) is available from some of these clearing houses. They are worth contacting to find out the function each performs.

CONDUIT. P.O. Box 388, Iowa City, Iowa 52244.

MICROCOMPUTER EDUCATIONS APPLICATION NETWORK (MEAN). 256 North Washington Street, Falls Church, Va. 22046.

SOFTSWAP. San Mateo County Office of Education, 333 Main Street, Redwood City, Calif. 94063.

ORGANIZATIONS

The organizations below deal with a variety of "computers in education" activities. Contact those that appear to share your interests.

CompuServe Information Service
5000 Arlington Centre Blvd.
Columbus, Ohio 43220
(614) 457-8600
Communications network for general purpose.

Dialog Information Services
3460 Hillview Avenue
Palo Alto, Calif. 94304
(800) 227-1927
Communications network with educational data bases.

Directory of Online Information Resources
CSG Press
11301 Rockville Pike
Kensington, Md. 20895
(301) 881-9400
Not a data base, but a directory to data bases.

ERIC
Educational Resources Center
National Institute of Education
Washington, D.C. 20208
(202) 254-07934

MicroSIFT
300 S.W. 6th Street
Portland, Oreg. 97204
(503) 248-6800
Clearinghouse for software.

Resources in Computer Education/Bibliographic Retrieval Services (RICE/BRS)
1200 Route 7
Latham, N.Y. 12110
(518) 783-1161
Data base on software for education.

The Source
Reader's Digest Educational Division
Pleasantville, N.Y. 10570
(914) 769-7000

Source Telecomputing Corporation
1616 Anderson Road
McLean, Va. 22102
Communications network with consumer services, data bases, and electronic mail.

General Organizations

Americal Educational Research Association (AERA)
1126 16st Street, NW
Washington, D.C. 20036
(202) 223-9845
Includes special interest group for CAI.

Association for Computers and the Humanities (ACH)
Queens College
Flushing, N.Y. 11367
(212) 520-7000

Association for Computers in Mathematics & Science Teaching
P.O. Box 4455
Austin, Tex. 78765

Association for Computing Machinery (A.C.M.)
1133 Avenue of the Americas
New York, N.Y. 10036
(212) 265-6300

Association for Educational Communications and Technology (AECT)
1126 16th Street, NW
Washington, D.C. 20036

Association for Educational Data Systems (A.E.D.S)
1201 16th Street, NW
Washington, D.C. 20036

Association for the Development of Computer-Based Instructional
Systems (ADCIS)
Western University Computer Center
Bellingham, Wash. 98225
(206) 676-2860
Goal: To facilitate communication between developers and consumers of
computer materials.

Boston Computer Society (BCS)
Educational Resource Exchange
Three Center Plaza
Boston, Mass. 02108
(617) 367-8080

Computer Technology and Reading
International Reading Association
800 Barksdale Road
P.O. Box 8139
Newark, Del. 19711
(302) 731-1600

Computer-Using Educators (CUE)
c/o Don McKell
Independence High School
1775 Educational Park Drive
San Jose, Calif. 95113

Dataspan
c/o Karl Zinn
109 East Madison Street
Ann Arbor, Mich. 48104

EPIE Institute
P.O. Box 620
Stony Brook, N.Y. 11790
(516) 246-8664
Educational technology consumer group.

ERIC Clearinghouse on Elementary and Early Childhood Education
University of Illinois
College of Education
Urbana, Ill. 61801
(217) 333-1386

ERIC Clearinghouse on Information Resources
Syracuse University
School of Education
130 Huntington Hall
Syracuse, N.Y. 13210

Educational Computing Consortium of Ohio (ECCO)
4777 Farnhurst Road
Lyndhurst, Ohio 44124

Educational Technology Center
c/o Alfred Bork
University of California
Irving, Calif. 92717
(714) 883-6945
Middle school computer materials.

Far West Laboratory
1855 Folsom Street
San Francisco, Calif. 94103
(415) 565-3035
Information service on many aspects of computers in education.

Human Resources Research Organization (HumRRO)
300 North Washington Street
Alexandria, Va. 22314

International Council for Computers in Education (ICCE)
Computer Center
East Oregon State College
LaGrande, Oreg. 97850
Educational users group.

Microcomputer Resource Center
Teachers College
Columbia University
New York, N.Y. 10027
(212) 678-3740

Minnesota Educational Computing Consortium (MECC)
2520 Broadway Drive
St. Paul, Minn. 55113
(612) 376-1101

National Audio-Visual Association (NAVA)
3150 Spring Street
Fairfax, Va. 22031
(703) 273-7200

National Council for the Social Studies (NCSS)
3501 Newark Street, NW
Washington, D.C. 20016

National Council of Teachers of English
Dr. Bernard O'Donnell
1111 Kenyon Road
Urbana, Ill. 61801

National Council of Teachers of Mathematics (NCTM)
1906 Association Drive
Reston, Va. 22091
(703) 620-9840

National Logo Exchange
P.O. Box 5341
Charlottesville, Va. 22905
Information and newsletters on the educational use of LOGO.

National Science Teachers Association (NSTA)
1742 Connecticut Avenue NW
Washington, D.C. 20009
(202) 328-5840

Softswap
San Mateo County Office of Education
333 Main Street
Redwood City, Calif. 94063
(415) 363-5472
Software exchange; "public domain" software.

Technical Education Research Center (TERC)
3 Eliot Street
Cambridge, Mass. 02138
Technical educators users group.

Young People's Logo Association (YPLA)
P.O. Box 855067
Richardson, Tex. 75085
(214) 783-7548
Information and newsletter on LOGO.

Glossary

Access Time: The time between the moment data is called for and the moment it is delivered from storage.

Address: A number that identifies a location in the computer's memory.

ALGOL: A high-level, procedural computer language designed for scientific applications.

Algorithm: A step-by-step procedure or strategy for solving a problem. In elementary mathematics children apply algorithms to compute sums, differences, products, quotients, square roots, and so on. They also learn algorithms for alphabetizing words. Many types of algorithms can be designed for computers to carry out.

Alphanumeric: Data consisting of any letter of the alphabet or any numeral or character.

Analog Computer: A computer which measures data that changes continuously, and which therefore can translate physical conditions like temperature into numbers. For example, it might measure temperatures or voltages and record them as quantities. Measured temperatures or voltages might then be used to represent variables in an equation. Graphs are often produced as the output. You might say that an analog computer measures continuously, whereas a digital computer counts discretely. Analog computers are used by scientists and engineers.

Array: An arrangement of data in a pattern which helps store and recall it easily. For instance, the addition/subtraction table is an array. An ordered set of variables and their values which are assigned space in the computer's memory.

Arithemetic/Logic Unit: That section of the computer that performs all the arithmetic and logical operations.

Artificial Intelligence: The study of the possibilities and implications of developing computer systems which can perform "intelligent" tasks, so that they appear to "think" like humans. This might involve playing games, interacting in a human language, or the like.

Assembler: A computer program that takes the user's higher-level language instructions and converts them into the computer's machine language, which it can "understand" and use. Instructions are translated item for item, so that the output has the same number of instructions as the original input.

Assembly Language: An intermediary computer language that uses mnemonics (memory aids) to write machine language instructions in a more understandable form.

Authoring Languages: High-level computer languages that are designed for use by those who wish to write CAI materials (e.g., teachers, or personnel trainers). See CAI, PILOT, COURSEWRITER.

Auxiliary Storage: See Secondary Storage.

BASIC (Beginner's All-Purpose Symbolic Instruction Code): A popular high-level computer language, widely available on most inexpensive microcomputers. While it is often the first language taught to children, there are other languages (see LOGO) that might be more appropriate.

Baud: A unit of speed of transmitting data; the number of bits of information that can be sent or received. One baud means one unit per second.

Binary: A system based upon only two possibilities. Computers can store information only as "off" (the absence of an electrical voltage) or "on" (the presence of electricity). Thus, patterns of electrical current represent binary codes in which "off" represents 0 (zero) and "on" represents 1 (one). A group of these, in turn, represent other characters, like letters (see byte). It should be noted that it is not necessary to understand the binary number system in order to use computers.

Bit (Binary digIT): Either of the numerals 0 or 1, the only numbers in the binary number system. Computers use these two digits to represent all data (see Binary).

Bubble Memory: A high-capacity storage device utilizing "bubbles" of magnetized areas which can move about in a magnetic field.

Buffer: A computer's temporary storage for data which balances or compensates for different operating speeds of various parts of a system, e.g., between a high-speed computer (CPU) and a slower printer.

Bug: An error in a computer program.

Bus: Three sets of wires that connect the hardware parts of a microcomputer. The control bus ensures correct control and timing, so that the parts operate together. The address bus ensures that each part sends and receives the correct information. The data bus transmits the values of that information.

Byte: A group of consecutive bits—often six, eight, or sixteen—which are treated as a single unit of information by the computer. A byte, then, represents one character—such as a letter, numeral, punctuation mark, special character (e.g., ⟩ or }), or function (e.g., a carriage return).

CAI (Computer-Assisted Instruction): A method of teaching which uses a computer to present individualized instructional materials. Students interact with the computer in a learning situation which might involve drill and practice, tutorials with different branches of study, simulations, or the like. Sometimes referred to as CAL (Computer-Assisted Learning).

Calculator: A device that performs arithmetical operations based upon data and instructions that are entered manually.

Canned Program: A program available from a library of programs.

Card Punch: An output device that punches holes in cards.

Card Reader: An input device that translates the holes punched in cards into electrical impulses which can be stored in the computer's memory.

Cathode Ray Tube (CRT):   The picture tube of a television set and the display screen for most microcomputers. A cathode ray (an electron beam) strikes a phosphorescent screen to display information such as text or graphics. Also called a monitor, display, or video screen.

CBI (Computer-Based Instruction):   The use of computers in education, either to teach (see CAI) or to help manage instruction (see CMI).

Central Processing Unit (CPU):   The "brains" of the computer, it consists of the arithmetic/logic unit and the control unit (see Arithmetic/Logic Unit, Control Unit).

Character: A letter, numeral, punctuation mark, or any other symbol used to represent information (see also byte). A computer stores and manipulates characters. The size of a computer's memory is designated as the number of characters it can store (see K).

Chip: See microprocessor.

CMI (Computer-Managed Instruction):   Use of computers in the management of instruction (as opposed to CAI programs that are designed to teach students). For example, computers might keep records, test results, and progress reports; they might generate materials; or they might test students and prescribe appropriate work.

COBOL (COmmon Business Oriented Language):   A high-level computer language developed for business applications and used in many sciences. A widely used procedural-level language.

Command: A instruction given to a computer.

Compiler: A computer program that translates a program written in a high-level language such as FORTRAN or Pascal into a machine language that the computer can "understand" directly.

Computer: A device capable of accepting information, processing that information by performing prescribed arithmetical and logical operations upon it, and producing the results of this processing.

Computer-Assisted Instruction: See CAI.

Computer Language: Instructions to a computer in a form it can "understand"; i.e., carry out. (See also Machine Language.) "High-level" languages contain English-like words and are easier to understand.

Computer Literacy: Knowledge of the technology, capabilities, applications (uses and abuses), limitations, and impact of computers. Often separated into two levels, computer awareness and full working knowledge.

Computer-Managed Instruction: See CMI.

Computer System: See System.

Control Unit: One of the two main components of the central processing unit, the control unit translates computer programs, directs the sequence of operations, and initiates correct commands to the computer circuits. It directs the step-by-step operation of the whole computer system.

Courseware: Software (computer programs) designed specifically for classroom use (see software).

COURSEWRITER: A computer language used to write CAI materials (e.g., those used for teaching or training).

CPI: Characters Per Inch

CPU: See Central Processing Unit.

CRT: See Cathode Ray Tube.

Cursor: A symbol, often blinking, which indicate where the next character will be displayed on the CRT. Often it can be moved around on the CRT to refer to or identify a location.

Cybernetics: The study of how humans and machines are alike; for example, comparing the brain and nervous sytem to electronic/mechanical communications systems.

Daisy-Wheel Printer: An impact printer whose characters are arranged on a circular printing component, resembling a daisy flower. Since it uses formed characters, it produces professional quality print (see Letter Quality).

Data: Any information to be processed by a computer program (as opposed to programs which are instructions that tell the computer how to manipulate or process the data).

Data Bank: A large collection of data. A large data bank may hold as much information as a large library. Often many people use common data banks.

Data Base Management System: Computer programs designed to store, maintain, and retrieve information (see also Data Bank).

Data Processing: A procedure for receiving information and performing a series of operations on it (e.g., rearranging, recording, sorting, etc.) to produce a result better suited for further use.

Debugging: Searching for and correcting errors in computer programs.

Digital Computer: A computer that operates on discrete data (see Bit) by performing arithmetic and logical processes on the data. Under the control of a computer program, it will input, store, manipulate, and output specific characters such as letters, numerals, or punctuation marks.

Disk: A device used to store magnetic information on a circular plate. A hard disk pack may store 300,000,000 characters (300 megabytes; about 300,000K).

Disk Drive: A mechanical device that can store information on, and retrieve information from, a disk or diskette. This information may consist of data or programs.

Disk Operating System: See DOS.

Diskette (floppy disk): Similar to the disk, but smaller and more flexible, with less storage density. Along with cassette tapes, the most common secondary storage device for microcomputers. The diskette permits more rapid retrieval of information. May store 400K or more characters. Permanently stored in a square jacket for protection, it resembles a phonograph record (especially the thin, flexible ones).

Documentation: Materials designed to aid the user of a computer program. It may include written directions and descriptions, examples, flow charts, listings of the program, sample outputs, and so on.

DOS (Disk Operating System): A language or program that operates the disk system, keeps track of storing and retrieving information, creates and opens files, copies files, and generally lets the computer know what devices are available and how to use them. It allows communication between the computer and the software and/or user.

Dot Matrix: A technique of printing characters (text) or graphics using small dots.

File: A collection of information that is treated as a unit; may be a data file (information to be processed by a program) or a program file (a computer program).

First-Generation Computer: The first electronic computers, which used vacuum tubes and electronic relay switches.

Floppy Disk: See Diskette.

Flow Chart: A diagram of the operations or steps which are to take place in a program, which helps one organize the solution of the problem and understand the program's logical structure. A flow chart usually consists of symbols such as arrows and geometric shapes, and human language.

Format: The way text is visually organized.

FORTRAN (FORmula TRANslation):   A computer language developed to help solve scientific and engineering problems. FORTRAN was developed in the 1950s and is still widely used.

GIGO (Garbage In Garbage Out):   The idea that the output or results of a computer program cannot be better than the quality of the input data. Unreliable or "bad" data will produce unreliable results.

Graphics: Any shapes, dots, lines, and colors that are drawn using a computer. May involve pictures, graphs, maps, diagrams, or the like.

Hard Copy: Printout on paper of data, programs, or solutions.

Hardware: The physical equipment of a computer system, consisting of electrical, electronic, magnetic, and mechanical devices. For example, keyboards, CRTs, printers, the central processing unit, circuit boards, primary storage, and card readers.

Heuristic: Describes an exploratory method of problem solving with repeated evaluations of progress toward the goal; for example, guided trial and error. (Contrast with Algorithm.)

High-Level Language: See Computer Language.

High Resolution: The ability of a cathode ray tube (display screen) to display highly detailed graphics such as pictures.

Increment: To add to or count; the amount a variable is increased.

Information Processing: Describes all the operations performed by a computer. The handling of information according to rules of procedure to accomplish classifying, recording, retrieving, calculating, or the like.

Information Retrieval: The storage and recall of large amounts of information (see also Data Bank).

Input: Data and programs to be processed by the computer. Also, the process of transferring data from an external source to an internal storage medium.

Input/Output Devices (I/O Devices):   The parts of a computer system that allow people to communicate with the central processing unit. Input devices insert data to be processed into the computer; for example, keyboards or card readers. Output devices include CRTs, printers, or card punchers.

Instructions: Symbols used to communicate with the computer, which constitute orders or directions. Computer programs.

Integrated Circuit: Electronic circuits and microscopic transistors etched into a tiny piece of silicon that help process information (see also Microprocessor).

Interface: An electronic link between components of a computer system that allows communication between these components and between the mechanical systems and humans.

I/O Devices: See Input/Output Devices.

Justification: Arranging characters to the left, right, center, etc., according to a prescribed pattern.

K (Kilobyte):   Used to represent the number 1024 (2 raised to the 10th power). The letter originates from the prefix kilo (1000). The size of a computer's memory is often stated in terms of a number of K of bytes of information; e.g., 48K. A diskette, or floppy disk, may store 200K characters.

Keyboard: An electric typewriter-like input device for typing information into a computer. Many microcomputers combine the central processing unit and the keyboard into one unit.

Keypunch: A device for punching holes into cards to be read by a card reader, which inserts the information into a computer.

Language: See Computer Language.

Letter Quality: Professional quality printing from a formed character printer (see Daisy Wheel Printer).

Library Functions: Mathematical functions whose form is stored in permanent memory; e.g., square roots and random numbers.

Library Routines: Programs available to users of larger computer networks. For example, many library routines are available for statistical analyses.

Light Pen: Used to select numbers, letters, or the like by pointing at a location on a CRT.

Line Printer: An output device that composes an entire line prior to printing; thus, an entire line is printed almost at once.

Logic: A system or pattern of problem solving in which things are done in a specific order in reasonable ways.

LOGO: A computer language designed by Seymour Papert at M.I.T., to be used by grade school children. Includes "turtle graphics." LOGO can be easily extended. It is said to encourage problem solving by children.

Loop: A series of steps or program statements that are repeated as a unit.

Machine Language: The language or instructions that a computer is constructed to carry out; usually binary code. The only language the computer can "understand" and respond to directly without first translating the input.

Magnetic Disk: See Disk.

Magnetic Tape: Secondary storage device that records information (data, programs) on cassettes or reels.

Mainframe: A large computer system with powerful capabilities.

Management Information Systems (MIS): Computer programs which store, organize, catalog, locate, retrieve, and maintain information. This supplies those in charge of managing an organization with the information necessary to efficiently organize and control the organization's operations.

Memory: A computer's storage. Usually it involves primary storage for rapid access to a limited amount of data, and secondary storage for larger amounts of data (see Primary Storage, Secondary Storage).

Menu: A list of choices exhibited in a computer program to guide the user.

Microcomputer: The smallest self-contained computer system, with a central processing unit consisting of a single chip or a small number of chips. Designed for single users.

Microprocessor (chip): A type of integrated circuit which contains microscopic switches etched into a small piece of silicon. These switches record the presence or absence of electrical current (see Binary). It is the computing equivalent of thousands of transistors and other electronic components and carries out the processing of the data. A handful of chips, each small enough to rest on a fingertip, contain most of the circuitry for a microcomputer.

Microsecond: One-millionth of a second. A small computer may add two numbers in a few microseconds.

Millisecond: One-thousandth of a second. The unit often used to measure the speed of secondary storage devices; e.g., a disk access might take 30 to 50 milliseconds.

Minicomputer: A medium-sized computer designed for a variety of uses, many languages, and several input/output terminals.

Modem (MOdulator/DEModulator): A device that allows information to pass from one computer to another over telephone lines.

Monitor: See Cathode Ray Tube. Also refers to a program that supervises the sequencing of operations by the computer.

Nanosecond: A billionth of a second. The fastest of modern computers can perform two additions every few nanoseconds; that means they are capable of executing about 100 million instructions in one second.

Network: Communication lines that connect various computer components together for large-scale computing and information sharing. A computer system consisting of a central computer and a number of users.

Nibble: Half a byte; four bits.

Number Crunching: A computer or computer program which is designed to perform large amounts of computation.

Object Code: Output from an assembler or a compiler which is directly usable by the computer. Also called object language.

Output: Information that is reported by a computer. Also, a device that allows the computer to report to humans (see Input/Output Devices).

Pascal: A high-level computer language that is becoming increasingly popular. It is more structured than BASIC, so programs are often more readable and clearly organized. It allows the user to extend the language by defining new procedures.

Peripheral Devices: Accessories and/or extra equipment that are added to the computer system to increase its capabilities. For example, game paddles, voice synthesizers, any input/output device, or printers.

Personal Computer: See Microcomputer.

PILOT: A computer language designed for use by those who wish to write CAI materials (e.g., teachers or those in business responsible for the training of personnel).

PL/1 (Programming Language 1): A modern computer language designed for scientific and commercial applications.

Primary Storage: Information handling devices that hold data and programs in memory during a program's execution (see RAM, ROM).

Printer: An output device for printing data onto paper.

Procedural Language: High-level programming language designed for the efficient expression of procedures which can be used to solve wide classes of problems. For example, COBOL, FORTRAN, PL/1.

Program: Instructions used to direct a computer to perform a specific set of operations so as to accomplish a given task. A plan for solving a program, written in a computer language so that it is "understood" by the computer (see also Software).

Programmer: A person who prepares a set of instructions (software) for a computer.

Punched Cards: Cards punched with holes to represent data.

RAM (Random Access Memory): A section of the primary memory of microcomputers. RAM chips store programs and data input from the keyboard or from secondary storage. It is called random access because it permits direct communication with any location in memory, and the time required is independent of the location of the last bit of information that was stored or retrieved. The location can then have information read from it or written into it. RAM can be used over and over again; but when the system is turned off, the data is lost. (Compare to ROM.)

Remote Terminal: An input/output device for communicating with computers which are located a great distance from the central processing unit. Communication systems such as telephone lines are often utilized.

Reverse Video: The ability of a video display (cathode ray tube) to display black characters on a white or green background.

ROM (Read Only Memory): A section of the primary memory for microcomputers. Retains certain information indefinitely (i.e., does not lose data when the system is turned off). Used to store programs that do not change, such as a BASIC language interpreter or disk operating system. (Compare to RAM.)

Scrolling: Moving text on a video display screen up or down.

Secondary Storage: A peripheral device used to store computerized data. Examples include magnetic disks or magnetic tapes and reels.

Second-Generation Computer: Appearing in 1959, these computers used transistors instead of vacuum tubes.

Simulation: A representation of "real life" physical conditions or situations through models. A mathematical model is used that gives the effect of a copy of a real action. Also, the use of such models to learn about the situations, especially when actual participation would be impractical or dangerous (e.g., flight simulation; investing in the stock market; prehistoric ecology).

Software: Computer programs which enable computers to process information and solve problems. Along with hardware, these constitute the computer system. Although it usually refers to professionally written programs, it sometimes is used to name any computer program. Examples include language translators that allow the use of BASIC, LOGO, PILOT, Pascal, and so on. Another type consists of CAI or CMI programs. A good library of computer software is necessary for worthwhile educational use of microcomputers.

Storage: See Memory.

String Variable: A series of bytes (letters, numerals, punctuation marks, etc.) which are grouped together and assigned a variable name, often denoted by the dollar sign ($), e.g., N$.

Structured Programming: A technique for designing and writing computer programs in which the program is constructed in independent segments arranged in a hierarchy, using a minimum number of branches and statement types so as to produce better organized, more readable programs.

Subscripted Variables: A set of values assigned a single variable name. Each variable is then denoted by a subscript; e.g., $A(1)$, $A(2)$, ... $A(N)$.

Syntax: In computing, this refers to the structure of instructions within a computer program; a syntax error is a mistake in programming procedure, such as a spelling error in a command word, or the omission of a needed number or space.

System: A computer and other electronic equipment, along with computer programs (software), which work together to input, process, and output data.

Terminal: An input/output device for entering data into a computer system and receiving information from it; e.g., teleprinters, keyboards, CRTs.

Third-Generation Computers: The most recent advance, these computers use integrated circuits (see microprocessor) and miniaturization to replace transistors, increase speed, and reduce size.

TICCIT (Timeshared, Interactive, Computer-Controlled, Instructional Television): A computer-assisted instructional system which provides individual instruction to many students simultaneously.

Time Sharing: A technique for organizing a computer system so that several people may use it at one time via terminals.

Translator: A computer program which translates a high-level language such as BASIC or PILOT into a lower-level language such as machine language.

TUTOR: An authoring language designed for writing CAI programs.

Variable: Something that may have several values and that can alter the outcome of a program.

Video Display: A view or display of data or graphics on a CRT (TV screen). Other displays do not use a CRT; e.g., plasma displays or LEDs.

Word Processing: Computerized typing and composing. Allows the user to list, repeat, edit, store, and print text. It can be used to rearrange words, sentences, paragraphs, and larger sections of text. It may include a dictionary that can check for misspelling.

Write Protected: Indicates that information cannot be written onto or erased from a disk. Involves an adhesive tab on the jacket of the disk.

Subject Index

See also the glossary for specific definitions, pp. 298–306.

A

Administrative applications, 59, 70
Alphabet, teaching 119, 120
Alphanumeric bar code, 41
ALU, see Arithmetic Logic Unit
Analog computers, 41
Analytic Engine, 32
Animation, see Graphics
Applications software, see Utilities programs
Arithmetic Logic Unit (ALU), 299
Artificial Intelligence, 44–49
Arts, computer applications, 163–166
Attendance software, 3
Authoring languages, 208, 236–277
see also Pilot
    criticism of, 241, 242
    definition, 237, 238
    references, 246, 247
    using, 238, 242, 243

Authoring systems, 208, 236-277, see Pilot
Automation, effect of 270

B

BASIC, 186–214
    graphics, 193–196
    problem solving, 200, 201
    references, 212, 213
    teaching, 187–206
"Big Track," 48
Binary numbers, 26
Bit (binary digit), 26
Blind, 17, 176
Braille, 177
Bug, 299
Bytes, 26, 27

C

CAI, see Computer Assisted Instruction

Author Index